dwelling, place and environment

dwelling, place and environment

towards a phenomenology of person and world

edited by

david seamon and robert mugerauer

1985 **MARTINUS NIJHOFF PUBLISHERS**
a member of the KLUWER ACADEMIC PUBLISHERS GROUP
DORDRECHT / BOSTON / LANCASTER

Distributors

for the United States and Canada: Kluwer Academic Publishers, 190 Old Derby Street, Hingham, MA 02043, USA
for the UK and Ireland: Kluwer Academic Publishers, MTP Press Limited, Falcon House, Queen Square, Lancaster LA1 1RN, UK
for all other countries: Kluwer Academic Publishers Group, Distribution Center, P.O. Box 322, 3300 AH Dordrecht, The Netherlands

Library of Congress Cataloging in Publication Data

Dwelling, place, and environment.

  1. Anthropo-geography--Addresses, essays, lectures.
2. Human ecology--Addresses, essays, lectures.
3. Dwellings--Social aspects--Addresses, essays, lectures
4. Phenomenology--Addresses, essays, lectures.
I. Seamon, David. II. Mugerauer, Robert.
GF49.D83 1985   304.2   85-13626
ISBN 90-247-3192-5

ISBN 90-247-3192-5 (hardback)
ISBN 90-247-3282-4 (paperback)

PRINTED IN THE NETHERLANDS

Contents

Part III. Place and dwelling

Part IV. Discovering wholes

Acknowledgments

We are grateful to the institutions and individuals who have supported our work on this volume. In particular, we would like to thank Mark Lapping, Ronald Hess, Bernd Foerster and Eugene Kremer for administrative and financial assistance; Mary Langman and Claire Waffle for secretarial aid; Harold Vandeventer for computer assistance; and Gary Coates and Lew Seibold for sympathetic interest and support. Particularly, we are grateful to Kathleen Neet-Seibold for her patience, concern and inspired typing. Robert Mugeraurer's work on the volume was facilitated by an appointment as a Visiting Scholar in the graduate school at the University of Texas at Austin. This volume was completed through a research grant from Kansas State University.

1. Dwelling, place and environment: An introduction

DAVID SEAMON and ROBERT MUGERAUER

Today, our modern Western world faces a paradoxical situation. At the height of our technological mastery, we often find ourselves separated from both the earth and our own human being. After many centuries of building our world, we meet an unsettling nexus of domination and homelessness. Confronting the powerful assumption that what matters is construction in space with our planet as raw material, we find an emerging need to take seriously what is ignored or discarded: not merely technological construction, but *dwelling*; not merely homogeneous and mathematized space, but *place*; not merely planetary raw material, but *environment*. A new attitude and approach are called for and underway as thinkers, builders, scientists and poets struggle to find a new way to face our situation. The essays of this volume are a contribution toward this effort.

In seeking a new way to see, think, understand and build, we must first question fundamentally what has happened and been assumed. Our current human dilemma is not simply a problem calling for new improved solutions. Indeed, the dilemma is not a problem at all, if by "problem" we mean an issue separate from us which must be confronted, disassembled, and solved. As the French philosopher Gabriel Marcel argues, we deal here with a "mystery" – a situation in which we are inextricably involved, and where we must call ourselves into question if we are to see again clearly.[1] The task is a questioning of who we are and what we truly want and need. We must ask what human dwelling on earth is and how it is possible to have a home.

To answer these questions, the essays of this volume, either directly or implicitly, turn to phenomenology, which offers a way of thinking rigorously and of describing accurately the complex relation between person and world. At the same time, phenomenology allows phenomena to be understood as they are without the reduction or distortion so often the result of positivist science or the many styles of structuralism. The phenomenological approach has made its way from philosophy to such diverse fields as psychology, philosophical anthropology, the history of religion and literary and art criticism.[2] At the same time, hermeneutics developed as a complementary approach emphasizing history, interpretation and language.[3] Now, a new phase has begun as a phenomenology and hermeneutics of embodied person and world considers the complexly integrated core of how we live. Just as medicine is in the midst of rethinking the nature of health, patient, and medical practice, so the environmental disciplines are reconsidering the nature of the person–environment relationship, particularly in regard to building and designing.[4]

The specific catalyst for this volume has been a series of special sessions on "Phenomenologies of Place and Environment," held at the annual meetings of the Society for Phenomenology and the Human Sciences (SPHS) since 1980. The purpose of these sessions has been to bring together scholars and practitioners whose work involves a phenomenological or hermeneutical approach to the person–environment relationship.[5] The focus has been on such themes as environmental ethics, sacred space, environmental behavior, sense of place, and a phenomenology of architectural design. Now, the time seems ripe to gather together what has developed from these sessions, since this work offers perspectives and discoveries that could have significant impact on the environmental disciplines, both at a conceptual and applied level.

As we speak of them here, the environmental disciplines include all fields which in one way or another deal with the relationship between human behavior and environment, particularly its geographical, ecological and architectural aspects. The disciplines most clearly central to such research are geography, environmental psychology and architecture. At the same time, philosophers, sociologists, urban designers, students of religion, and so forth are experimenting with a qualitative, descriptive approach to environment and environmental experience. In this volume, we have sought to highlight this broad range of researchers, and authors include three architects and an urban designer (Dovey, Saile, Bognar, and Violich); four geographers (Relph, Hill, Seamon and Buttimer); three philosophers (Mugerauer, Grange and Zimmerman); and two psychologists (Lang and Jager). Music, physics, and the phenomenology of religion are each represented by one contributor (Schafer, Bortoft and Brenneman, respectively).

In choosing the essays presented here, all of them specially requested for this volume, we have been encouraged and heartened by the way in which themes among the essays resurface and resonate. Though our request for essays was broad and open-ended, we found that topics such as seeing, authenticity, interpretation, wholeness, care, and dwelling ran as undercurrents throughout. Our major hope is that each essay plays a part in revealing a larger whole of meaning which says much about a more humane relationship with places, environments and the earth as our home.

Part I. Beginnings and directions

At the start, we recognize the tremendous debt this volume owes to philosopher Martin Heidegger (1890–1976), whose ontological excavations into the nature of human existence and meaning provide the philosophical foundations for many of the essays, particularly those in Part I of the volume. Above all else, Heidegger was regarded by his students and colleagues as a *master teacher*. He not only thought deeply but was also able to show others how to think and to question. Since he, perhaps more than anyone else in this century, provides the instruction for doing a phenomenology and hermeneutic of humanity's existential situation, he is seminal for phenomenological and hermeneutical research in the environmental disciplines. He presents in his writings what conventional scholarly work, especially the scientific approach, lacks; he helps us to evoke and understand things through a method that allows them to come forth as they are; he provides a new way to speak about and care for our human nature and environment.

The essays of Part I immediately demonstrate the important influence of Heidegger's thought in establishing the philosophical underpinnings of the volume. Edward Relph's opening essay, though directed nominally to the ontological foundations of geography as a discipline, has significance for all researchers concerned with people's existential relationships with world, including the earth's geographical aspects. Borrowing from Heidegger, Relph points out that people are always immersed in an environment and world. One phenomenological aim is to understand the nature of this immersion, which provides the touchstone and background for any formal, scientific consideration of environmental elements and interconnections. This style of understanding, says Relph, is grounded in *wonder:* "a compassionate intelligence that seeks to see things in themselves." Wonder is often the heart of genuine phenomenological seeing. A primary concern in our selecting the essays for this volume was the degree to which they evoked this "sense of wonder about the world as we experience it."

Drawing on several of the same Heideggerian themes as Relph, Kimberly Dovey in his essay considers the phenomenon of authenticity, a topic crucial to much phenomenological endeavor. Dovey concludes that authentic environmental meaning is not a condition of the physical world but, rather, is a situation "of connectedness in the relationship between people and their world." Environmental authenticity is a modern dilemma because only today do technological, economic and social structures exist which sever finished products from the processes which produced them. In earlier times, the designer of place was usually the builder; and make, user. Bonds between form and process, surface and depth, perception and action were more readily maintained. Artifact, building and landscape more often arose from direct wish and need; the result was a meaningful connection between thing and human world. The question Dovey leaves us with is how today's buildings and environments can again evoke a sense of place and authenticity. Several later essays offer concrete suggestions for fostering a renewed environmental integrity.

Robert Mugerauer's essay brings attention to another crucial Heideggerian theme – the significance of language in our encounter with the world. Mugerauer argues that the world is not a brute given nor a construction of consciousness. Rather, world and language are given together; depending on how we make contact with and describe the world, so it reveals itself to us. The need is to find "fitting words" through which "the environment is able to appear." Mugerauer speaks of an *environmental hermeneutics* – i.e., a way of interpretation which evokes "what things are and how they are related to other things in the webs of particular lives and places." In discussing the reciprocity between local language and essential qualities of place, Mugerauer speaks of authentic meaning in the same way that Dovey speaks of authentic architecture and landscape.

The last essay in Part I by Joseph Grange integrates and extends themes of the earlier essays, using the notion of *place* as one means for examining the person–environment relationship. Grange explores "person" here by considering the role of the body in making and giving meaning to the world. Presenting the four themes of posture, orientation, feel and comprehension, Grange concludes that we are first of all bound *bodily* to our world. Next, by considering the way that the environment engages people, Grange explores its material, social and built dimensions and attends to the crucial, multifaceted exchange and engagement between body and environment, nature as one and nature as many, self and others, natural and human worlds. An openness of both body and environment, says Grange, is an existential foundation of human immersion in the world.

Each of the four essays in Part I considers the reciprocal ways in which person houses world and world houses person. The essays suggest that this reciprocity is multidimensional, extending from the most elementary level of physical embodiment to the cultural realm of intellectual, affective and symbolic meanings. At the same time, the world begins with its base of nature and extends to include personal, interpersonal and built dimensions. The essays suggest that any authentic link between these various strata of people and world involves a fit which allows person and world to be what they are as, at the same time, they reflect and are reflected in each other.

Part II. Environment and place

A phenomenology of environment and place examines three major themes: first, the essential qualities and interconnections of human environmental experience; second, essential qualities of environment, such as sound, topography, light, and spatial qualities, which promote a particular character of place and landscape; third, the larger context of societal and symbolic environments fundamental to place. R. Murray Schafer's essay overviews the sonic environment, or *soundscape*, as he calls it. Unlike the objects of visual perception which generally have physical form and, therefore, permanence, the world of sound is fleeting and supports a way of knowing much different from that of vision: "seeing is analytic and reflective. Sounding is active and generative." Schafer suggests that the dominance of sight in the modern world has led us to lose contact with the soundscape. For example, modern architecture, particularly in its use of glass, "divided the usually perceived world from its aural, tactile and olofactory accompaniments." Schafer asks how we can regain contact with the soundscape and use it as a vehicle for the enhancement of human experience.

Miriam Helen Hill's essay introduces a phenomenology of the blind person's environmental experience. Her conclusions, especially those arising from the comments of blind freedom-fighter Jacques Lusseyran, suggest that human perceptual capabilities are much richer and more powerful than most sighted people realize. The foundation of any thorough encounter with the world, argues Hill, is grounded in the body, whose sensibilities she depicts in terms of object perception and body as preconscious but intelligent subject. This multifaceted bodily awareness concretely demonstrates the more abstract notions of orientation, feel and comprehension of which Grange spoke earlier.

These essays by Schafer and Hill consider how embodied person and environment interrelate and merge experientially. Schafer argues that technological developments have dramatically changed the soundscape, while Hill points out how the blind person's perceptual world, though lacking in vision, is still complete and whole. These essays also suggest that with self-conscious understanding and intention, our experiential bonds with the world can widen and deepen. In turn, the environment and world as experienced can expand in dimensions and meanings.

The next three essays in Part II focus on the cultural and symbolic dimensions of environment and place. As Relph explained in his opening essay, places are qualitatively different from landscape or space in that they "are constituted in our memories and affections through repeated encounters and complex associations." In the last three essays of Part II, various dimensions of place are explored, from the sense of place evoked by Yugoslavian coastal towns to the quality of sacredness associated with the holy wells of Ireland and the natural landscape of the American Southwest. A key question is how the researcher as outsider can find a way to empathize with place and make contact with its special character, which for the insider of that place is generally taken-for-granted and not explicitly articulated.

Francis Violich's essay examines the sense of place for four towns on the Dalmatian coast of Yugoslavia. These towns have dramatically contrasting characters, in spite of certain shared features such as similar size, architecture and natural vegetation. Violich suggests that a key to the differences can be found in varying land–sea interphases, which he describes in terms of four metaphors: "urban arena," "ladder," "open arms," and "urban ship." In reaching this conclusion, Violich conducts a firsthand reading of the four sites, walking through each village, carefully looking and reflecting, and recording his insights in written and graphic form. His approach serves as one innovative model for studying places in sympathetic, qualitative fashion.

The essays by Walter Brenneman and David G. Saile give attention to the spiritual qualities of environment and place. Brenneman examines Ireland's holy springs, more commonly called "wells." He argues that these wells consolidate two different forces: the *sacred* and *loric*. The former, Brenneman points out, is a centrifugal force and underlies all universal religions, patterns and structures – for example, myths and rituals repeated in the same way and times throughout a sacred world, as, for instance, the Catholic Mass. In contrast, loric power is centripetal, drawing itself in toward a center. In terms of a sense of sacred place, Brenneman argues, the loric power is crucial because it endows a particular site with uniqueness, as with the Irish holy wells. Only much later, once Catholicism had gained power in Ireland, did the wells become a symbol of the sacred. For a phenomenology of place, Brenneman's most intriguing point is that loric power generates a sense of intimacy, yet that intimacy is "completely hidden to those who possess it." Like Violich, Brenneman provides a valuable guide for exploring this intimacy and describing it explicitly.

David G. Saile's essay on Pueblo dwelling in the southwestern United States echoes several of Brenneman's themes, effectively demonstrating the juncture of sacred and loric powers at a community and regional scale. Focusing on insiders and outsiders' sense of Pueblo dwelling and place, Saile describes the elaborate way in which environmental elements such as mountains, lakes, caves, springs, shrines, village layout and buildings fit together to provide a landscape fostering and reflecting a profound sacred meaning. Saile suggests that each particular place and site possesses its own special loric quality, yet underlying the uniqueness are sacred themes and patterns more or less common to all Pueblo groups. Through his discussion of outsiders' views of the Pueblo world, Saile also demonstrates how readily descriptions of that world can be distorted and thus elaborates Mugerauer's theme of the relation between environment and language.

In the last essay of Part II, Botond Bognar examines a way in which phenomenology might be used in the architectural design studio. He argues that conventional studio teaching too often presents architectural design as a problem to be solved scientifically or aesthetically. Instead, Bognar argues that a more sensitive design might arise if students were first introduced to an experiential approach to environment and design – i.e., coming to realize how spaces, landscapes and places work or do not work in terms of human experience and behavior. In the last part of his essay, Bognar describes a series of exercises he conducts with beginning design students to sensitize them to the human meaning of environment and place. His essay suggests one way in which an empathetic awareness of environmental and architectural experience might be used practically to promote more sensitive environmental design. As Violich, Saile and Bognar indicate in their essays, a heightened awareness of places and the people who live in and use them may help in the creation, protection, and regeneration of successful environments. Saile, Brenneman, and Bognar's essays give attention to means for establishing an understanding of places, while Violich suggests practical thematic implications such as readability, freedom of choice, formal contrast, cultural heritage, and so forth. The suggestion is that phenomenological examination of place provides innovative conceptual angles to the person–environment relationship and also provides insights into a style of design and planning more in touch with the spirit of place.

Part III. Place and dwelling

Especially as thought by Heidegger, dwelling involves the process by which a place in which we exist becomes a personal world and home. Dwelling incorporates environments and places but extends beyond them, signifying our inescapable immersion in the present world as well as the possibility of reaching beyond to new places, experiences and ideas.

The essays in Part III examine place and dwelling as both a state of being and process. The first essay by Richard Lang considers dwelling as embodied inhabiting. Echoing themes from Grange, Lang considers the home as an extension of bodily existence; he looks at one aspect of the home — the door — as a phrasing for access and disclosure. The door, Lang argues, concretizes and reflects the experience of transition, "animating in a visible manner the dialectic of inside and outside." In a similar way, Bernd Jager examines the relationship among body, house and city. Like Grange and Lang, Jager emphasizes the significance of physical embodiment, particularly through architectural expression, in establishing a sense of familiarity and dwelling. Both body and built environment, says Jager, are visible as at the same time they foster vision. In this portrayal, Jager points to a useful new way of phrasing the intimate relationship and immersion between person and world: the physical world is what one sees, but it is also the foundation and context for that seeing. The embodied world, therefore, has a primary role in sustaining particular modes of human being and becoming. The designer has the responsibility to create a built environment which projects and supports a civilized seeing and a humane inhabitation.

The next essay by David Seamon examines the phenomenon of changing places and therefore considers dwelling and place from the viewpoint of temporal process. Using the "Emigrant" novels of Swedish novelist Vilhelm Moberg, Seamon probes the experience of leaving one world and settling another. A major conclusion is that appropriate dwelling involves a suitable balance between home and journey, memory and expectation, past and present. The essay also illustrates the use which imaginative literature can have in phenomenological inquiry. In the last essay of Part III, Michael E. Zimmerman points to the future and asks practically what dwelling is and what it might become. He argues that we must not take Heidegger's philosophy too easily and superficially, particularly in regard to what dwelling requires. What is needed, says Zimmerman, "is more profound understanding of who we are, so that we can behave more appropriately on earth." Heidegger's "letting beings be" must not become a slogan for planning and policy but, rather, a beacon which leads us to a deeper awareness of self and world.

Part IV. Discovering wholes

A central aspect of phenomenology is the identification and description of *wholes* – i.e., complexes of pattern and meaning which outline the underlying, continuing order of things, processes and experiences. Several of the earlier essays have explored various environmental wholes – for example, Relph's outline of the components of geographical being-in-the-world or Hill's picture of the underlying dynamics of blind persons' environmental experience. These wholes may relate more to the environment – as in Schafer's soundscape or Violich's land–water relationship. On the other hand, the wholes may be closer to the "person" pole of the person–environment relationship, as with Grange and Lang's emphasis on bodily inhabitation.

In the phenomenologist's quest for wholes, specific environmental elements or experiences are the base for wider generalizations about behavior, landscape, meaning, and so forth. The search is for underlying *structures* – networks of relationships marking out essential dimensions of the thing, event or experience. These structures incorporate a series of intrastructural connections and tensions which in their various combinations generate particular modes and contexts of meanings, behaviors and experiences.[6]

In the first essay of Part IV, Anne Buttimer examines the use of symbols as one means for searching out wholes. Her focus is the symbolism of water, which, she says, is an integral component of any complete understanding of human dwelling. Analyzing written materials from different times and places, Buttimer directs attention to the themes of identity, order, and niche as one way of portraying water symbolism as a whole. To suggest the practical value of these three themes, Buttimer indicates their use in facilitating dialogue between the lay public and experts in water management.

The last essay in the volume, Henri Bortoft's discussion of counterfeit and authentic wholes, summarizes much of the discussion on method and meaning highlighted in earlier essays. Particularly, Bortoft says much about a phenomenology of dwelling; he extends to all human looking and seeing the theme of authenticity discussed by Dovey in relation to environment. What are wholes, asks Bortoft, and in what way must we work to see and understand them? Beginning with the example of the hologram, Bortoft moves to a phenomenology of authentic interpretation. A whole is neither the sum of its parts nor some entity beyond its parts. Rather, the whole comes to presence through a careful reading of the parts. Bortoft discusses Goethe's way of science as one means for discovering and interpreting wholes. Then, returning to Heidegger, Bortoft argues that a science of authentic wholeness would not only promote a clearer seeing of phenomena but also generate a deeper compassion and reverence for nature and the environment.

Commonalities

Many common themes crisscross the essays of this volume and point toward a whole whose core is authentic knowing, doing and being, especially in regard to nature, place and dwelling. In identifying this core of the essays more precisely, one can say that a first major focus is *seeing and saying:* How can we deepen and extend accurate, concerned contact with the phenomenon we study? How can we find words that thoughtfully describe the phenomenon. Such seeing, as Bortoft particularly emphasizes, is more than intellectual: it involves a holistic, intuitive dimension related to dedication, reciprocity, and a wish to see. How to foster such heartfelt seeing, particularly in education, is a question crucial in today's times of homelessness and environmental degradation. Several of the essays point to practical ways through which researchers can incorporate a deeper, more encompassing mode of understanding.

Clearly, this mode of seeing and understanding requires a substantive focus, which in most general terms here is the *person—environment relationship*. All the essays in the volume deal with some aspect of environment, place or environmental experience. The aim is an accurate sighting of the underlying structures of the particular environmental aspect, be it soundscape, spatial behavior, settling, or whatever. A major conclusion indicated by the essays is that the nature of place and environmental experience is considerably more subtle, complex and multidimensional than conventional positivist or structural portraits suggest. The human component of the person—environment relationship ranges in modes of experience from the basic perceptual and bodily sensibilities described by Grange and Schafer to the styles of heightened, refined awareness suggested by Hill and Bortoft.

In the same way, environments, landscapes and places are multifaceted in character, projecting a range of world which extends from tangible sense data to less visible qualities such as atmosphere, spirit, and sacredness. A phenomenology of the person–environment relationship must work to delineate this extraordinary range of environment and environmental experience. The aim is an ordered presentation which remains faithful to the nature of particular places, events, and experiences yet relates their meaning to a wider pattern of underlying structures and interconnections.

A third underlying theme of the essays is *harmony*, which appears here in a variety of ways – for example, between seer and thing seen, person and world, theory and practice, dwelling and building, and natural and human environments. One particularly important reciprocity here is between theory and practice, thinking and doing – i.e., how can scholarly sightings relate to the world of policy and design; and, in turn, how can that world of practice support and extend authentic seeing? Heidegger's thinking, as evidenced especially in the essays of Dovey, Bognar, Zimmerman and Bortoft, has direct bearing here. The indication is that a major point of union between theory and practice is in design, through which sensitive seeing and building grounded in dwelling would strengthen the world ecologically, humanly, and spiritually. Each of the essays in larger or smaller measure contributes to some aspect of this integration, either through implications directly relevant to design or through extending awareness of various aspects of the person–environment relationship.

Notes

1. Gabriel Marcel, *The Mystery of Being* (London: Harvill Press, 1950), vol. 1, pp. 211–212.
2. On the history of phenomenology, see Herbert Spiegelberg, *The Phenomenological Movement* (The Hague: Martinus Nijhoff, 1982). On phenomenology and psychology, see Herbert Spiegelberg, *Phenomenology in Psychology and Psychiatry* (Evanston: Northwestern University Press, 1972); Amedeo Giorgi, Anthony Barton and Charles Maes, eds., *Duquesne Studies in Phenomenological Psychology*, vol. IV (Pittsburgh: Duquesne University Press, 1983). On philosophical anthropology, see Marjorie Greene, *Approaches to a Philosophical Biology* (New York: Basic Books, 1968); Helmut Plessner, *Philosophische Anthropologie* (Frankfurt: S. Fischer, 1970). On phenomenology and the history of religion, see Mircea Eliade, *Cosmos and History* (New York: Harper and Row, 1959); Gerardus van der Leeuw, *Religion in Essence and Manifestation*, 2 vols. (New York: Harper and Row, 1963). On phenomenology and literary criticism, see Robert Magliola, *Phenomenology and Literature* (West Lafayette, Indiana: Purdue University Press, 1977). On phenomenology and art criticism, see Robert Rosenblum, *Modern Painting and the Northern Romantic Tradition* (New York: Harper and Row, 1975). For an excellent discussion of method and epistemological

commitment in the human sciences, see Donald Polkinghorne, *Methodology for the Human Sciences* (Albany: State University of New York Press, 1983).

3. For an introduction to hermeneutics, see Richard E. Palmer, *Hermeneutics* (Evanston: Northwestern University Press, 1969); Josef Bleicher, *Contemporary Hermeneutics* (London: Routledge and Kegan Paul, 1980).

4. For a phenomenological approach to medicine, see Edmund Pellegrino, *Humanism and the Physician* (Knoxville: University of Tennessee Press, 1979); Richard M. Zaner, *The Context of Self: A Phenomenological Inquiry Using Medicine as a Clue* (Athens: Ohio University Press, 1981).

5. The first of these special sessions was organized by philosopher Steven Skousgaard for the 1980 annual meetings of the Society for Phenomenology and Existential Philosophy (SPEP) in Ottawa, Canada. Since then, sessions on the phenomenology of place and environment have been held under the aegis of SPHS and participants have included philosophers, geographers, architects, psychologists, and urban designers.

6. See Maurice Merleau-Ponty, *The Structure of Behavior* (Boston: Beacon Press, 1963); David Seamon, "The Phenomenological Contribution to Environmental Psychology," *Journal of Environmental Psychology* 2 (1982): 133; Amedeo Giorgi, "The Relationships Among Level, Type, and Structure," in Amedeo Giorgi, Richard Knowles and David L. Smith, eds., *Duquesne Studies in Phenomenological Psychology*, vol. III (Pittsburgh: Duquesne University Press, 1979), pp. 81–92.

7. One invaluable contribution to the harmonization of theory and practice not represented in this volume is the attempt by architect Christopher Alexander and colleagues to establish a "Pattern Language" – i.e., a set of universal, interconnected elements and qualities which underlie successful human places, be they regions, cities, towns, neighborhoods, or buildings. In one sense, Pattern Language can be described as an implicit phenomenology of design elements supporting a sense of place. Alexander's work is a crucial complement to many of the present essays, and the reader is directed to the following books by Alexander, all published by Oxford University Press, New York: *A Pattern Language* (1977); *The Timeless Way of Building* (1979); *The Oregon Experiment* (1975); *The Linz Cafe* (1981); *The Production of Houses* (1985). For a discussion of Alexander's latest work, see Steven Grabow, *Christopher Alexander: The Search for a New Paradigm in Architecture* (London: Oriel Press, 1983); Pete Retondo, "An Uncommon Bench: A Small Building by Architect Christopher Alexander and Associates," *CoEvolutionary Quarterly* 10 (1984): 78–85; James Shipsky, "Christopher Alexander: Theory and Practice," *Architecture* 74 (1984): 54–63. For one evaluation of the practical effectiveness of Pattern Language, see Dorit Fromm and Peter Bosselmann, "Mexicali Revisited: Seven Years Later," *Places* 1 (1983–84): 78–90.

Part I

Beginnings and directions

2. Geographical experiences and being-in-the-world: The phenomenological origins of geography

EDWARD RELPH

The beginning of academic disciplines lies in curiosity about the nature of the world, and especially in attempts to give order to this curiosity by finding ways to direct it. Such efforts can often be traced back to the philosophers and scientists of ancient Greece, and certainly the first formulation of geography as a coherent body of knowledge can be ascribed to Eratosthenes, the Greek librarian at Alexandria from about 234 to 196 B.C., who apparently coined the term to refer to the description of the earth.[1] While there are doubts about whether the 'geography' of Eratosthenes meant the whole earth or just regions of it, and about whether descriptions were to be written or presented cartographically, it is clear that from its inception geography has served to satisfy a deep curiosity about what the world is like elsewhere.

The history of geography is well established. Why, then, might it be necessary to examine the phenomenological origins of geography and people's relationships with their geographical environment? Surely in this context, "phenomenological" can refer to little more than the unordered everyday experiences of the type which the work of Eratosthenes transcended? To return to such experiences seems tantamount to a dismissal of two-thousand years of scientific geographical achievement.

This is not the case. Phenomenology does indeed have to do with pre-scientific experience, but this is not its only concern. Heidegger, whose thinking provides the basis for many of the ideas in this essay, described phenomenology as "the process of letting things manifest themselves."[2] The similarity of the words notwithstanding, phenomenology is quite unlike biology, theology or other '-ologies,' because it neither characterizes its subject matter in advance nor indicates the object of its research.[3] Phenomenology is a way of thinking that enables us to see clearly something that is, in effect, right before our eyes yet somehow obscured from us – something so taken for granted that it is ignored or allowed to be disguised by a cloak of abstractions. For Heidegger this "something" was preeminently *Being* – the fact that things exist at all. The elucidation of Being requires not a rejection of scientific knowledge so much as an attempt to understand the relationships between scientific and prescientific consciousness.

Consider the phenomenon of curiosity. In *Being and Time*, Heidegger suggests that curiosity "seeks restlessness and the excitement of continual novelty and changing encounters."[4] It was curiosity which led Eratosthenes to measure the earth's circumference; it was curiosity which drove subsequent generations of men and women to seek the source of the Nile and to explore the continental interiors. Curiosity is a kind of dissatisfied knowing that always pushes on to further questions, and it is therefore a distinctive feature of scientific forms of inquiry. But by asking questions and offering answers, conventional science also dispels wonder. Wonder is the mark of a prescientific attitude – that is, of a compassionate intelligence that seeks to see things in and for themselves. Heidegger's term for wonder is "marvelling," within which there is an admiration for the earth with its myriad places and landscapes. What we understand of the world derives both from wonder and from curiosity.

An account of the phenomenological origins of geography is, perhaps, an astringent academic exercise. Some geographers and other students of the environment may be deeply interested in such a task, but it is unlikely to arouse widespread enthusiasm. This lack of interest is unfortunate. The experiences of places, spaces and landscapes in which academic geography originates are a fundamental part of everyone's experience, and geography has no exclusive claim to them. Indeed, one of the first aims of a phenomenology of geography should be to retrieve these experiences from the academic netherworld and to return them to everyone by reawakening a sense of wonder about the earth and its places. To do this can nevertheless provide a source of vitality and meaning for geography by casting it in its original light, where 'original' has the dual meaning of 'first' and 'new.'

The question of the phenomenological origins of geography can be addressed by an examination of the relationship of human beings to their world and the connections between this relationship and various geographical concepts such as region and place. Accordingly, this essay has two major sections. The first is an account of being-in-the-world, which is the prescientific (i.e., everyday, immediate or original) relationship that people have with their surroundings. This section is based on Heidegger's discussion in

Being and Time of environmentality.[5] The second, longer section examines the connections between scientific geography, being-in-the-world, and a geography of wonder that we know through direct experience. This discussion draws on the work of the French historian, Eric Dardel, who examines geographic experience, or as he calls it *géographicité* – the ties of region, landscape, space and place that link people to the earth.[6]

Being-in-the-world

The geographer's quest, writes Yi-Fu Tuan, is for understanding of "man-in-the-world."[7] This focus makes immediate sense, in so far as geographers have conventionally dealt with the relationships between, for instance, human settlement patterns and topography. Tuan, however, intended more than the study of material linkages, for he qualified his conclusion by explaining that "the phenomenologist studies neither 'man' in the abstract, nor the 'world' in the abstract but 'man-in-the-world'."[8] There is, in other words, something about his phrase "man-in-the-world" which is not immediately obvious. Like many such expressions taken from philosophy, it enfolds a wealth of meaning and subtlety. In particular, it points to being-in-the-world, a phenomenon to which Heidegger devoted much of *Being and Time*. Being-in-the-world is the basic state of human existence, and it indicates the fact that everything which exists has an environment.[9]

Heidegger presents being-in-the-world as a unitary phenomenon with three constitutive elements.[10] First, there is "being-in," a kind of relationship that is full of concern and marked by ties of work, affection, responsibility, interest and memory; or it may be characterized by deficient modes of concern, such as leaving things undone and neglecting responsibility. Second, there is the entity which has being-in-the-world as a feature of the way it is; this entity is the self. Third, there is the "in-the-world." This notion is more difficult and needs explanation. The "world" for Heidegger is not nature, nor the sum of things which happen to surround us. "The world comes not afterward, but beforehand;" we do not specifically occupy ourselves with the world, for it is so self-evident and so much a matter of course and we are so implicated in it that we are usually quite oblivious to it.[11]

As the taken-for-granted sphere of activity and interest that embraces existence, the world has two forms – *presence-at-hand* and *readiness-to-hand*.[12] To think about the world or the entities within it as abstract things is to render them subject to observation, to make them the object of casual curiosity and to distance oneself from them. This attitude, for Heidegger, makes the world present-at-hand. This phrase is his expression for self-conscious, perhaps disinterested reflection, or any attitude in which there occurs a feeling of separation from matters. Thus, in asking, "How can this city be explained as a geographical phenomenon?", or, more mundanely, "How do I find my way to the new city hall?", the relationship is one of presence-at-hand. An element of self-awareness inserts itself between me and my world. This can happen because I choose to be detached and disinterested, because I encounter something unfamiliar which causes me to stop and reflect, or because I am overtaken by a mood of alienation.

A more fundamental mode of being-in-the-world is readiness-to-hand. By virtue of making, considering, participating, discussing, moving around, producing something, attending to something and looking after it – by virtue of all such activities – beings are always and already in a world with which they are concerned.[13] No matter how much we may reflect and abstract, we are already in a direct and immediate relationship with the world. In this concernful relationship, things are ready-to-hand. Heidegger writes: "What we 'first' hear is never noises or complexes of sound, but the creaking wagon, the motor-cycle. We hear the column on the march, the north wind, the woodpecker tapping, the fire crackling."[14] In this readiness-to-hand, there is no self-conscious reflection about what or how things are. One already knows.

For Heidegger, the primordial form of readiness-to-hand lies in using. Wood to a carpenter, stone to a sculptor, an engine to a mechanic – each is a relationship which is not merely spatial but which radiates meanings that derives from grouping, adjusting and using things. Things which are encountered as ready-to-hand in use Heidegger calls "equipment."[15] This term illustrates the practical value of things and implies that their use always occurs in a context. The pen and paper I use are equipment. I pick up my pen, uncap it, write with it not thoughtlessly but with at most a gentle, scarcely conscious effort of thought that acknowledges the special qualities of this pen and paper and allows me to adjust my writing slightly to accommodate them. The pen and paper as equipment are simultaneously part of a context which includes a desk, a lamp, books, and so on.

Is the world entirely comprised of ready-to-hand equipment and present-at-hand entities? Heidegger does not address this question directly, though many of his examples and comments indicate that there is another aspect to the world as we experience it. When he writes, for example, of the noise of the motorcycle, or of going for a stroll in the woods, it is clear that this motorcycle and these woods are not theoretically observed and present-at-hand. Yet neither are they precisely ready-to-hand equipment. They are perhaps best understood as part of a ready-to-hand context or background that is seen and sensed in its everyday immediacies, and which embraces equipment, but which cannot itself be actively used. This background is, to adapt a phrase of Heidegger's from a slightly different context, "inconspicuously familiar."[16] In other words, it is so well known to us that we accept it as being what is is, and though we may notice the seasonal changes in the forest, or the daily round of activities on the street in front of our house, we do so without any present-at-hand attitude that distances us from them.

For the purpose of this essay, the important aspects of being-in-the-world are presence-at-hand and the readiness-to-hand of equipment and its background. These aspects can easily be misunderstood, so a caution is warranted. Presence-at-hand and readiness-to-hand are not Heidegger's terms for objectivity and subjectivity, and they are not alternative attitudes which we can choose to adopt or to reject at will. Rather, as the phrases themselves suggest, they are descriptions of different modes of closeness and involvement with the world which are necessarily part of existence. It makes no sense to criticize or to promote either one by itself, for both attitudes are part of the unitary whole of being-in-the-world.

Geography, geographical experience and being-in-the-world

Being-in-the-world embraces the fact that there is always and already an environment for each of us before we become curious about the earth and the location and character of its different places. What then is the connection between being-in-the-world and geography? Is geography an elaboration of certain aspects of being-in-the-world that renders them present-at-hand? Can the concepts of academic geography be traced back to more fundamental forms of existence? To address these questions, it is necessary to bring forward that aspect of being-in-the-world most clearly associated with geographical thought, and which I have described above as the world of background or context revealed through circumspection. "Bringing forward" here means that the connection between being-in-the-world and geography will be examined. In order to emphasize this connection, the world of background can be considered in terms of geographical experiences of regions, landscapes, spaces and places.

An initial clarification of what is meant by "geographical experiences" can be achieved by considering William James's remarks about religious experience.[17] James argued that abstract definitions of the essence of religion are unsatisfactory because there are so many spiritual understand-

ings (love, fear, the infinite, and so forth) that we can only conclude that
"religion" is a collective noun. Instead, James sought to clarify religion
through a study of personal religious experience. Institutional religion has
to do with churches and ritual; it is "an external art, the art of winning the
favour of the gods."[18] Personal religion has to do with individuals' experience of whatever they consider divine – be it ecstasy, awe or matters
of conscience. Churches and rituals have some role in such experiences but
in the end such influences are secondary, since the founders of churches
and sects were originally motivated by their own experiences and faith. In
personal religion "the relation goes direct from heart to heart, from soul to
soul, between man and his maker," and for this neither ceremony nor institution is needed.[19] In order to grasp the varied character of personal
religion, James reformulated it as "religious experience;" that is to say, he
brought forward those aspects of personal religion which could be described clearly and communicated to others.

Geographical experience is a less familiar term, though possibly a more
ordinary phenomenon than religious experience. It refers to the entire realm
of feelings, acts and experiences of individuals in which they apprehend
themselves in a distinct relationship with their environment. These experiences are not as intense as those of the divine, but neither are the two
always mutually exclusive: the gods are regularly encountered in views from
mountain tops.[20] Like those of institutional religion, definitions of academic
geography pose problems. The practitioners of geography have rarely
agreed on the aims and methods of their subject, which is now variously
defined as a rational science of locations, the study of person–environment
relations in space, the study of spatial organization, and so on. What geographers do in their research and writing has no identifiable common focus.
It can only be concluded that geography has no single definition but is a collective noun embracing a variety of approaches and aims.

On first consideration, the relationship between academic geography and
being-in-the-world is tenuous and limited. It is tenuous because much of
present-day geography is technical and far removed from everyday experience – it is virtually impossible to see any connection between, for example, investigations of mechanisms for the geographical transmission of
economic fluctuations and the readiness-to-hand of equipment. Further, the
relationship is limited because only a small fraction of the population has a
detailed knowledge of academic geography and, therefore, few people are
able to make the connection between it and their personal experiences of
places and landscapes. Geographical experiences, however, do not suffer
from this obscurity. Though they are not commonly known by name, they are

experiences which everyone has and which require no textbooks or special methods to be appreciated. They go directly from place to person and from person to place. Eric Dardel, in his book, *L'Homme et la Terre: Nature de la Réalité Géographique*, discloses the main aspects of geographical experience in terms of what he calls *géographicité*, which can be translated as "geographicality."[21] Geographicality is grounded in an original wondering about environment and is "the distinctive relationship which binds man to the earth . . . his way of existence and his fate."[22] It is universal, necessary and taken for granted: "Geographical reality demands an involvement of the individual through his emotions, his habits, his body, that is so complete that he comes to forget it much as he comes to forget his own physiognomy."[23] Geographicality is, therefore, unobtrusive, inconspicuously familiar, more lived than discussed. It is, in fact, a naming of the geographical forms of being-in-the-world.

Academic geography is an expression of a self-concious, present-at-hand curiosity about the world. In order to organize their information and observations, geographers have traditionally employed four concepts – region, landscape, space and place.[24] These themes, however, are not just geographical concepts. In a rather different guise, they are the contexts and subjects of geographical experiences, and in a different aspect again they are parts of being-in-the-world. Heidegger wrote at length about spatiality and region, and somewhat more elliptically about place. Of course, the terms space, place, region and landscape do not have the same meaning in each of these contexts, but initially there does seem to be an interconnection; the words, at least, slip easily from geography to geographical experience to being-in-the-world.

Region

Long considered by geographers to be the distinguishing concept of geography, "region" has recently fallen from fashion perhaps because it is not a concept which lends itself to the mathematical and statistical analyses now in favor. A geographical region is defined as a part of the earth that is distinctive from other areas and which extends as far as that distinction extends.[25] It is characterized by internal similarities of landforms, cultural history, settlement forms, climate, or a combination of all of these. Thus, one can refer to the region of New England, the semi-arid region of British Columbia, or the prairie region of Canada. A region is, in short, a particular way of classifying geographical information.

From the perspective of geographical experience, it is possible to identify with and to feel oneself in a clear relationship with a region. One can be a Southerner or a New Englander, and these identifications mean more than being from a particular region – they imply something about speech and personality. Identity with a region in this way may be rather superficial and involve simplifications of personal and place differences, but it does precede any academic, geographical attempt to classify regions. Eric Dardel writes that the world is structured into regions of lived-meaning around the place where one lives.[26] There is our home region, the area up north with its lakes and forests, and the region down east with its fishing villages. Each of these regions has its own name – the Golden Horseshoe, Muskoka, Cape Breton. The distinctive characteristics and boundaries of each region, however, are not exactly defined; there is no need for such definitions, since the regions are known already in experience.

Tuan uses "region" in a very different sense, though still in the context of geographical experience. In *Space and Place*, he writes: "Every person is at the center of his world, and circumambient space is differentiated in accordance with the schema of his body. As he moves and turns, so do the regions front-back and left-right around him."[27] Space as experienced is broken into regions that are given structure and shape by the form of our bodies. These extended bodily regions are in the first instance wholly personal, but it seems that the world, too, can take on these values. Tuan asks, therefore, if cities have front and back regions, and answers, yes, at least in some cases, such as traditional Chinese cities.[28]

In *Being and Time*, Heidegger is quite explicit that "region," as he uses the term, is not formed by things present-at-hand together.[29] Rather, a region refers to the fact that the things we use as ready-to-hand have specific places to which they belong, but there are many such places for any one thing; it is these places circumspectively kept in view which constitute the thing's region. As a simple example, my pen could be in my pocket, on my desk or in a drawer – these places together comprise its region. At the same time, a region of being-in-the-world comprises far more than a sort of unself-consciously known sum of possible locations for things ready-to-hand. To illustrate this point, Heidegger gives the example of the sun, whose light and warmth are in everyday use and ready-to-hand, and which has its own places which we call sunrise, noon, afternoon, sunset, and midnight. These places are indicators of, and give form to "celestial regions," which, Heidegger continues, "need not have any geographical meaning as yet . . . The house has its sunny side and shady size; the way it is divided up into rooms is oriented toward these, and so is the arrangement within them, according to their character as equipment. Churches and graves, for instance, are laid out according to the rising and setting of the sun – the regions of life and death . . .''[30] Thus, existence itself has regions and it both gives to and receives from these an orientation and a structure.

Landscape

''The geographic landscape,'' wrote Carl Sauer, ''is a generalization derived from the observation of individual scenes.''[31] It is, in effect, an average landscape of a region and the most visible part of regional character. In this sense, 'landscape' is a technical term used in the analysis of visual environments. It may be comprehensive, embracing both ordinary details and exceptional features, but there is no doubt that landscape in academic geography is present-at-hand. One of the commonest metaphors used by geographers for landscape is that it is a text or book that can be read and interpreted.[32] This metaphor indicates that landscape is to be approached with a measured and detached gaze of curiosity and with skepticism about why things look as they do. Landscapes in academic geography are thus seen more as objects for interpretation than as contexts of experience.

The landscapes we experience are always specific scenes, such as the landscape I see through my office window, or the skyline of Manhattan from the Staten Island Ferry. Landscapes include trees, lawnmowers, garbage bags, trucks, people, and clouds in all their particular manifestations. Strictly speaking, there is no such thing as 'landscape' – there is only *this* landscape, here and now. Furthermore, for all their visual and sensed immediacy, the landscapes of geographical experience are indeterminate phenomena. They cannot be embraced, nor touched, nor walked around. As we move, so the landscape moves, always there, in sight but out of reach. A landscape includes a multitude of things, of equipment, yet it cannot be reduced to these things. Eric Dardel wrote that ''a landscape is something more than a juxtaposition of picturesque details; it is an assemblage, a convergence, a lived-moment. There is an internal bond, an 'impression,' that unites all its elements.''[33] The bond to which Dardel refers is one of human presence and concern; landscapes, therefore, take on the very character of human existence. They can be full of life, deathly dull, exhilarating, sad, joyful or pleasant.

The word 'landscape' has little popularity except perhaps in the meaning of pleasant scenery. Landscapes are usually regarded without a word in mind for them and are presumably seen as aspects of the visual environing world.

In such seeing, they are encountered either as equipment or as inconspicuously familiar background, though these two realms are not neatly separated categories of experience. "Landscape is not, in its essence, made to be looked upon," claims Dardel, "but, rather, is an insertion of man into the world, a site for life's struggle, the manifestation of his being and that of others."[34] In such experience, landscape is part of what Heidegger understood to be the fundamental relationships of human beings to their world — that of use and of equipment which is ready-to-hand. We know landscapes, in other words, because we go hiking in the mountains, because we drive through streets on the way to work, because we encounter landscapes continually in the course of going about our daily affairs. We know them because they reveal the state of the weather and the passage of the seasons, because they harbor the places of our memories, because they are the visible matrix of where we live.

As inconspicuous backgrounds, landscapes retreat from attention. Heidegger gives an example when he writes of a street as equipment for walking: "One feels the touch of it at every step as one walks. It seems that nothing could be closer and more ready-to-hand. And yet it is more distant than the acquaintance one sees at a distance of twenty paces. The street retreats, as it were, into the background."[35] For much of the time, landscapes stay as unobtrusive backgrounds to other more important concerns, but occasionally they are brought forward into our awareness. For instance, in certain affective states, or in "moods," as Heidegger calls them, we may be predisposed to notice the world around us.[36] Perhaps this awareness is because we feel healthy and cheerful and the world seems to reflect our happiness; conversely, we may feel afraid and depressed and the dark streets and looming hills echo our fear. Landscapes may also become conspicuous when they become unusable.[37] An accident on the highway delays our journey and we notice for the first time the harshness and hardness of the crash barriers, the size of the direction signs, the separation of the highway from the adjacent landscapes. Or perhaps a familiar landmark is destroyed and its sudden absence draws our attention to the whole scene of which it was a part. In such moments, we are reflectively aware of landscapes as integral aspects of our being-in-the-world.

Space

In modern academic geography, space is that of the surface of the earth, usually assumed to be devoid of topographic anomalies. Space is, in effect, geometric. This interpretation of space enables the relative locations of cities, industries and transportation routes to become issues for geometric analysis. It is now widely held that geography is *the* science of space, by which it is meant that geography has a special claim to investigate spatial patterns and processes by using the established methods of science. In this meaning, space is an extended surface for the distribution of things present-at-hand, and no more than that.

In geographical experience, space is rarely encountered in such a pure and abstract way. Perhaps in huge human-made plazas designed to be geometric, or in looking down from an aircraft at a grid pattern of roads and fields, some element of this present-at-hand space is visible. But even in these cases, the spaces are always colorful and conditioned – much more than black lines on a white background. Dardel makes a clear distinction between geometric space of the sort taken over by scientific geographers and what he calls *geographical space:* "Geometric space is homogeneous, uniform, neutral. Geographical space is differentiated into that of the prairies, the mountains, the oceans, the equatorial forest . . . Geographical space is unique; it has its own name: Paris, Champagne, the Sahara . . . it has a horizon, a surface form, a color and density."[38]

Dardel examines five aspects of geographical space, and while these are not mutually exclusive, they are distinctive and recognizable in experience. Material spaces are those of cliffs, fields, city skylines, or sand dunes; those spaces partake of the character of the surrounding surfaces and manifest themselves directly to us as distances to be travelled in terms of the time and effort needed to climb hills or to drive across cities. Telluric space is that of depth, solidity and durability; it is the space of caves and exposed rock. "Here," wrote Goethe of an outcrop of granite, "I rest directly on a foundation which reaches into the deepest regions of the earth. In this moment the inner forces of the earth act directly upon me."[39] The space of water is formless and filled with motion. It invites special responses: the ocean offers distant horizons with their sense of adventure, a river escapes to the sea, a waterfall provides a subject for almost endless contemplation. Even more brilliant and shifting than water is the space of the air, of skies changing with cloud, mist, sunshine and rain. It can be rent by thunder, heavy with the promise of snow, eerie as the mist rises.

The geographical spaces of matter, depth, water and air are all 'natural' – that is, they are not of people's making but are found or given, and they are open or exposed. Constructed, human-made spaces – Dardel's fifth aspect of geographical space – are, in contrast, usually enclosed, offering a sense of security from the outside world. Since built spaces are human-made, they convey human purposes directly through their forms and surfaces. In Dardel's terms, they are "human intentions inscribed on the earth."[40] They include the spaces of building, of city streets and squares, of fields and fences, of an isolated farm gathering space around itself.

Geographical space is a fusion of these specific spaces of earth, air, water and human artifacts with the moods and imaginings through which we experience them. We project our attitudes and beliefs so that a cave can be a place of security or of threat, depending on our particular intentions and needs. A clearing in a forest can seem like a room or a site for magic or simply a relief from the darkness of the spaces beneath the trees. Constantly changing with weather and season and time of day, ordered by human intentions and experiences, geographical spaces are rich and complex: "the real space of geography delivers us from the infinite abstract space of geometry or of astronomy. It places us in a space of our own dimensions, in a space which gives itself to us and responds to us."[41]

It is this form of spatiality as part of being-in-the-world that Heidegger described in *Being and* Time.[42] Existence (*Dasein*) brings things closer, renders them ready-to-hand. Here, the remoteness or closeness of what is ready-to-hand need not correspond with objective distances of things present-at-hand. The house next door is a few meters away, yet it is utterly remote because my neighbor is unfriendly. Space as we encounter it immediately in experience "lacks the pure multiplicity of the three dimensions."[43] Space is not in the subject nor is the world in space but space is in the world as part of everyday experience. Human existence is spatial and its spatiality embraces closeness, separation, distance and direction as modes of existence. This existential spatiality is so complete that Heidegger suggests that a special kind of mental effort is required to see the world as present-at-hand in space or to see things as somehow distributed in a space that is given in advance.

Place

Although place is closely related to space and landscape, its experiential dimension is qualitatively different from that of landscape or space. The latter are part of any immediate encounter with the world, and so long as I can see I cannot help but see them no matter what my purpose. This is not so with places, for they are constructed in our memories and affections through repeated encounters and complex associations. Place experiences are necessarily time-deepened and memory-qualified. In geographical experience, a place is an origin; it is where one knows others and is known to others; it is where one comes from and it is one's own: "Before any choice there is this 'place,' where the foundations of earthly existence and human condition establish themselves. We can change locations, move, but this is still to look for a place; we need a base to set down our Being and to realize our possibilities, a *here* from which to discover the world, a *there* to which we can return."[44]

Geographical experience begins in places and reaches out across spaces to landscapes and the regions of existence. Specifically, it begins in the place in which I live as the center of my world, though there may be other places which serve as foci of meaning for me. Relationships to places need not be strong and positive; sometimes there is a strong affection (topophilia) for particular places, but this may be paralleled by an aversion (topophobia) for other places. Belonging to a place, feeling part of it, gives many people a positive sensation of security, yet for others it may be oppressive and restrictive. Whether we know places with a deep affection or merely as stopping points in our passage through the world, they are set apart in time and space because they have distinctive meanings for us.

How different this is from the traditional geographical idea of place, which means little more than location, though this may embrace an integrated complex of phenomena, such as street patterns, economic activities and local customs.[45] Places defined in this formal way are to be described and analyzed, their internal and external order revealed. Clearly, the academic-geographical attitude to places is one of presence-at-hand, in which the geographer is distanced from the meanings of place experience.

"When space is discovered by just looking at it," wrote Heidegger, "[it is] neutralised to pure dimensions. Places – and indeed the whole circumspectively oriented totality of places belonging to equipment ready-to-hand – get reduced to a multiplicity of positions for random Things."[46] This is an accurate description of the achievement of scientific geography, in which places have become points and mere locations. For Heidegger, place is the context of things ready-to-hand that is itself ready-to-hand. Though Heidegger did not develop this meaning of place in detail, it does seem to be fundamental to his understanding of being-in-the-world. Joseph Fell writes in a commentary on *Being and Time* that "the Being of the human being, his essential nature, is Place, the ground or clearing within which there can be disclosure of beings as what they are."[47] And to support this view he quotes from one of Heidegger's later essays: "*Dasein* names that which should first be experienced, and thence properly thought of, as Place – that is, the locale of the truth of Being."[48]

In all of Heidegger's writing there is an element of metaphor because he is trying to disclose experiences which are subtle and usually have no names. When he writes of region, space, and place, we must be careful to keep this element of metaphor in mind and not to impose our prior understanding of these words onto this thinking. Then, perhaps, we can grasp the possibilities for geographical experiences as they are carried back into the realm of being-in-the world. Understood from an experiential perspective, landscape, region, space and place appear as overlapping aspects of the fundamental unity of human beings with their total, indivisible and mundane environments. They are geographical modes of existence.

Redressing an imbalance

Scientific geography, geographical experience, and being-in-the-world are unified in a field of concern. Though they present themselves in different ways, they are inseparable. Hence it is possible to trace, for example, connections between landscape as an object of technical, academic analysis and landscape as an aspect of being-in-the-world. The presence-at-hand of academic-geographical concepts and approaches may have a different character from geographical experience, but it would be a mistake to understand the two as alternatives in opposition to one another. Rather, they are related in a complementary tension in which both can contribute to our understanding and appreciation of the world.

Nevertheless, an imbalance has apparently developed within this tension and unity, and abstract technical thinking has begun to submerge geographical experience either by making the latter seem relatively trivial or simply by obscuring it with generalizations. Heidegger states that environments can be defined simply in terms of their observable features but that "when this happens the nature which . . . assails us and enthralls us as a landscape remains hidden."[49] Immediacy of experience is thus not destroyed but concealed from us. With formal scientific approaches, this concealment is perhaps unavoidable, and Heidegger comments further: "The botanist's plants are not the flowers in the hedgerow; the source which a geographer establishes for a river is not the springhead in the dale."[50] There is not necessarily any difficulty in this; we simply have to accept that it is not possible to maintain simultaneously a detached scientific attitude and and to be open to geographical experience. When one achieves significant priority over the other, however, as scientific curiosity now has dominance over geographicality and wonder, then important possibilities for existence are denied.

This imbalance became the start for much of Heidegger's later thinking. For instance, he wrote that "All distances in time and space are shrinking. Man now reaches overnight, by plane, places which formerly took weeks and months of travel . . . Yet the frantic abolition of distances brings no nearness; for nearness does not consist in shortness of distance."[51] And elsewhere: "The power concealed in modern technology determines the relation of man to that which exists. It rules the whole earth."[52] Dardel saw evidence of this same imbalance within geography, and declared: "Geographical experience often has to turn its back on the indifference and detachment of formal geography."[53]

The problem now is to find a way of redressing this situation. Heidegger indicates clearly and repeatedly that there is no easy answer. One cannot identify the various aspects of being-in-the-world, classify them, and develop policies and educational programs to communicate them, for this is to render them present-at-hand and thereby to change their essential character. In the context of geographical experience, people cannot be trained to marvel at landscapes, nor to love their places and their planet. On the other hand, love of place and of the earth are scarcely sentimental extras to be indulged only when all technical and material problems have been resolved. They are part of being-in-the-world and prior, therefore, to all technical matters. What Heidegger argues for is a "thoughtful" and "careful" attitude to the world, and he uses these words in their exact meanings. This attitude "demands of us not to cling one-sidedly to a single idea nor to run down a one-track course of ideas," and adopts a composure toward all forms of technical thinking that understands their necessity but denies their right to dominate us.[54] In geography and other environmental disciplines, this composure will require, at the very least, a heightened awareness of the character and qualities of one's own geographical experiences and an attempt to convey to others the fundamental importance of marvelling at the places of the earth.

Notes

1. E.H. Bunbury, *A History of Ancient Geography* (New York: Dover, 1959), chap. XVI.
2. M. Heidegger, letter in W.J. Richardson, *Heidegger: Through Phenomenology to Thought* (The Hague: Martinus Nijhoff, 1967), p. xiv.
3. M.Heidegger, *Being and Time*, J. Macquarrie and E. Robinson, trans. (New York: Harper and Row, 1962), p. 59.
4. Heidegger, *Being and Time*, pp. 214–217; quotation on p. 216.
5. Heidegger, *Being and Time*, pp. 95–107.
6. Eric Dardel, *L'Homme et la Terre: Nature de la Réalité Géographique* (Paris: Presses Univer-

sitaires de France, 1952). Translations from this book are mine.

7. Yi-Fu Tuan, "Geography, Phenomenology, and the Study of Human Nature," *Canadian Geographer* 15 (1971): 191.

8. Ibid.

9. I use the term "existence" throughout this essay as the equivalent to Heidegger's expression, *Dasein*.

10. Heidegger, *Being and Time*, pp. 78–79; see, also, John MacQuarrie, *Martin Heidegger* (Virginia: John Knox Press, 1968), pp. 15–19.

11. M. Heidegger, *The Basic Problems of Phenomenology*, A. Hofstadter, trans. (Bloomington: Indiana University Press, 1982), p. 165. This work is based on lectures given by Heidegger in 1927 and therefore parallels and elaborates ideas expressed in *Being and Time*.

12. Heidegger, *Being and Time*, p. 67 and p. 101. See also M. Gelven, *A Commentary on Heidegger's Being and Time* (New York: Harper and Row, 1970), pp. 56–57.

13. Heidegger, *Being and Time*, p. 83.

14. Ibid., p. 207.

15. Ibid., p. 97.

16. Ibid., p. 137.

17. W. James, *The Varieties of Religious Experience* (London: MacMillan, 1961), pp. 39–41.

18. Ibid., p. 39.

19. Ibid., p. 40.

20. See the various examples given by James, *Varieties of Religious Experience*, p. 69 and pp. 310–312.

21. Dardel, *L'Homme et la Terre*, p. 1.

22. Ibid.

23. Ibid., p. 47.

24. This should be self-evident for geographers, but for support see J.A. May, *Kant's Concept of Geography* (Toronto: University of Toronto Press, 1970), p. 201, p. 204, and pp. 210–213; D. Harvey, *Explanation in Geography* (London: Edward Arnold, 1969), p. 187 ff.; R. Hartshorne, *Perspectives on the Nature of Geography* (Chicago: Rand McNally, 1969).

25. Hartshorne, *Perspectives*, p. 130.

26. Dardel, *L'Homme et la Terre*, p. 15.

27. Yi-Fu Tuan, *Space and Place* (Minneapolis: University of Minnesota Press, 1977), p. 41.

28. Ibid.

29. Heidegger, *Being and Time*, p. 136. The translators' footnote indicates that the German word *Gegend*, translated here as "region," has no exact English equivalent.

30. Ibid., p. 137.

31. C.O. Sauer, "The Morphology of Landscape," in *Land and Life*, J. Leighly, ed. (Berkeley: University of California Press, 1967), p. 322.

32. See, for example, P. Lewis, "Axioms for Reading the Landscape," in *The Interpretation of Ordinary Landscapes*, D.W. Meinig, ed. (New York: Oxford University Press, 1979), pp. 11–32.

33. Dardel, *L'Homme et la Terre*, p. 41.

34. Ibid., p. 44.

35. Heidegger, *Being and Time*, pp. 141–142.

36. Ibid., pp. 172–173.

37. Ibid., pp. 103–105, where these issues are discussed in terms of conspicuousness, obtrusiveness and obstinacy.

38. Dardel, *L'Homme et la Terre*, p. 2. The following discussion is a summary of pp. 9–41.

39. Goethe, cited in ibid., p. 21.
40. Ibid., p. 40.
41. Ibid., p. 35.
42. Heidegger, *Being and Time*, p. 134–148.
43. Ibid., p. 145.
44. Dardel, *L'Homme et la Terre*, p. 56.
45. F. Lukermann, "Geography as a Formal Intellectual Discipline and the Way in Which it Contributes to Human Knowledge," *Canadian Geographer* 8 (1964): 167–172.
46. Heidegger, *Being and Time*, p. 147.
47. J. Fell, *Heidegger and Sartre: An Essay on Place and Being* (New York: Columbia University Press, 1979), p. 63.
48. Heidegger, cited in ibid., p. 47.
49. Heidegger, *Being and Time*, p. 100.
50. Ibid.
51. M. Heidegger, "The Thing," in *Poetry, Language, Thought*, A. Hofstadter, trans. (New York: Harper and Row, 1971), p. 165.
52. M. Heidegger, *Discourse on Thinking*, J.M. Anderson and E.H. Freund, trans. (New York: Harper and Row, 1966), p. 50.
53. Dardel, *L'Homme et la Terre*, pp. 127–128.
54. Heidegger, *Discourse on Thinking*, p. 54.

3. The quest for authenticity and the replication of environmental meaning

KIMBERLY DOVEY

Two intriguing phenomena pervade the creation and experience of the modern environment.[1] On the one hand, there is a growing preponderance of places, buildings and things that are commonly called *fake* or *inauthentic* – for example, plastic flowers, false shutters, staged touristic environments, pseudo-vernacular buildings, and mock woodwork. On the other hand, there is a strong cultural trend involving a search for an *authenticity* which seems to be missing in these examples, a desire to have the "real" thing and to deride any synthesized substitute. It is not easy to say why such themes are so current, yet I take it as a social fact that a heartfelt quest for authenticity proceeds.[2] To accuse someone, their possessions or home of being inauthentic implies a strong moral judgement and arouses righteous indignation. The purpose of this essay is to explore this dual phenomenon of the production of fakes and their systematic elimination.

To accomplish this aim, the essay first examines the phenomenon of fakery, which is interpreted as the replication of environmental meaning through the manipulation of appearances – a situation which frequently breeds doubt and deception in person–environment interaction. Yet the quest for authenticity and the search for "real" meaning through "honesty" of form often leads to the destruction of that which it seeks by inducing fakery. The argument is that both fakery and the quest for authenticity are symptoms of a deep crisis in modern person–environment relationships and of a mistaken belief that authenticity can be achieved through the manipulation of form. However nebulous and ambiguous this notion may remain, authenticity is a property not of environmental form, but of process and relationship. As process, it is characterized by appropriation and an indigenous quality. As relationship, it speaks of a depth of connectedness between people and their world. Authentic meaning cannot be created through the manipulation or purification of form, since authenticity is the very source from which form gains meaning.

Transformations of form and meaning

To clarify the nature of authentic meaning, I begin by examining the transformations of form and meaning through a seemingly trivial example: the case of false window shutters (Figure 1a–1d). In the past, window shutters served as a boundary control device for the regulation of temperature, ventilation, light, sound, views, and social interaction. In this original context, shutters were integrated with the everyday life of the places they enclosed by virtue of the dialectic between opening and shutting. Their form evolved from this context of boundary control (Figure 1a). As other kinds of boundary control became popular, however, shutters were cut off from these functional roots. In the first stage of this disjuncture, the shutters are built to shut but not actually to be used. Their connection with life inside the building is severed and their role becomes purely visual and static (Figure 1b). In the third stage, this static visual role is concretized as the shutters become fixed to the wall, the possibility of "shutting" now entirely denied (Figure 1c). A last stage is achieved when the correlation in size between shutters and windows is lost such that they would not cover the windows if they did shut (Figure 1d). At this point, the shutters have become blatantly unshuttable and purely decorative. But have these shutters become inauthentic and if so at what point?

If one asks this question of authenticity in terms of a formal analysis, then the critical transformation would appear to occur at Figure 1c, when the shutters become unshuttable. Yet the fixing of the shutters is only a concretization of a deeper transformation already occurring in Figure 1b. Here, although the shutters are formally indistinguishable from the original, they are no longer shut and are entirely decorative. The shift between Figures 1a and 1b is a transformation of the relationship between the dweller and the form, involving a loss of integration between the shutters and the everyday life of the place. At the same time, there is a transformation of the formative process: whereas the original shutter form derives from action in everyday life, the latter forms derive from the visual image of "shutters."

There are, then, two kinds of transformation: one which occurs with the loss of use and integration with everyday life; another which occurs with the loss of shuttability. Caught between these transformations is the ambiguous case of the shutters in Figure 1b which are either authentic or inauthentic,

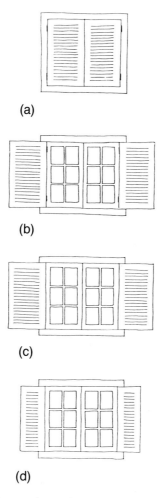

Figure 1. Transformation of form and meaning: The example of shutters

depending on whether one views them as formal or usable objects. This ambiguity is not a trivial matter because it leads to a clearer understanding of authenticity. As the replicated shutters become less and less like the original, they lose meaning. This is why derision tends to fall on the blatant and unambiguous examples like Figure 1d. If the shutters do not connote ''shutting,'' they lose some of their original meaning. Yet if they do connote ''shutting,'' they achieve this meaning through deception.

This transformation of the shutters is not an isolated example, as one can see by considering the household fireplace. Originally an important center of domestic heat and social contact, the fireplace was also a symbolic and spiritual center of family life. When the heating function is usurped by modern technology, the intangible need for a center to replace the hearth persists and often leads to representations – fireplaces that are mere show, or, indeed, cannot be used at all. As with the shutters, the crucial transformation occurs when the form loses its integration with the everyday life of the place – in this case, its use in heating and gathering. Once again, the replication stems from the attempt to preserve or create a shared meaning, using a prop that has lost its role in everyday life. My argument, then, is that the phenomenon of fakery is essentially a replication of meaning. For the shutters, this meaning is inextricably bound up with "shutting;" for the fireplace, with "heating and gathering." Meaning is thus the foundation of fakery, and replications are forms that attempt to carry authentic meanings. Replications succeed by virtue of their very ambiguity and sophistication – i.e., by their success at masking their own transformation. It is important to understand, then, that *inauthenticity emerges out of the very attempt to retain or regain authenticity*.

There is, however, a problem with this argument in as much as "shutting" and "decorating" can both be valid functions of environmental form. Within a context of "style," shutters can in time become part of a culturally shared image of "window," as fireplaces become part of the image of "living room." The meaning of these environmental elements cannot be recreated easily when they have their functional roots severed technologically. The paradox is that while our attempts to retain the meaning of "shutting" with fixed shutters may be inauthentic, our attempt to retain the meaning of "window" by the very same means may be authentic to the degree that the shared meaning is evoked.

Involvement and appropriation

A resolution of this paradox requires a deeper understanding of the kinds of meaning which emerge in person–environment interaction, and a fundamental distinction between the use-based meaning of "shutting" and the image-based meaning of "decorating." Useful in this regard is Heidegger's distinction between *Zuhandenheit* (readiness-to-hand) and *Vorhandenheit* (presence-at-hand), which he argues are ontological categories or modes of Being in terms of which aspects of our world appear to us.[3] *Zuhandenheit* is the mode of Being of implements (*Zeug*) which we use and with which we actively engage. The meaning of the implement emerges from what it is "for." *Vorhandenheit*, on the other hand, is the condition of an object that stands in a theoretical visualized relationship to the subject; it is not used but rather stands available for our consideration.[4] Thus, the meaning of a hammer is found in its use for "hammering," just as a pen is for "writing," a bridge for "bridging" or a house for "dwelling." The locating of the meaning in the "for" makes it highly dependent on the context, thus meaning is inextricably bound up in connections with other implements and the world at large.[5] In the case of the hammer, for example, the meaning is connected to the shape of the hand, the strength of the arm, the structure of the nail and the wood, and all of the events leading up to and flowing from the act of hammering. Returning to the shutters example, we find the meaning emerging from the activity of shutting, which in turn has links with that which is shut out and in, with the cycles of day and night, with seasons and weather, with the uses and views of rooms, and so forth. Only in the context of everyday use does the shutter gain its meaning. False shutters are an attempt to retain or regain this meaning through the replication of appearance. In this attempt, however, the meaning relationship is shifted from *Zuhandenheit* to *Vorhandenheit*, and the shutters become objects for contemplation. Heidegger clearly gives ontological priority to the action-based over the contemplative, since we are involved in the world first by virtue of our concern for that world. Further, it is through this concerned involvement that our world is disclosed and appropriated:

> The hammering does not simply have knowledge about the hammer's character as equipment, but it has appropriated this equipment . . .; the less we just stare at the hammer-Thing, and the more we seize hold of it and use it, the more primordial does our relationship to it become . . .[6]

Appropriation is a difficult yet vital notion here, since it embodies the dual qualities of both caring for the world and taking from it.[7] As caring, appropriation speaks of our primary involvement in the world, our concern. This caring or concern is not a moral attitude for Heidegger; rather, it is ontological – i.e., a fundamental aspect of existence.[8] Further, appropriation is more than just a utilitarian concern; it involves a respect and preserving of the world in its own right. It is through this care that the world is disclosed. A second part of appropriation is the notion of taking, which is close to the etymological root as seen in the Latin *appropriare* – "to make one's own."[9] Taking, in this sense, is a kind of incorporation of the world into ourselves. As our world discloses itself through our concern, we take this disclosure into our Being. Appropriation is closely related to the process of identification. As we open ourselves to the world of things and places, we bring them meaning through our care and concern, and at the same time these things and places lend meaning to our sense of identity. Appropriation is rooted, therefore, in a concerned action through which we appropriate aspects of our world as anchors for our self-identity.

The importance of the concept of appropriation for the understanding of authenticity lies in this emergence of meaning through action. Our successive appropriations and identifications from past experience form a kind of ontological ground of meaning. In as much as experience is culturally shared, so are these meanings. This ground of shared meanings constitutes the very experience that the fake tries to replicate. Insofar as the fakery succeeds, it conceals an attendant doubt and deception. At the same time, this doubt and deception breeds unreliability into our acts of appropriation – the very acts that generate meaning in the first place.

Deception

One way to understand the problem of deception is to explore the effects of deceit in human relationships. Honest interaction is the foundation of social life because effective communication requires some integrity between the surfaces and depths of people's behavior. Lies spread uncertainty and alienation through a social system, since each lie sows seeds of doubt into all future statements by the liar. When we feel that we cannot rely upon surface appearance, we have two options: either we separate ourselves from the source of deceit, or we adopt an attitude of mistrust and engage in an investigative operation directed towards the discovery of a deeper reality. Both consequences of deceit contaminate the social system, since separateness leads to social fragmentation and alienation, while the investigative approach engenders a web of new lies in the cover-up operation.

Although deceit is by no means so clear in relationships between people and their environment, the consequences are similar. On the one hand, criticisms of fake things and places are a means of separating oneself from his or her world. On the other hand, the insistence on having the "real" thing requires an investigative operation, a search for the clues indicating authenticity. This investigative attitude is itself a kind of separation from the phenomenon, a stance of *Vorhandenheit* that reduces the thing or place to an object. It involves not our openness to the disclosure of the thing or place, but rather a kind of empirical testing. Just as fabrications are invented to cover up previous deceit in human relationships, so environmental replication becomes more and more sophisticated in order to thwart investigations and capture "real" meaning. A further consequence is that this objective attitude colors our experience of the authentic originals since they, too, must be tested first and experienced second. The result is that specific doubts about fakery lead easily to a more general doubt about the authenticity of our world.

From another perspective, however, one could argue that if the deceit really works then the consequences are not significant. Jencks writes that "when synthetic wood and stone can be manufactured which outperform and are visually indistinguishable from their natural counterparts, then it becomes pedantic and efféte to insist on having the 'real' material."[10] This possibility is indeed a problem and the insistence on a kind of technical authenticity is often full of pedantry. There are, however, reasons for rejecting Jenck's argument. First, it assumes a purely visual *Vorhandenheit* relationship of people to their world – a view that is prominent in the enclaves of architectural criticism.[11] Second, Jenck's argument is elitist in that it ignores the preferences of lay people, assuming they do not care to know whether they are inhabiting a stage set. Yet people *do* care. No one wants to be deceived – not by people, places, things or materials. Despite their isolation from the design process, most individuals desire to know about their world at depth. They can accept all kinds of faked things and perhaps even learn to love them so long as they are not deceived by those things. For example, the use of synthetic stone can be an authentic means of decorating a house, yet one would not want to buy or become attached to the house in the mistaken belief that the stone was "real." While it may be pedantic to insist on having the "real" stone, it is not pedantic to insist upon knowing the difference. This awareness is fundamental to the way in which people experience their world.

Experiential depth and environmental purity

Although deception is the source of the moral problem of inauthenticity, the issue is more complex. The differences between the original and its replication are more than just categorical. They involve differences of experiential depth – differences in the richness of possible environmental appropriations. To understand this point, consider the case of an artificial surf beach in Phoenix, Arizona (Figure 2). Here, identical waves roll in at identical intervals to wash upon imported sand. There are no crabs to nibble one's toes, no sharks, undertows, tide lines or driftwood. There are no shells to be found in the sand, no rock pools to be explored, no sea breezes and no salt air.

Figure 2. Artificial beach, "Big Surf," Phoenix, Arizona

There is nothing inherently "bad" about the artificial beach, but it is useful for a discussion of authenticity because its designers have gone to such lengths of replication without the remotest possibility of deception in the desert context. The difference between an original beach and the replica is largely that of *depth* – this includes spatial depth, historical depth, depth of diversity and of learning opportunity. The original meaning, although anchored in the forms of sand and waves (which have been replicated), is also bound up with salt, breezes, crabs, undertows and intangible forces of the ocean (which have not been replicated). Any original beach is a learning environment par excellence, offering a significant opportunity for a sense of connectedness with the natural world and an enhanced understanding of one's place in nature.[12] In short, the original beach embodies a depth of process, a depth of learning opportunities, and it engenders a depth of emotional commitment and appropriation.

There is no moral problem with the artificial beach, since there is no deception. Rather, it is the comparative poverty of the beach in terms of experiential depth and its attempt to claim so much meaning that gives rise to our judgements of inauthenticity. Only because it begs to be compared to the original do we bother to criticize. Yet I do not mean to argue that the artificial beach cannot be cared for and appropriated. When we grow up in such places or spend a lot of time in them, they become part of our everyday world, our "home." Their forms become anchors for our self-identity. No doubt the artificial beach is popular and well-loved, and may one day be preserved as an authentic part of Phoenix history. So long as we are not deceived, we can genuinely appropriate the technically inauthentic.

An important question remains, however: To what extent does the replica come to serve as a surrogate for the original? This is an important issue because synthesized substitutes are designed from a stereotyped and purified image of the original. The original always embodies far more chaos, "defects" and diversity than its duplicate. From a myriad of original forms, a selection is made which purifies and petrifies the meaning – a selection which meets socio-culturally defined expectations and reflects ethnocentric views. This is a particular problem for children who may well come to regard the original as a defective version of the surrogate. If they are to form their conceptual categories (such as "beach") from purified replicas of those very categories, then an incestuous cycle may begin that inhibits the ability to encounter the prototypical world in its originality.

The environmental purity and lact of diversity stemming from the replication of meaning can also be taken a step further, resulting in the purification of everyday life itself. This pattern occurs through another, more subtle confusion of categories. Consider the case of pseudo-vernacular landscapes – the design of housing or commercial developments to simulate a bygone era. *Pointe Benicia* is such a housing development in the "historic" town of Benicia, California. Although the architectural forms of this development appear to be traditional and diverse, they are actually generated from a few basic designs laid out in village-style around an artificial lake with mechanically bubbling brooks and wooden footbridges (Figure 3). Such places are increasingly common and popular today, based upon a widely shared nostalgia for a more stable, picturesque and authentic past.[13] Such environments, however, do not represent a real past that consumers have ever experienced but, rather, a mythical image of "harmonious village life." This image is a stereotype, stripped of its oppressions and hardship. Yet as shallow as it is, this stereotype is generally perceived as involving a *public* environment – i.e., the houses and shops *as well as* the streets, squares, and other public spaces. When the meaning which is anchored in these forms is replicated today, however, the place in a legal sense generally becomes *private*. This transformation gives rise to the realm of the "pseudo-public" – i.e., places with public meanings yet private control. In the original square, street or marketplace, freedom of access and use was at least public-

Figure 3. The pseudo-vernacular, "Pointe Benecia," Benecia, California

Figure 4. The pseudo-public, "Pointe Benecia," Benecia, California

ly negotiable. Yet in the pseudo-public realm, all kinds of political and deviant behavior can be proscribed and access denied at the whim of the owner. At *Pointe Benecia*, signs have appeared to keep out non-residents who are lured by the "village" (Figure 4). Clearly, the pseudo-public realm can appear without the pseudo-vernacular, but in association with such styles it becomes particularly confusing because it draws its meaning and success from its role as a surrogate public place. In this way, the shallowness of experience and purity of form occurring with the replication of meaning can also extend to the creation of a political and behavioral purity of everyday life. The result is a subtle and unself-consciously deceitful erosion of public life.

Authenticity as indigenous process

I have described several distinctions between the original and the replica which I believe are important to the problem of authenticity – distinctions of relationship, category and experiential depth. I now want to consider a distinction of process. In all of the examples outlined above, the original and the replica embody fundamentally different kinds of formative processes which converge upon the same formal result. For instance, the original beach emerges organically from its geographical context, while the artificial beach is a technological product based on a purified stereotype. Both processes have their own kind of order: the former, growing in place, is intrinsic; the latter, derived from an external image and imposed, is extrinsic. The intrinsic forming process I will call *indigenous*. Although we commonly associate "indigenous" with the traditional and primitive, the etymological root means "produced or born within," thus indicating a somewhat wider meaning.[14] Indigenous processes, therefore, are those where form is "inborn" and are opposed to processes which are derived and imposed from without to fit some wider order. A formative process is indigenous when the form emerges out of the everyday life and context of the place. Thus, the shutters evolved from the dynamics of boundary control; the fireplace from the nature of fire, heat and gathering; the beach from the interaction of land and sea; the medieval village from the dwelling traditions of that society.

Our association of the indigenous with the traditional and the past, although narrow, is not unfounded, since the issue of authenticity is a peculiarly modern one. To a traditional society, where the processes of environmental change are integrated with everyday life, there can be no dispute about origins – no doubt about depth. Only as modern industrialization separates us from the process of production and we encounter the environment as a finished commodity, does the problem of authenticity emerge. As Relph claims, the problem of authenticity and the replication of meaning is strongly linked to the modern spread of technology, rationalism, mass production and mass values.[15] At the same time, the quest for authenticity is also a modern phenomenon; as MacCannell argues: "the final victory of modernity . . . is not the disappearance of the nonmodern world, but its artificial preservation and reconstruction . . . ."[16] At home, this quest takes the form of the eradication of fakery, but increasingly the quest is conducted away from home in the form of tourism. "For moderns," says MacCannell, "reality and authenticity are thought to be elsewhere: in other historical periods and other cultures, in purer, simpler lifestyles."[17] This search for authenticity in the past and the exotic is lamentable, both because it purifies and commoditizes that which it seeks, and because the seeds of authenticity are always available at home. In as much as authenticity is rooted in indigenous process, it is only found and generated in the dwelling practices of everyday life.

Ambiguities of authenticity

It is important to understand that when I speak of indigenous process, I am not speaking of a kind of place, but rather a kind of process. This distinction raises some important ambiguities, since the same place can often exhibit a range of processes and, therefore, aspects of both authenticity and inauthenticity – for example, an owner-built house of mock stone. My last example illustrates some of these ambiguities as well as the impact of the modern search for authenticity on the traditional world.

The Dogon are a tribal group in Mali who have long been famous for their highly developed cultural systems and the aesthetic appeal of their artifacts and habitat.[18] The *Togu Na* ("House of Men, House of Words"), a place of communal decision-making, is a characteristic building type with a thick straw roof set on open columns. Images of tribal significance such as masks, animals and fertility symbols often appear on the columns and surrounding rock faces. The changes wrought by modernism in recent years have been many, including an influx of Western tourists eager for snapshots of primitive life. Many of the young men have deserted the villages for the cities and some have returned disillusioned. A *Togu Na* in Banani, one of the more accessible villages, was rebuilt in 1975 by these young men. It is adorned with clay figures in great profusion which, according to Spini and Spini, represents "an attempt to give the tourists a superficial account, by means of the most striking images, of the masks and animals, but no longer as a coded message, just simple notional lists."[19] The images are not only multiplied but "introduced with expressive violence typical of other African civilization."[20] On a nearby *Togu Na*, there is a sign requesting money for photographs and in yet another the space once reserved for the ritual dressing of the masks is now given over to non-traditional dance displays. Finally, some of the "men's houses" have been de-gendered as Western women are permitted to enter.

The transformation here has much in common with the examples presented earlier: from a process which is integrated, intrinsic and indigenous; to one which emphasizes display and other-directedness. This display comes as a direct response to the tourists – indeed, it is an attempt to mirror and embellish their very expectations.[21] At the same time, the *Togu Na* is transformed from a "men's house" to a "commercial enterprise" while pretending to remain a "men's house." In its outside influence, commoditization, and misrepresentation, this process has become inauthentic. Yet there are two important ambiguities to confuse the issue. First, the Dogon themselves decided to rebuild in this way, so in a sense it is an inborn process. Although there was outside influence in the forms that they chose, this influence was not imposed from without. In this light, the rebuilding may be considered an authentic commercial enterprise grounded in an indigenous response to economic need and the opportunity of tourism. Second, the production of the display may actually be playing a very important role in protecting the authenticity of the Dogon culture and habitat. If the tourists' search truly destroys the authenticity which they seek, then the belief that they have found the real thing ends both the search and the destruction. To deceive outsiders with a fake display may then be an authentic form of defence against the ravages of tourism. This protective function of fakery is a crucial ambiguity which has also been noted in relation to urban conservation, the pseudo-vernacular and the natural environment.[22]

Modernism has also brought its pressures on the Dogon in other ways. In the plains villages, the pillars of the *Togu Na* are generally wooden and carved with the forms of breasts as fertility symbols. These carved pillars are now quite valuable commodities on the world art market, and they are frequently stolen by tourists and art dealers. One of the responses of the Dogon to this threat is to disfigure their own sculptures by cutting off part of the breasts.[23] With their commodity valued destroyed, these sculptures are safe from Western museums and living rooms. But what of their authenticity? To us, with our fetish for form, this disfiguration appears to empty the pillars of meaning and value. We would never disfigure the things we love to prevent theft. Yet clearly for the Dogon, the pillars have intrinsic value that goes deeper than appearance and is not entirely annulled by the disfiguration. If authenticity is not to be located in form but in process, as I have argued, then perhaps even the disfiguration is an authentic preservation of meaning. And here, perhaps, is another distinction: while inauthenticity is an attempt to regain lost meanings through the replication of form, authenticity involves the power to retain the meanings without the form because it is the very well-spring that brings meaning to form.

Authenticity as connectedness

The concept of authenticity is a truly ambiguous one, yielding to varying in-terpretations when viewed in different ways. These ambiguities are only a problem, however, when one insists upon locating authenticity as a condi-tion to be found in the physical world. With this point in mind, I want to offer some tentative ideas of how one might conceive of authenticity in the modern world – not as a condition of things or places, but rather as a condi-tion of connectedness in the relationship between people and their world. Consider one dictionary definition of "authentic": "reliable, trustworthy; of undisputed origin, genuine."[24] Here, we find three aspects of meaning. "Undisputed origin" implies a *connection* between the form of the phenomenon and the processes that produce it. Thus, wood cannot be authentic except as the product of the processes of growth in a tree. This relationship is a temporal connection between past and present, process and product. "Genuine" similarly implies that the phenomenon which looks like wood is not a plastic replication – that there is a *connection* between the surface and the depth of the material world. This link implies a kind of spatial integrity where if one were to penetrate the surface appearance, then a richer version of a reality that is not different in kind would be disclosed. The third aspect of authenticity, the "reliable, trustworthy" component, is once again a temporal *connection*, this time between present and future, perception and action. In as much as we must act in everyday life on the basis of the perceptual surface of the lived-world, authenticity renders this world both reliable and trustworthy. It is, therefore, a part of the meaning of wood that it can be cut, nailed, carved, painted and burnt – that it will carry certain loads and gain a certain patina with time.

These three aspects of authenticity are never separate and together iden-tify different kinds of *connectedness* between the everyday world and those deeper realities and processes that created it and those consequences

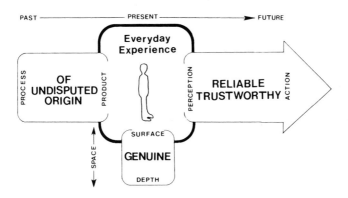

Figure 5. Transformation of form and meaning: The example of shutters

which flow from one's engagement with it. In this sense, authenticity is a property of connectedness between the perceived world and the believed world. It connects us spatially with the places in which we dwell and temporally with the past and the future (Figure 5). Authenticity is a condition of integrity in person–environment relationships. This connectedness is not a perceptual phenomenon; its deeper significance lies not in its connection of appearance to reality, but in its connection of people to their world. Authenticity is, then, a way of being-in-the-world, a connectedness born of our acts of appropriation. It is a spatio-temporal rootedness which enriches our world with experiential depth.

Just as authenticity is not to be found in the world of things, neither is inauthenticity. The tendency to speak of inauthentic things or places, to locate the problem of authenticity in the physical environment, is very much misplaced. Inauthenticity is rather a disconnectedness of the larger system of person–environment interactions, a disease of this system. The fundamental paradox and the source of the greatest ambiguity is that *inauthenticity emerges out of our very attempts to find and recreate a lost authenticity, a lost world of meaning.* Inauthenticity is an attempt to resurrect meanings, but it results in their very destruction. The problem lies not in the searching, which is genuine; but in the misplaced belief that authenticity can be generated through the manipulation of appearance. Authenticity has the indigenous quality of being inborn. So long as the search is conducted "out there," in the exotic and the past, beyond the world of everyday life, it seems bound to be frustrating and perhaps destructive. Authentic places and things are born from authentic dwelling practices in everyday life. Their order flows "bottom up" rather than "top down."

The search for authenticity stems from a serious disconnectedness in the ecology of person–environment relationships that one might call homelessness. This comes not only from the absence of a place to dwell, but also from having the dwelling experiences that constitute home cut from beneath one's feet by rapid advances in industrialization and technology. Much of what passes for inauthenticity is evidence of our attempts to regain a sense of home through synthetic surface effect. This manifestation of inauthenticity in the form of fakery is a replication of meaning. It is a lure for our false hopes and an attempt to capture our hearts by deceit. It is a cosmetic solution for a deeper schism in the system. Our attempts to eradicate fakery from the environment are not only superficial but also often misplaced and dangerous. Misplaced, because the "fakes" often have quite authentic aspects about them, most notably their role in protecting the truly authentic. Dangerous, because if we eradicate the most blatant and least deceitful places, then we encourage their replacement by more sophisticated and more deceitful versions of the same thing. It is well to remember that our scorn never falls upon that which truly deceives us. Our decrying of the inauthenticity of places and things is all too often a pedantic effort to lend our lives a surface effect of authenticity while a deeper disconnectedness from the places which we inhabit remains unchallenged.

Notes

1. The author would like to thank Sandra Gifford, David Seamon, Robert Mugerauer, Lars Lerup, Johanna Drucker, and Dean MacCannell for commentary on various drafts of this essay.
2. Two provocative critiques of the authenticity of places to which this paper owes a good deal are Edward Relph, *Place and Placelessness* (London: Pion, 1976); and Dean MacCannell, *The Tourist: A New Theory of the Leisure Class* (New York: Schocken, 1976).
3. My primary source is Martin Heidegger, *Being and Time*, John Macquarrie and Edward Robinson, trans. (New York: Harper and Row, 1962). Secondary sources include George Steiner, *Martin Heidegger*, (Harmondsworth: Penguin, 1978); Vincent Vycinas, *Earth and Gods: An Introduction to the Philosophy of Martin Heidegger* (The Hague: Martinus Nijhoff, 1961); and Karsten Harries, "Fundamental Ontology and the Search for Man's Place," in *Heidegger and Modern Philosophy*, Michael Murray, ed., (New Haven: Yale University Press, 1978), pp.65–79. The problems of translating Heidegger are enormous and the terms *Zuhandenheit* and *Vorhandenheit* have been variously rendered as "ready-to-hand," "handiness," and "at handness," in the former case; and "present-at-hand," disposability," and "on handness" in the latter case. To avoid confusion, I retain the original terms.
4. See, in particular, Heidegger, *Being and Time*, pp. 97–102; Steiner, *Martin Heidegger*, pp. 89–90; and Vycinas, *Earth and Gods*, pp. 34–37.

5. Heidegger, *Being and Time*, p. 97.
6. Ibid., p. 98.
7. See Edward Relph, *Rational Landscapes and Humanistic Geography* (London: Croom Helm, 1981), chap. 10; and Harries, "Fundamental Ontology."
8. Vycinas, *Earth and Gods*, p. 41.
9. Walter W. Skeat, *A Concise Etymological Dictionary of the English Language* (New York: Perigree, 1980).
10. Charles Jencks, *Architecture 2000: Predictions and Methods* (London: Studio Vista, 1971), p. 117.
11. This relationship is evident in the predominant style of discourse conducted in the major architectural journals. Buildings are evaluated and reputations made and lost largely on the basis of published photographs, which reduce buildings and places to a *Vorhandenheit* relationship.
12. Heidegger, *Being and Time*, p. 100.
13. See Adrian Forty and Henry Moss, "A Housing Style for Troubled Consumers: The Success of the Pseudo-Vernacular," *Architectural Review* 167 (1980): 72–78; and David Lowenthal, "Past Time, Present Place" Landscape and Memory," *Geographical Review* 65 (1975): 1–36.
14. From the Latin *indu* (within) and *gen* (to be born, to produce), Skeat, *Concise Etymological Dictionary*. Note also the connection with Heidegger's notion of "autochthony;" see Martin Heidegger, *Discourse on Thinking*, J. Anderson and E. Hans Freund, trans. (New York: Harper and Row, 1966), pp. 47–51.
15. Relph, *Place and Placelessness*.
16. MacCannell, *The Tourist*, p. 8.
17. Ibid., p. 3.
18. See Marcel Griale, *Conversations with Ogotemmeli* (London: Oxford University Press, 1965).
19. Tito Spini and Sandro Spini, *Togu Na: The African Dogon "House of Men, House of Words"* (New York: Rizzoli, 1977), p. 74.
20. Ibid., p. 76.
21. See James Duncan, "The Social Construction of Unreality: An Interactionist Approach of the Tourist's Cognition of Environment," in *Humanistic Geography: Prospects and Problems*, David Ley and Marwyn Samuels, eds. (Chicago: Maaroufu Press, 1978), pp. 269–282.
22. See Donald Appleyard, "Introduction," in *The Conservation of European Cities*, Donald Appleyard, ed. (Cambridge: M.I.T. Press, 1979), pp. 8–48; Forty and Moss, "A Housing Style for Troubled Consumers;" and Martin Krieger, "What's Wrong with Plastic Trees?" *Science* 179 (1973): 446–455.
23. Spini and Spini, *Togu Na*, p. 104.
24. *The Concise Oxford Dictionary*, sixth ed. (Oxford: Clarendon, 1976).

4. Language and the emergence of environment

ROBERT MUGERAUER

Environment, it would seem, is well understood. The environmental disciplines, ranging from environmental psychology and behavioral geography to architecture and regional planning, have investigated the human experience of environment. These disciplines have analyzed how the environment impacts people's experience and how perception and technology shape the environment. Clearly, much has been done which is correct.

Because the matter is complex, however, I would like to inquire, more basically, how it is possible that we sensuously experience and perceive the environment and then scientifically study both that experience and the environment itself. I argue that scientific knowledge of environment is possible only because there is a prior experience in which the environment appears as holistically intelligible. We always find ourselves in the midst of an already interpreted environment; from this placement we both deepen our understanding and make mistakes. Further, both the primary interpretive experience and the secondary scientific abstraction are themselves possible only because *the environment and people always and already are given together in language.*

Such a claim in no way denies the importance of environmental knowledge gained through a study of sensory experience; it only points out that we first encounter environment as what stands around us, already interpreted and understood by way of language. Our topic, therefore, needs to be environment and the experience of language, or, language and the emergence of environment.[1]

This essay explores how mistaken assumptions underlying the common views of environment and language render these views theoretically and practically inadequate. By thinking through instances where both realism and idealism fail to provide the necessary understanding and instances where we fail or succeed to encounter language and environment existentially, one can specify the manner in which language and environment belong together and dwelling is possible. As a result, one can find a more fundamental position from which to describe and interpret the phenomena of language and environment. One can show how language enables environment to emerge, which also enables us better to understand the places and manner in which we attempt to dwell.

Landscape described by language

How, then, do environment and language belong together? Since we live in the midst of the world and are familiar with our surroundings, even if not in the way required for scientific analysis, we should be able to make sense out of our environment. After all, we control and manipulate our natural setting; we make our way, without any perceptible effort, in our daily course; we are curious, often pleased, by new and varied places. In short, we are quite at ease with the idea that the environment simply is there as a given to be dealt with matter-of-factly.

Imagine a landscape which we want to understand, describe, and interpret. This landscape would be a dimension of the environment in which we live and which the environmental disciplines takes as their subject matter. Samuel Woodworth Cozzens described such a landscape as he traveled through the American Southwest in the 1800s:

> Imagine, if you can, a valley or plain eighty miles in width, and extending for hundreds of miles on either side of you. It is a valley, only because you are surrounded by interminable ranges of mountains; it is a plain, only because there are mountains before you and mountains behind you . . . . It is a mass of cañons, ravines, ridges, gullies, chasms, and mountains, piled one above another in inextricable confusion, in all conceivable shapes, towering above and around you on all sides . . .

> The walls are perpendicular, and of a blood-red color. No vegetation is anywhere to be seen; nothing but the stones around us, and the grayish white alkali on the surface of the plain on which we stand, with its surroundings of crags, pinnacles, towers, and mesas of rock rising far above us, until their summits pierce the clouds on the one side, and this black, yawning abyss just before us . . . .

The gloom increases with every step. The walls around assume in the darkness a thousand grotesque and misshapen forms. The obstacles in our pathway become more frequent and dangerous. The darkness becomes more and more intense. We can no longer see the path for more than four or five feet ahead of us.

Now, as it abruptly turns an angle, we lose sight of it altogether, and we feel as though the next step might precipitate us into – what? And so we go on, hesitating, doubting, fearing, until, after hours of tedious toil, such as I hope never again to experience, we finally reach the bed of the river that has worn this mighty wrinkle in the face of Mother Earth.[2]

Given Cozzens' description, we might easily agree that the place should be called, as he tells us it is, *Journada del Muerte*, – the Journey of Death. We might suppose that he has given a straightforward, routine description of a perceived – albeit, particularly nasty – environment. Such a reconnoiter could be preliminary to any environmental study. Indeed, environmental disciplines have epistemological assumptions in such a case; these assumptions are necessary to account for how scientific inquiry is possible. We could suppose, for example, that Cozzens' environment is the given data. Understood either as a directly given reality or as the raw stuff from which sensations and then perceptions are formed, the idea is the same: the physical environment is the basic given; human consciousness sensuously encounters it and describes it with language. Our language and ideas represent that brute given to us so that we can operate on it in more sophisticated ways – for example, as science and technology do. Such is a common working assumption; it lies behind our regular methodology of doing research in environmental perception and of gathering data for other empirical studies. Again, we assume that language describes a prior given – the environment.

Things, however, are not so simple. Further reflection shows that language does not regularly follow and report what simply is there. This observation indicates that the environment is *not* a brute given, either as a well-defined reality or as the raw stuff from which well-defined perceptions regularly derive. Recall Cozzens' account. From the description, we would expect that the landscape reported is some random stretch of Arizona or New Mexico, perhaps unusually noxious. Strikingly, however, his landscape is not such a place; rather, it is the *Grand Canyon*! Surely, Cozzens did not "miss seeing it." Yet, somehow, the Grand Canyon, as the Grand Canyon we know, did not get into the language and description of a traveler who was taking special care to describe what he saw and experienced.

To be sure, Cozzens did describe the landscape from the point of view of a traveler; that is, it appears as what he is traveling through. That is why features which impede progress, cause disorientation, and even provoke fear are in the fore. It is this *traveling through* which largely explains why language which we would claim appropriate to the landscape was absent. In contrast, the Grand Canyon today is most often thought of as a feature to *travel to*. By way of our language of the scenic, the Grand Canyon emerges as an awsome view – that is, a object for aesthetic experience. Whether the language of scenery and tourism was available to Cozzens is another matter; the point here is that it does not occur or bring "the scenic" to mind. The shock of the difference between what we and Cozzens see and say travels in several directions: the environment we assume as given to us was not given to him; at the same time, the environment given to him is not there as a "fact" for us. There is nothing obvious, to be merely reported, even in so obvious a landscape. Moreover, what Cozzens encountered in traveling through and what we encounter in traveling to the Grand Canyon are both different from the environment which indigenous peoples encounter as they dwell there rather than travel – a point about which more will be said shortly.

Another example of varying interpretations of environment can be drawn from the travel diaries of pioneers who followed the Oregon Trail in the early 1800s.[3] After travelers from the East and Midwest had journeyed for six weeks from Independence, Missouri, and moved from oak and hickory forests to the edge of semi-arid highlands, they encountered a totally new landscape: the escarpments and sedimentary bluffs along the Platte River in western Nebraska. First, large rock formations were seen about fifteen miles away, then more and more appeared until five miles away a mountain came into view. This sandstone mass was more than thirty miles long with three spurs coming almost to the river. Not at all softened or rounded with vegetation, the rocks were severe, an impression enhanced by the clear air.

For people historically from the forested landscape of Europe, the sight of these bluffs was a shock beyond anything the travelers might have expected. Consider the account which the traveler John Bidwell wrote in 1851:

> the scenery of the surrounding country became beautifully grand and picturesque – [the bluffs] were worn in such a manner by the storm of unnumbered seasons, that they really counterfeited the lofty spires, towering edifices, spacious domes, and in fine all the beautiful mansions of cities.[4]

Similarly, in the diary of another traveler, A. Delano, the bluffs appeared as a veritable collection of the world's architecture:

Here were the minarets of a castle; there the loopholes of bastions of a fort; again the frescoes of a huge temple; there the doors, windows, chimneys, and the columns of immense buildings appeared in view, with all the solemn grandeur of an ancient, yet deserted city, while at other points Chinese temples, dilapidated by time, broken chimneys, rocks in miniature made it appear as if by some supernatural cause we had been dropped in the suburbs of a mighty city − for miles around the basin this view extended, and we looked across the barren plain at the display of Almighty power, with wonder and astonishment.[5]

What is happening here? Not mere playfulness or delusion. In fact, the travelers report, self-consciously and with embarassment, that such architectural impressions were forced upon their minds. The Reverend Sam Parker and Israel Hale say that they "could not help" perceiving the environment as they do.[6] In this situation, language is lacking; the landscape's essential characteristics stay concealed. Because the environment can not become manifest through an adequate language, it comes forth, instead, in the language which is available from traditional pastoral poetry and landscape painting. This available language shows the landscape in light of doctrines of the sublime and picturesque, or in light of an archeologically derived belief in the cyclical passage of human play and vanity, complete with congruent ruins and references from the Bible and classics.

The impressions of these travelers complement Cozzens' experience of the Grand Canyon. While in the passages quoted above, Cozzens did not see the Canyon as an aesthetic object but, instead, in the language of a smooth or terrifying journey, these travelers on the Oregon Trail see and think through a language of historical-moral-aesthetic contemplation. In fact, this same phenomenon is found in Cozzens' writing. On another occasion he writes:

Cathedrals of hugh size, castles, rotundas, amphitheatres with domes and towers, are on every hand, while yonder, rising a thousand feet in the air, is a strange resemblance to a mighty organ, with its pipes consisting of hugh columns of green, white, blue, brown, and pink sandstone towering high above you, with the tops worn by the winds and waters into points seemingly like needles. Count them: there are forty . . . . Yonder stands a castle, with its towers and spires hundreds of feet in height, its walls of blue gray limestone mixed with white and red granite, beautifully mottled with shales of every color. Seemingly but a few miles in front of us we readily imagine we are about approaching some enchanted castle, where we shall not fail to find the rest, as well as food, which we so much need . . . .[7]

In short, what happened to Cozzens and the travelers on the Oregon Trail is that though they encounter an environment, they have only the language from their own heritage and landscape with which to think about and describe it. They see and say only what they are able to: a landscape unavoidably informed by Western European interpretation, rooted in Biblical, classical, and post-Cartesian perceptions.

Landscape created by language

The above discussion leads us to reject our initial assumption that the environment simply is there, complete with its meanings independent of our experience, to be passively described by language. We might, therefore, replace this assumption with its opposite – that is, that human consciousness is the radically creative, autonomous reality. In other words, we might replace the assumptions of a naive realism with those of idealism and suppose that external reality is merely a confusing physical stimulus which needs to be ordered and categorized by human consciousness before we have what we call "environment." Here, the mind and language would form or impose order, and the perceived environment would be a human or cultural product, constructed *via* language and symbol. This idealist argument would explain how people, especially from different cultures, do not experience, perceive, or describe the same environment even when they encounter the same physical stimulus. This situation would also seem to explain why, for example, Cozzens did not see the Grand Canyon as we do, and why a positivist and a humanistic scholar would have different descriptions of the same landscape: they each apply different conceptual schemata and linguistic categories to what they encounter.

Upon more careful examination, however, we find that an idealism is not adequate for understanding the environment either. Consciousness does not "create" environment by means of language – a point demonstrated in acknowledging that there may be objective features of the environment which we fail to see and understand. Even while we may differ as to what is perceived, and even if we add connotations or nuances to what basically is there, we can be wrong.

One illustration of this disharmony can be had by considering another example from the American Southwest. North Europeans have brought to

America a subtle language with which to describe places where water comes and goes. In English, we have words like "stream," "creek," "brook," "gully," "gulch," "ditch," "ravine," and so on. The idealist assumption might be sustained insofar that such words are successful in ordering environments of the East and Southeast. We can live in and understand water landscapes in Tennessee or Vermont with this language. In other environments, however, these words can fail, as they sometimes do in the Southwest, often with disastrous results. Not that there are no streams, creeks, and gullies in the Southwest – obviously, there are. There are also, however, *arroyos*. Arroyos are watercourses with intermittent flows, where after a hard rain, large volumes of water suddenly come into and pass through what otherwise looks like an "always-dry" place. Most often, these arroyos are called "creeks" and "gullies" in English. In other cases, the correct name, "arroyo," may be used, but with no understanding of what an arroyo is. Thus misunderstanding arroyos as creeks and gullies, Anglos continue to build towns on top of arroyos, as if the landscape were similar to Pennsylvania's. The result is that these towns are flooded, their people and buildings washed away.

Ironically, the clearest cases where the assumption fails but nonetheless persists often occur where the word "arroyo" is used to label genuine arroyos, but where the true character of arroyo itself is masked by language and thus not really understood. This happens, in Austin, for example, with streets labeled *Arroyo Seco* because of the adjacent "dry creek or ditch;" or with *El Arroyo*, a restaurant which is partially built within the depression of an arroyo.[8] Obviously, the crucial issue is not mere labeling, or correctly identifying landscape features. Rather, with the words, "creek," "gully," or especially with "arroyo" understood merely as a Spanish word for a creek or gully, we have an instance of the failure of mind and language to create the meaning of a landscape.[9] Further, the effort of consciousness to constitute and form environment actually results in misperception or mistakes about what really is. What seems to emerge in fact conceals or obscures environment. In these situations, language and perception fail reality.

Landscape and language always already given together

We can conclude that environment is neither a brute given to be recorded passively in seemingly objective, scientific language nor a raw material to be organized according to coherent cultural patterns by an actively creative, trans-subjective language. Rather, there must be some middle way which has as its assumption that words need to be "fitting words." With such appropriate language, environment is able to appear. We are able to hold on to landscape through language and thereby see, understand, share, and live. Put another way, we ask a wrong or misleading question if we inquire whether it is language or environment which comes first. Specifically, the question errs practically and theoretically because it assumes that language and environment are given independently of each other and that the issue is which is prior and thus able to determine the other. Asking this erroneous question leads us to mistake what happens in the emergence and study of environment. In fact, language and environment *always already are given together*. We always find ourselves in the midst of environment already given and interpreted by way of language. The crucial question becomes how language and environment are already given together.

To move toward an answer to the question, first consider a passage from García-Márquez's *One Hundred Years of Solitude*. This passage depicts the situation of environment and language being given together or not at all. The author describes the simultaneous loss of environment and words in the village of Macondo in a way which acknowledges both the proper essence of things and the power of language:

> One day [Aureliano] was looking for the small anvil that he used for laminating metals and he could not remember its name. His father told him: "Stake." Aureliano wrote the name on a piece of paper that he pasted to the base of the small anvil: *stake*. In that way he was sure of not forgetting it in the future. It did not occur to him that this was the first manifestation of a loss of memory, because the object has a difficult name to remember. But a few days later he discovered that he had trouble remembering almost every object in the laboratory. Then he marked them with their respective names so that all he had to do was read the inscription in order to identify them . . . . With an inked brush he marked everything with its name: *table, chair, clock, door, wall, bed, pan*. He went to the corral and marked the animals and plants: *cow, pig, hen, cassava, caladium, banana*. Little by little . . . he realized that the day might come when things would be recognized by their inscriptions but that no one would remember their use. Then he was more explicit. The sign that he hung on the neck of the cow was an exemplary proof of the way in which the inhabitants of Macondo were prepared to fight against loss of memory: *This is the cow. She must be milked every morning so that she will produce milk, and the milk must be boiled in order to be mixed with coffee and milk*. Thus they went on living in a reality that was slipping away, momentarily captured by words, but which

would escape irremediably when they forgot the values of the written letters.[10]

By describing the normal life and the loss of environment, García-Márquez describes how we experience the world: what is given is understood and held on to by way of language. That there are walls and lizards about us means nothing if we are blank in the face of what we are given; our letters and words are meaningless scribbles if isolated from their power of disclosing and holding reality for memory. Indeed, this blankness would be such an oblivion that it is hard to imagine how, in such a case, wall, lizard, or world would be given at all. Words, including names, are not merely labels, but the evocation of what things are and how they are related to other things in the web of particular lives and places. And more than names and words, there is language itself, which is not any fanciful artifact, but that which has the power to articulate and join humans to plants, animals, and activities in a surrounding world. The entire fabric of a people's meaningful world – the total environment – comes along with the whole of that people's language.

García-Márquez's fragment of a story shows us the power of language: the essential features of an environment become manifest insofar as they are brought forth and held in language. Language comes into its own as language not insofar as it either passively records or actively creates (which are actual though partial and derivative powers of language), but insofar as it fittingly brings forth and holds for thought the essential features of the environment.

In finding confirming evidence for this thesis, we need to remember the failures as well as the successes of language and environment being given together. Failures are only possible where the relationship is possible. In the example of the Grand Canyon, for instance, we saw a failure: neither the landscape we now call the Grand Canyon nor language adequate to bring the Canyon forth were present to the traveler; both were absent together. Further, there is no good reason to assume that what we see and say today is at all adequate either, as compared to what emerged for indigenous peoples. In the arroyo example, the builders of the Anglo world in the Southwest do not live in the language where the emergence of crucial features occurs; even though they appropriate the word "arroyo," they have not lived the event of the unexpected surge of water and of finding the sense of the phenomenon located by means of the proper words. Without such disclosure, they think instead only of a dry creek bed.

Travel literature is full of such cases because when we cross into strange language and landscapes, we frequently fail to "live in" an already properly interpreted manifestation of environment. The European encounter with the Arabian Desert provides an example parallel to the already cited case of the arroyo. While the desert heat and lack of water may have been expected by early travelers, over-attention to those very characteristics obscured or blocked the appearance of a more complex reality. Particularly striking are cases where the supposition of the desert as an "ever dry place" shattered in the experience of desert flooding. Consider the account Charles Doughty gives in his *Travels in Arabia Deserta*, which records the revelation – to him – of the unexected possibility of a flood in the desert. Following desert custom, Doughty uses the story form to relate an incident which befell Ghroceyb, one of his desert traveling companions, who had been amidst the seemingly familiar landscape of rock and sand:

> It was a dangerous passage, and Ghroceyb returning had been in peril of his life: for as he rode again over the *Harra* [vulcanic country] there fell a heavy rain. Then he held westward to go about the worst of the lava country; and as he was passing by a sandy *seyl*, a head of water came down upon him; his [riding camel] floundered, and his matchlock fell from him; Ghroceyb hardly saved himself to land, and drew out the [riding camel] and found his gun again.[11]

A flood in the desert! How could this be? What is a *seyl?* The answers to both questions are given together. Doughty is able to interpret the unexpected event only when he learns at one and the same time the meaning of the Arabian *seyl* and the Arabic word "*seyl.*" The passage quoted above holds the experience of desert as the scene of flashflood in the word "*seyl,*" which means, as Doughty here learns and puts into his own words, "the dry bed" wherein "sometimes, being suddenly flushed by rain in its upper strands, a head of water flows down with dangerous fulness and force; and men and cattle overtaken are in danger to perish therein."[12] Not only do the meanings of the landscape's features and its language emerge at one and the same time; there is no point in trying to separate them because what is disclosed to Doughty, simultaneously, is what *seyl* and the word "*seyl*" mean.

This example shows that while oblivion and occasional insight plague and reward the traveler in new lands, the loss and gain of understanding through language are pervading features of all our lives. Recall the citizens of Macondo in their struggle to live in their village. The same point is made by the incident of the traveler Ghroceyb who was swept away, according to

Doughty's story. Separate from the issue of the emergence of language and landscape for Doughty, what about Ghroceyb? Did his action fail adequately to live up to what he understood of the desert? Did he forget what his language told him, or was he simply caught unaware?

Whatever the case, these examples make clear that the phenomenon of disclosure of landscape through language is not limited to the experience of strange or new environments. For example, when we Americans read a passage in our native language or repeat an old cultural articulation, we often find it obviously descriptive or true precisely because we do not notice, much less question, what happens there. Thoreau writes:

> From a hilltop near by, where the wood had been recently cut off, there was a pleasing vista southward across the pond, through a wide identation in the hills which form the shore there, where their opposite sides sloping toward each other suggested a stream flowing out in that direction through a wooded valley, but stream there was none. That way I looked between and over the near green hills to some distant and higher ones in the horizon, tinged with blue. Indeed, by standing on tiptoe I could catch a glimpse of some of the peaks of the still bluer and more distant mountain ranges in the northwest, those true-blue coins from heaven's own mint, and also of some portion of the village.[13]

What could be more obvious? Thoreau speaks of the beauty of the wilderness and of its harmonious belonging between the sky and the village. His description seems what we or anyone would and could say if we took the time or had his writing skills. A look at history, however, reveals that what happened here was something new – something which Thoreau, artists such as Church and Cole, and photographers such as W.H. Jackson and E. Watkins, brought to language and visual articulation. This new situation is now so thoroughly given to us and taken for granted that only a historical retrieval of earlier language–landscape manifestation shows that our understanding has not always been so.

Though a full review of the issue is not possible here, it can be noted that as heirs to our Western tradition, most Americans in the 18th and early 19th century saw the natural landscape as horrible and cursed, as something to be overcome physically and spiritually.[14] The American east coast was, in the words of William Bradford as he disembarked from the Mayflower, a "hideous and desolate wilderness."[15] The wilderness was the opposite of paradise, understood as the dark and threatening realm of demons and savages, a consequence and sign of evil and man's fall from divine grace.

Wilderness was good only as the scene or opportunity for enlightened moral conquest. Hence, the cultivated environment – natural landscape over- come – was good; wilderness was hostile and repugnant. Only gradually did writers, artists, and photographers give voice and delineation to the natural environment as symbol and even vivifying source of natural, moral, and spiritual values.

For our purposes, here, the point is that the mountains appear to us the way they do precisely because language, with the help of Thoreau and other noted figures, enables mountains to shine forth as attractive rather than repugnant – attractive just because they do mediate between the human community and heaven and are part of an environment where the wild and the civilized are balanced in fruitful encounter.

That language historically enables understanding also is seen in our sec- ond example where travelers encountered the amazing bluffs on the way to Oregon. At one level, the fanciful reduction of the landscape to more familiar terms is interesting insofar as it shows the need for interpretive categories. No matter how interesting, however, these categories still do not disclose the bluffs. The real lesson is that, as compared to the Native Americans em- powered with adequate language, those pioneers were not granted the land- scape. Indeed, insofar as it has been achieved, an adequate emergence re- quired a struggle over hundreds of years to get the bestowal in Thoreau, Leopold, and other such articulators of landscape. The struggle is the achievement and heritage of American art and literature.

Certainly, it could be argued that what has been achieved with such great difficulty also is fleeting. Does what Thoreau says seems obvious or just out of date? Either way, it may be that such an understanding of environment has passed away – either by forgetfulness or as commonplace – and is scarecly missed. Today, many people see the earth as nothing more than raw material and relegate the words of Thoreau to history or quaintness.

Dialect as revealing environment

Lest the use of poetic or literary examples be misleading, it should be said that not only rare or "high" language brings environment forth. The reason for examining poetry or literature is simply that we often find there paradigmatic examples of language as a most powerful and fulfilled event of bringing forth environment. A more pervasive source is the living local or traditional language of an indigenous people – i.e., their *dialect*, which also gives the essential features of landscape. Dialect holds together *local en-*

vironment and *mother tongue, place* and *local language*. It is not accidental that the rise of scientific-homogenous languages coincides with systematic or universal geography as the study of homogeneous space and with a decline in the reality and interest in dialect and regions, or that the new view of the relation of language and environment is connected with a renewed study of dialect, place, and region.

It is difficult to cite a good example which is intelligible to all readers, since we do not share a common home ground or dialect. Any translation of genuine dialect into standard academic English removes the specific disclosure which comes in the dialect as such. The point is that where dialect continues to function and has not been reduced to a quaint or curious specimen, its interpretation of the environment is what makes possible a coherent, meaningful, and valued way of life for those who share the dialect. This is why there is a different way of being for each local place, people, and dialect. For example, a place and manner of being are disclosed to an indigenous group with the word, "hollow." To those in the lived realm of the hollow, it is the scene where mountain, valley, water, sky, wind, plants and animals all have specific relations to those who belong there and who with their deep family roots, are part of a web of difficult but profound possibilities and rhythms. These possibilities and rhythms are quite unlike those available to outsiders, whether the latter be coal mine owners, social workers, sociologists, or even people of the Hudson River who live their own lives by way of valley/"valley." "Hollow" as hollow is not a site for commercial profit, government aid to the needy, or doing research; nor is it a valley or basin. It is a particular, congruent world where in the earth's indentation, all that belongs together in enduring hardship and in celebration reverberates in its own style appropriate to the muffled sound associated with what is hollow. Perhaps we can catch a hint of this in the words of Hannah Morgan as she talks about her Appalachian home in Harlan County:

> I was back home, up the hollow, I was looking at the pines. I was hearing the wind coming at them, and hearing them say "yes, we're here," and singing and singing. I was hearing my great-grandmother just before she died, telling me about these pines – how brave they are, and proud, and full of hope: evergreens.[16]

The significance of dialect is further confirmed by cases where language and environment are lost and are known to be lost. This occurs, for example, when we are in a landscape which has no special meaning for us, but which, we know, was a rich and flourishing scene for a complex culture. Clearly, those who lived in that scene built, worshipped, had customs, and so on – all of which occurred in close conjunction with the environment. For that to have happened, these people must have understood the environment's essential features, interpreting them properly and fully, and evolving an indigenous way of life as a way of inhabiting just that place. A specific instance again can be found in the Grand Canyon. Lying near the upper reaches of the Grand Canyon, Havasu Canyon was the tribal home of the Havasupe for a thousand years, but appeared to many European–Americans not as a place to live but as a possession and site for aesthetic experience, as is clear from the comments of a turn-of-the-century official, whose words echo some of the other Anglo descriptions of the area:

> The Grand Canyon of the Colorado river is becoming so renowned for its wonderful and extensive natural gorge scenery and for its open and clean pine woods, that it should be preserved for the everlasting pleasure and instruction of our intelligent citizens as well as those of foreign countries. Henceforth, I deem it just and necessary to keep the wild and unappreciable [sic] Indian from off of the Reserve . . . .[17]

In contrast, those who lived in Havasu Canyon understand it not as an object for visitors, or as property to be sold, but as the opening in the earth where, and by means of which, they lived. Thus, earlier traditional indigenous views and newer understandings of language and environment conflict. Even what the land itself is is disputed: native Americans hold that the land is sacred bearer of life, including the human; dominant European–Americans, that it is a commodity to be owned. In other places, current disputes over whether to mine reservation lands witness the continuing displacement of the one interpretation by the other. The struggle of the displaced people is heard in the words of Lee Marshall, a Havasupi speaking at a government hearing in an attempt to recover the canyon as the tribal home:

> We want our freedom from the park lands and forest lands which surround our reservation. Land doesn't talk; wild plants don't talk; wild animals don't talk; even the beauty of our canyon doesn't talk, but our Great Spirit and mother nature have a way to care for them . . . . Wild plants, wilderness, forests, wild animals and fowls of the air were put on this mother earth for a purpose; that purpose was that men could gather and eat and save what they can. Even our ancestors' bones are

dug, placed in glass containers and displayed on shelves to tell a story to canyon visitors of prehistoric creatures roaming our lands.[18]

The loss of such at-homeness happens all over the world today. When indigenous people are displaced or relocated, their language no longer brings forth their traditional environment, except in memory, dream, or legend; nor do these people have a new language in which a new environment can emerge, with the result that they become speechless and homeless. Those who come after, either to displace or simply replace them, have not the language which enables living properly there, nor yet a new language adequate for the occasion. Western technological society does not contest the loss in richness and intelligibility of life and environment; indeed, the sense of loss is a source of wonder from which we can learn. Lévi-Strauss captures this loss of an earlier event of environment brought forth in language in *Tristes Tropiques*, the very title of which names a sadness of and for the tropics:

> I had wanted to reach the extreme limits of the savage; it might be thought that my wish had been granted, now that I found myself among these charming Indians [who referred to themselves as Mundé] whom no white man had ever seen before and who might never be seen again . . . . Alas! they were only too savage . . . . There they were, all ready to teach me their customs and beliefs, and I did not know their language. They were as close to me as a reflection in a mirror; I could touch them, but I could not understand them.
>
> But if the inhabitants were mute, perhaps the earth itself would speak to me . . . perhaps it would answer my prayer and let me into the secret of its virginity. Where exactly does that virginity lie . . . is it this tree, this flower? They might well be elsewhere. Is it also a delusion that the whole should fill me with rapture, while each part of it, taken separately, escapes me? If I have to accept it as being real, I want at least to grasp it in its entirety, down to its last constituent element.[19]

At this point in his expedition, language breaks off for Lévi-Strauss – neither the natives nor the environment are understood. He is forced back into his own language and into himself and thereby out of the jungle. While he does write a biographical account, by his own admission he is able to little more than explore his adventures with the strange peoples and landscape as part of his effort as a connoisseur of his own consciousness.[20] In Lévi-Strauss' account, we hear of two language-given experiences of one physical location. Those experiences are so different, despite all points of contact, that we can not but recognize two distant language-landscapes. In one, place genuinely emerges as home for the Mundé; in the other, there is nostalgia for such a lost belonging and an inevitable restlessness which takes the form of a renewed search for language and environment.

Today, we experience homelessness and even intensify it at the same time that we seek its cure. Our task for tomorrow is to turn away from any homesickness for an environment which can not be ours, and from any self-imposed imprisonment in our own subjectivity in order to begin to become at home by letting our own proper language and environment emerge. The first step in this task is to better understand language as the emergence of environment.

Environmental hermeneutics

The environmental disciplines need to investigate further, as a foundational issue upon which their possibility rests, how it is that person and environment are both given together in language. Indeed, often it is hardest to see what is most obvious because it is such a profoundly assumed basis for our experience. We are so sophisticated as scientists in directly interpreting and thus experiencing the environment that we proceed without noticing the epistemological and metaphysical foundations of our perceptions. We jump in describing, sorting, analyzing, and synthesizing mountains, rivers, meadows, and so on. We lose sight of the fact that this work proceeds at a secondary level — it is a secondary abstraction from the environment in the midst of which we live without reflecting or without scientifically describing. We do science by analyzing in greater detail and at a different level what we are in the midst of — which is what is given to us as subject matter. We forget, even as scientists, that he subject matter we analyze — environment — already is given to us and interpreted in language. Thus, environmental disciplines are possible only insofar as they critically work from our historical interpretation of environment, which itself is possible only insofar as mountains, rivers, meadows and the rest already show themselves, in language, to us as they are.

Such a fundamental area of study is not what has been done earlier as a result of either "realist" or "idealist" methodologies. Where environmental disciplines see language as *reporting* environmental features or the spatial patterns of cultures in an environment, what follows is analysis and correlation of those relationships and patterns. Where these disciplines see language and culture as *creating* the environment as a meaningful system, they systematically correlate language-symbolic-cultural forms and spatial environmental descriptions and meanings. Not that either of these methodologies are to be disparaged or their value denied. Rather, such procedures need to be supplemented and grounded by a third project, barely underway, which utilizes the empirical research already done and which moves simultaneously behind and beyond it.

Since language enables us to hold a basic interpretation in mind, we can proceed from there to different scientific interpretations, including the critical retrieval of other and earlier cultural environments. We call this new science which is beginning *hermeneutics*, or more specifically, *environmental hermeneutics*. Environmental hermeneutics is the interpretation of the essential ways in which (1) human-cultural ways of dwelling and (2) essential features of environment occur historically, for specific places and languages, for specific regions and dialects. This new study would be not only a mapping, no matter how correct or complex, but even more importantly, a new regional-dialect discipline which would interpret the emergence, persistence, and changes of the relationships of language-scape and landscapes (and other dimensions of culture and environment). Such an approach is difficult to explain briefly and adequately. What really is required is undertaking the project in classes, workshops, and research papers. At least, though, it is possible to specify some basic characteristics of this new way of interpretation. One can indicate at least four dimensions:

(1) Environmental hermeneutics entails *understanding what a specific, "local" language is saying*. Though we might begin by mapping differences in word usage, it is not adequate to end with a mere listing and classifying, but with a reflective listening to the saying of environment, where we work out the meanings as carefully as we would for a great poem or novel.

(2) Environmental hermeneutics involves understanding the ontological aspects of the language event. In addition to and beyond the interesting, idiosyncratic, and expressive aspects of language understood by way of sociology and psychology, and apart from the categorical knowledge of linguistic science, the primary subject-matter of environmental hermeneutics *is the being or reality of environment* – whether natural or cultural. The goal is understanding the essential environmental characteristics which are disclosed and concealed in the local language. The focus is not on environment in general, or on homogeneous space, but on particular regions, places, and features of environment.

(3) Environmental hermeneutics goes on to *describe the essential features of the environment* which shows itself as it is (or fails to, insofar as

it remains concealed). Also, care is taken to *describe the way in which this happens for a particular language*. Such a project must be scientific in the sense of a theoretically grounded craft practiced by a community of master interpreters who also are learners – a community which can critique, refine, and share their understanding with each other and with students.

(4) Environmental hermeneutics insists that *the first three emphases must be allowed their historical dimension*. Fuller interpretation and understanding are possible only where it is recognized that, over time and in different epochs of language, essential features of environment are both disclosed and concealed in complexly intelligible ways. "Mountain," for example, may, in different historical languages, enable mountains to emerge as the scene of paradigmatic actions of the gods, as a despicably desolate and humanly useless tract, as the creation and sign of the Judeo–Christian God, as a material object to be known by scientific method and manipulated with technology, as an exquisite source of sublime feelings, as a sign of God's favor and blessing on a people and nation, as a reservoir or stockpile of raw material, as a place where the earth stands firm and endures for mortals, and so on. In these larger historical-linguistic contexts, the features we name "gorge," "ravine," "shale," "pine," and so on, take on vastly different meanings and possibilities. We briefly saw this happen with the Grand Canyon.

Taken together, these four dimensions of environmental hermeneutics indicate how it is that language enables the environment to come forward into experience. It is clear that understanding environment by way of language is part of a change which puts a renewed focus on such themes as place, dwelling, and regional geography. In this regard, an environmental hermeneutic would be both an area of specialization in itself (as a regional-dialect discipline proper) and a foundation for other areas of environmental study.[21]

Hence, its peculiar focal character: environmental hermeneutics concentrates on and illuminates its own special concerns; at the same time, it does so precisely because it gathers together a variety of approaches currently practiced in philosophy, literary criticism, geography, architecture, regional planning, anthropology, traditional studies, art history, and history of religion. In the end, environmental hermeneutics would be the gathering place where we could see how environment emerges and can be understood.

Notes

1. The position developed here derives from the work of Martin Heidegger. See, for example, his *On the Way to Language* (New York: Harper and Row, 1971); and *Poetry, Language and Thought* (New York: Harper and Row, 1971). Perhaps the best access to the topic is Walter Biemel, *Martin Heidegger* (New York: Harcourt, Brace, Jovanovich, 1976).

2. Samuel Woodworth Cozzens, *The Marvellous Country or Three Years in Arizona and New Mexico* (Boston: Shephard and Gill, 1873), pp. 100–107. I would like to thank J. Gray Sweeney for pointing me to this quotation and for his stimulating insights into the "aesthetics of nature."

3. The account of the Oregon Trail experience used here is taken from Paul Shepard, *Man in the Landscape* (New York: Alfred A. Knopf, 1967), chapter 8, especially pp. 238–243.

4. Ibid., p. 240.

5. Ibid., p. 241.

6. Ibid., pp. 242–243.

7. Cozzens, *The Marvellous Country*, pp. 101–102.

8. For accounts of events during a recent major flooding of arroyos in Austin, Texas, see *The Austin American-Statesman*, issues for Memorial Day, 1981, and the week following.

9. The crucial difference is in the contrast between "arroyo" and the words "dry creek," "creek", or "gully;" in other parts of Texas the word "draw" would help considerably, but that word is not used in central Texas. For the basic distributions of these words, see Terry Jordan, "The Texas Appalachia," *Annals of the Association of American Geographers* 60 (1970): 409–427; and E. Bagby Atwood, *The Regional Vocabulary of Texas* (Austin: The University of Texas Press, 1962).

10. G. García-Márquez, *One Hundred Years of Solitude* (New York: Harper and Row, 1970), pp. 48–49.

11. Doughty, *Travels in Arabia Deserta* (New York: Random House, 1910), p. 251.

12. Ibid., p. 671.

13. Henry Thoreau, *Walden* (New York: Holt, Rinehart and Winston, 1962), p. 71.

14. See, for example, Marjorie Hope Nicholson, *Mountain Gloom and Mountain Glory* (New York: W.W. Norton and Co., 1959); Roderick Nash, *Wilderness and the American Mind* (New Haven: Yale University Press, 1967); Vincent Scully, *The Earth, The Temple, and the Gods* (New Haven: Yale University Press, 1962); Clarence J. Glacken, *Traces on the Rhodian Shore* (Berkeley: University of California Press, 1967); Robert Rosenblum, *Modern Painting and the Northern Romantic Tradition* (New York: Harper and Row, 1975); J. Gray Sweeney, *Themes in American Painting* (Grand Rapids, Michigan: Grand Rapids Art Museum, 1977).

15. William Bradford, *Of Plymouth Plantation, 1620–1647*, S.E. Morison, ed. (New York: Knopf, 1952), quoted in Nash, *Wilderness*, p. 24.

16. Robert Coles and Jane Hallowell Coles, *Women of Crisis*, vol. I (New York: Dell, 1978), p. 104.

17. Letter from W.P. Hermann, Grand Canyon Forest Reserve Supervisor, November 9, 1898, quoted in Stephen Hirst, *Life in a Narrow Place* (New York: David McKay, 1976), p. 2.

18. Lee Marshall, "A Master Plan for Grand Canyon Village by the Havasupai Tribal Council", quoted in Hirst, pp. 260–261.

19. Lévi-Strauss, *Tristes Tropiques* (New York: Pocket Books, 1977), pp. 374–376.

20. Ibid.; see especially pp. 80 ff.; pp. 382–387; pp. 427–435; pp. 473–ff.

21. There is a large literature in language geography, folklore and history on the topic of en-

vironment and language. For an accessible overview, see Terry G. Jordan and Lester Roundtree, *The Human Mosaic* (New York: Harper and Row, 1982), bibliography to chapter five. But the vast majority of research has thus far concerned itself with the accurate and scholarly collection and analysis of the material. The interpretation of the modes in which language discloses the environment remains to be done. Though a survey of the field is not appropriate here, the following works are worth mention: Richard Weiss' work on Swiss folklore, house form, and landscape in *Volkskunde der Schweiz* (Zürich: Eugen Rentsch, 1984) and *Häuser und Landschaften der Schweiz* (Zürich: Eugen Rentsch, 1973); Gerhard Hard, *Die "Landschaft" der Sprache und die "Landschaft" der Geographen* (Bonn: Ferd. Dümmler, 1970); Hard, "Mundartforschung und Mundartgeographie", (*Saarbrücker Hefte* 21, 1965), pp. 27–50; George Steiner, *After Babel* (New York: Oxford University Press, 1975); Joel Garreau, *The Nine Nations of North America* (Boston: Houghton Mifflin, 1981). On landscape thought from the viewpoint of the body and philosophical anthropology, see Marjorie Grene, "Landscape," in Ronald Bruzina and Bruce Wilshire, eds., *Phenomenology: Dialogues and Bridges* (Albany: State University of New York Press, 1982), pp. 55–60.

5. Place, body and situation

JOSEPH GRANGE

Without place, there would be neither language, nor action nor being as they have come to consciousness through time. Suppose there were no place. There would be no 'where' within which history could take place. 'Where' is never a there, a region over against us, isolated and objective. 'Where' is always part of us and we part of it. It mingles with our being, so much so that place and human being are enmeshed, forming a fabric that is particular, concrete and dense. This essay attempts to weave, unweave and weave again the threads of place.

How can one in a thematic way explore such a phenomenon? I adopt as axiomatic the proposition that the spiritual arises from the physical. This essay, therefore, examines two themes: first, the body as flesh; second, the environment as engaged human situation. In one sense, this method is circular in that it seeks to repeat itself in ever-widening reflections of understanding. Circular, however, does not mean logically false; it suggests intensity by means of nearness of relations.

Thematic development does not exhaust the question of method. Organization is not the same as mode of investigation. My method will be that of phenomenology. By this much used, even abused term, I mean the effort to let those things which show themselves show themselves from the very way in which they show themselves.[1] The seeming repetition in this definition is deliberate: it enforces Husserl's dictum, "back to the things themselves." Consciousness and its content, however purged of misrepresentation, is all that human beings possess. This essay relies solely on the *Logos* – i.e., the structure and meaning of the two themes to be explored.

The body as flesh

With its hangover of metaphysical dualism, the word 'body' scarcely suits

the purposes of this essay. 'Body' suggests density and mass, with the attendant connotations of the body that I seek to overcome. Human beings are
not weighed down by their bodies, nor are our bodies at the mercy of a push-
and-pull environment. Another, more valid term is required.

I adopt the word 'flesh,' whose sensuousness shocks us into remember-
ing the fundamental activity of the human body: to feel the world and to
house the environment in our being. Flesh speaks of the living, not the dead.
It inscribes itself in passion, which, both active and passive, writes our contribution to the world. If the body is seen as flesh, the ways in which place
arises as the active, emergent soil of value begin to reveal themselves. First
and foremost, flesh and place merge to form a matrix of value. This axiological function shifts in relation to the domination of environment or
human body. The exact balance of contributions is not the major concern
here, and the behavioral sciences are quite correct in stressing their role as
arbiter and investigators of such calculations. Their findings are important
but cannot be allowed to reduce the interplay of flesh and place to that of
mere external mechanics.

The human body is value and always is 'already there.' Flesh is dia-
phonous, the sheer transparency that feels the contours of every context,
registers it and expresses the consequent values. A clutched hand speaks
of tension; open arms of warmth and welcome. The rigid walk of the urban
pedestrian reveals the dense, impacting weight of city walls; the lambent
grace of the stroller in the meadow shows the lightness of a natural space.
The huddled man in the storm contrasts with the easy, open graciousness
of the city man at home in his familiar neighborhood streets. There is, in
other words, a language to the human body, a style that we learn to read
even as we forget how we do it. If place is ever to be seen in its concrete-
ness, the implicit, subconscious prose and poetry of human flesh requires
explicit articulation.

How does fleshly articulation take place? There would seem to be four
elemental structures that our bodies deploy in order to found place: *posture,
orientation, feel* and *comprehension*. These structures are like gestures con-
noting the active, fleshly role of our bodily being. They are described
separately but are to be understood together. They comprise the way in
which human flesh establishes place within an environment.

Posture founds our relationship with the world. We are equipped with a
backbone, which means that we face the world straight ahead. In addition,
our eyes are so fixed that the space in front of us dominates our consciousness. The world appears before us, elicits our attention, demands our
concern, beckons or discourages our participation. Spinal column and

ocular setting determine our first reaction to place. The result is a double and simultaneous reaction: on the one hand, 'what is' appears initially to be on the vertical–horizontal axis; at the same time, 'what is' shows itself always in the first place to be straight ahead, over there, over against us. Posture initiates us into place *as distant.*[2]

This initial, primary distancing creates enormous difficulties for any satisfactory philosophy of the environment, and its consequences for ecology are only now being recognized. Still, this postural setting of place is invaluable because it allows us to see the world as a space upon which the drama of action is engraved. It encourages observation which, in turn, generates forethought and reflection. Place, therefore, arises out of flesh as disengagement and neutrality. What a strange birth for that which is most intimate with us! It is this phenomenon of distance arising from posture and vision that also leads to a sense of separation from nature. Without this sense of difference, we would be engulfed by our environment – drowned in an ever-shifting and thickening viscosity of sensations. The human ego would never emerge as an autonomous force, and planaria and *homo sapiens* would be on the same level. More to the point of this essay, no built environment could ever be created. Engagement with nature requires a primary disengagement.

Orientation marks an initial movement back into the matrix of environmental relations but does so in the most reserved of ways. When we are in place, we know where we are. Where does this 'where' come from? It springs most intimately from our own flesh. How so? Reflection on the everyday, ordinary words used to describe our gestures of orientation yields an astonishing fact: we do not immediately notice color, shape or motion. A phenomenological analysis demonstrates that orientation flows most directly from our initial postural structure. We elaborate upon the meaning of distance and say, "far away," "very close," "near to hand" or "over there." We structure our place through distance and this culminates in the act of orientation. Distance introduces us to nearness which in turn forces upon our flesh all the modalities of intimacy as well as estrangement. The human body as flesh is the cradle of spiritual being. All the elaborate metaphors of spirituality – nearness to God, banishment from the Garden, the Pilgrim's long journey – are already engraved in our flesh which anchors our knowledge in the concretely real.

In orientation, we know where we are. What is this knowledge that forces itself upon our somatic being? Surely it is not precise or factual in a sophisticated empirical sense. Neither is it logical in any theoretically refined way. I suggest that the knowledge of whereness is the intimate distance of place derived from the somatic stance of our being. In the most literal sense, this knowledge is the *ground* on which we stand. Our incarnate being evaluates place; from that act of orientation, all knowledge grounded in truth arises. The 'where' of knowledge is rooted in our flesh, a mode of knowing that discriminates the near through the distant. This act of orientation allows the human body to structure its environmental feel.

Feel is both a noun (structure) and verb (gesture). I intend the word in both senses, for the human body is both substantive and active. By 'feel' I do not mean intense affect such as that experienced in raw emotional states. Rather, I refer to the dim, throbbing backdrop that supports orientation. To say something is far away is at the same time to sense the vastness of space. Vastness is a word whose precision derives from the interiority of our bodies: we feel vastness *from out of our flesh*. 'Over there far away' makes sense only if it originates in the recesses of our body. We sense vastness because our body feels its own limits and thereby grasps the 'feel' of voluminous space.

The human body viewed externally is dense and impacted, literally 'crammed' with organs, bone and tissue. Felt from within, however, the body is an open space – so much so that we tend to take it for granted. One need only recall the sense of thickness and obstruction felt during sickness to know that in its normal, healthy state, the body seems not to be there. This transparency is what creates the 'feel' of an environment. Our body as flesh resonates with its situation. Surroundings can be felt as gloomy, bright, light, threatening, overwhelming or enticing. It is a sign of the remarkable delicacy of our somatic being that an almost limitless range of values can be detected by the nuanced 'feeler.'

Reflect on the language of touch. We say, "hard," "smooth," "grainy," "bumpy," "thick," "oily," "harsh" and so forth. How does flesh come up with such precise values? Physiology traces with astounding deftness the ways and byways of neurological operations. Its presentation of casual explanation is one of the accomplishments of our age. But what of the meaning signified by this incarnate evaluation of a place? Does it not suggest that the human body, as flesh, is always and everywhere an echo of what is. This echo lets the hollowness of the body show itself from itself. The hollow allows echoes. We have come a long way from the density of matter to the openness of the human body as experienced in a living manner. This journey is made possible only by letting the body show itself from itself. What is most characteristic of the human body in its gestures of *feel* is what one can term 'inherence in otherness.' This mode of being brings the distant near and allows intimacy to take place. Place, in effect, is intimacy through the mystery of the body.

Comprehension must be understood in its root sense – a seizing which is at the same time an act of bringing together into unity of definiteness the disparate parts of posture, orientation and feel. The human body understood as a mystery of openness always acts as a 'one,' though it can be explained as a series of parts – a 'many.' How one arises out of the many can perhaps never be known. The fact remains, however, that the act of comprehension creates a sense of unity, however dim and implicit, that is characteristic of place.

Another way of understanding this comprehending quality of the body is to recall Heidegger's insistence that every mood is a way of understanding, and every understanding carries with it a mood.[3] The body feels the mood of a place as bright or lowering, as spacious or cramped, as filled with possibility or deadened with hopelessness. This union of affect and understanding can be seen more concretely in the concept of meaning as contrasted with that of truth understood scientifically. The positivist conception of truth is yoked to verification – i.e., something is 'true' when it can be verified through appropriate sense-observations. This matching of hypothesis, theory and observation results in the identity of truth with procedure. Phenomenologists point out that meaning does not emerge through the identification of method and theory. Rather, meaning shows itself in labyrinthine ways – sometimes like a sudden light, at other times through slow successive levels of uncovering. Poetry is paradigmatic insofar as the words, upon rereading, continually yield up new levels of meaning. Meaning is the outcome of the fusion of understanding and mood. Comprehension as the unifying seizure of a manifold environment is the somatic counterpoint of that process. Comprehension is why place always has a mood, and the mood of a place is always at some level intelligible. In comprehension, the gestalt of posture, orientation and feel shows itself as a pattern of meaning.

What is definitive about comprehension is that it is always singular and unique. What is cramped for one person may be cozy for another. Does this mean that there is no 'objective' truth in comprehension? If truth is confined to science, then the answer is affirmative. But meaning is not opposed to truth. It resides at a level other than positivist definitions. How, then, can one universalize such meanings? Is it possible to come up with a yardstick or standard by which to judge place?

These questions mark a critical juncture in this essay. The question now must be asked, what drives human beings to judge place? By what right or power do we assert our domination of place such that we can judge it? Suddenly, if we pay attention to this question, everything is turned upside down.

More specifically, it is we who are turned upside down. We have questioned our vaunted right to judge. This questioning is actually a refusal to accept the dominant positivist attitude that has continued to shape our thinking since the rise and success of science. In questioning our right to judge place, we do two things. First, we assert that place is not dependent on our judgment. We can not always measure values from our standpoint. We refuse the anthropocentric vision. Second, we do not declare nihilism or cultural relativism to be our appointed lot. How can this be so? The answer is to be found in the axiological quality of the human body as flesh. We cannot avoid 'feeling' the value of place, orientating ourselves to it through posture, and registering its meaning through comprehension. Our body and the environment are one, a position that is not novel. It has a long, distinguished heritage, involving such thinkers as Plato, Spinoza, Whitehead and Merleau-Ponty. It only seems novel because of the rise in dominance of our objectivist–positivist consciousness. We have demonstrated the incorrectness of the subjectivist orientation by reason of the value-laden openness of the body.

What of the other side of the critical problem – the extreme objectivism of rigid empiricism? How are we to eliminate that side of the dilemma? What is wrong with positivism is what it makes of the object facing us. It reduces this object to shape, extension and, where necessary, motion. This extreme quantification of place strips the world of Being and value. In place of a textured environment holding worth in itself, we are given a blank array of objects whose only significance lies in their measurability and observability. Anything else is the contribution of the subject deciding the particular value of the particular place and its objects. This mode of empirical thinking destroys the possibility of the emergence of meaning; any qualitative evaluation of place is said to be the product of subjective reaction. Truth is confined to correctness – the correct equation of theory and results; the identification of 'what is' with bare numerical formulae; and, at its extreme limits, the assertion that Being is an empty word and better laid to rest on the metaphysical junk heap.

The objective side of the critical problem suffers the same fate as its subjective partner when confronted with the fact that the body as flesh is already there in the environment. One can pretend that the human body is not there or wish that it were there as a calculator attuned to the assumed quantitative reality. A double-edged sword cuts the Gordian Knot that has withheld place from human inquiry since the rise of modern science. Both edges of that sword are honed by a phenomenology of the body. First, there is the discovery that body as flesh is a kind of intentional openness, an *a priori* condition of any analysis whatsoever. The echoic and hollow structure of the body demands that it be understood as an abode of meaning, an active process of housing significance. Furthermore, this inherence in the otherness of place – an unavoidable fleshly fate – can be understood analytically as having certain movements or rhythms. Posture, orientation, feel, and comprehension establish layers of meaning which, in turn, build up a sediment of perception which it is our duty to understand and not explain away.

The other edge of the sword is, quite simply, the devasting question asked earlier. By what right, entitlement, or virtue do we judge place? Suppose place judges us? This question throws us out of the circle of the critical problem. It dissolves the subject/object dichotomy and centers our task of understanding in a different region. This different region is not a 'new' one, nor is it the outcome of a novel methodology that generates an arcane terminology or an *outré* vision. There is nothing 'mystical' about what has been so far said. Any sense of surprise comes from meeting the obvious because our consciousness is occluded by the dominant methodologies of our time – subjectivism and objectivism. Asking the question about our entitlement to these positions throws us into the rawness of what is. But 'what is' has always been. The where of place encountered phenomenologically shocks us by its intricacy. The human body, however, is equally intricate and deft at disclosing the many meanings of place. All we have done is to let that fleshly poetry show itself in its basic gestures. This second edge dislocates because it forbids us the comfortable confines of our familiar pattern of circular questioning – is it 'objective' or 'subjective'? Instead of the pleasant but fruitless game of arguing the primacy of one side over the other, we challenge the entire routine. The question – what is place? – shocks us.

Environment as engaged human situation

Every metaphysician worth his salt has tried to name the basic elements of "what is." For Plato, it was "The Ideas;" for Spinoza, "Substantia;" for Whitehead, "actual occasions;" for Leibniz, "monads." I choose the term "situation" because of its resonance, which has both the ring of the existential tradition and the more universal tone of naturalism.[4] It combines the deep human concern of continental thought with the scientific realism of American pragmatism. Even more important is its root significance: *situs*, the womb out of which arises what is; *situs*, the embracing bay that harbors the possibilities of life; *situs*, the site of what was, what is, what can be, what will be.

Every situation was first of all a site − a place within which things could happen and events could occur. At the outset, the primary feature of any environment whatsoever is *openness*, almost the same quality as the body as flesh. But the openness of environment has a different shape and texture; it, first of all, shows itself as *roundedness*. We have no word to capture succinctly the sense of envelopment without suffocation that I wish to suggest here. The German has *Umwelt*, the French *milieu*. We have to work through many senses of 'round' to understand the richness of environment.

One can begin with the vague suggestiveness of the word 'environment' itself. Environment is verbal and bespeaks activity. The verbal form − 'to environ' − means to surround, which indicates that every environment is what it is because of an exterior that marks off what is *outside* and an interior that shelters and defines what is *inside*. To be environed is to be one thing and not anything else. It is to be definite, to have a form so as to come into being as this particular such and such and so and so. Environment gives identity an opportunity to become and is, therefore, maternal. As active process, environment embraces without choking off possibility. Situation is to be understood in this sense of roundedness. *Urbi et orbi*, now the Papal salutation; formerly, the Roman mode of addressing humankind. Both *urbs* and *orbis* announce a definitive shape. Roundedness is built into both the City and the World, and, by extension, the Body Human and the Body Politic.

How does one reconcile the enclosed with the open? This question restates the problem directly. We faced a similar problem at the outset of our discussion of the human body. There, the strange dialectic between distance and nearness reconciled a seeming opposition. To elaborate fully and concretely the relation of the closed and the open, we must envision environment as showing itself in three ways: first, as *physical*, the world of nature; second, as, *social*, the world of human relations; third, as *built*, the world of human creation.

We begin with nature. 'Physical' here does not mean the inert *materia* deployed by Newton and Descartes to make sense of the material world. We go back further to the Greek experience of *Phusis* and there encounter the primary Western experience of nature.[5] For the Greek who spoke *Phusis*, nature appeared as 'Power,' but of a particular kind. The specific things of nature arose from a self-emerging power which was always awesome − overpowering, in fact. It is undoubtedly the reverence for this power which speaks through the early nature poetry of Hesiod. Nature as physical was alive, and blossoming forth with instantiations of 'what is.' Further, this power was 'all round,' though for the most part intensely located at sites that possessed particular strength − for example, the grottoes, streams, caves, mountains and other places that enraptured the Greek mind. It is easy to dismiss this experience as primitive, the dregs of a superstitious mind. Such dismissal would be perfectly in accord with the modern temperament; it would also cause us to lose the sense of environment I am trying to describe.

The Greek experience of the physical world of nature reflects almost precisely the sense of rounded openness I mentioned earlier. Recall our problem: how does the presumably closed yield the open? The Greek solution is exceptionally subtle. Nature is seen as power that emerges out of itself. That is to say, the being of nature is to give, and every environment is an environment by reason of its generosity. We now term an environment a situation characterized by generosity, but previously we defined environment as an engaged situation. How does engagement work? To be engaged is literally to be involved with; to be entwined around, through and with another. In another sense, to be engaged is to be 'busy.' The busyness of nature has to do with generosity – indeed, one of the most mysterious forms of generosity.

> *When Phusis is busy with generosity, it is engaged with its own being. This situation, understood as physical environment, involves emerging into otherness. Identity generates difference.*

The second way in which environment shows itself is as *social*. Here, the path to understanding the relation between the closed and the open is made easier by the work of the so-called 'Third-Force' psychologists like Abraham Maslow, Gordon Allport and Carl Rogers. These thinkers argue that the fundamental aim of therapy is to clear a place for their client's being. The entire act of psychotherapy revolves around the continual nurturing and maintenance of a sphere of freedom.[6] Further, this region of openness is to be experienced by a *person*. This person is characterized by autonomy, having a sense of the bounded, the self-ruled, the closed. Here, the paradoxical relation of the closed and the open appears again, but this time revolves about the conscious use, maintenance, and recognition of freedom. The limiting bonds such as mores and traditions that arise in the course of social evolution serve a double function. First, they routinize life's habits so that what is necessary for survival attains an almost automatic status. This thickening of life's aims binds up creativity. Laws, customs, symbols and traditions regulate the activities of the person so that survival is assured. The past assumes a kind of massiveness such that the future tends to repeat what was. Here lies the conservative function of social bounding. Yet all around and within this structure of conformity lurks the possibility of freedom which, as Whitehead said, "dwells in the interstices of society."[7] This potential freedom is the second function of limiting social bonds and lends itself most accurately to our analysis of place. Social place must contain two elements: first, a protective routine shielding humans from the devastating intrusion of novelty; second, an openness that allows, even encourages, freedom and its outcomes.

This double function of social order means that on an initial level individuals and social orders relate through antagonism. We have, however, already employed the term 'engagement' as a more accurate rendering of the situation. When antagonism matures into engagement, social relations are lifted to the level of discourse and dialogue. The place of the social environment, when appropriately structured, is characterized by the virtue of *civility* – words replace force, conversation and debate push compulsion to the edges of the environment. In other words, a 'city' arises in the midst of antagonistic turmoil and engagement, which, though at times acrimonious, more frequently takes on the characteristics of reason. People are autonomous and, in that sense, closed off, but they are open to reason which is always an invitation to participate in the shared life of mind. Reason seeks only to persuade, never to dominate. When reason dominates, it has degenerated into ideology. The autonomy of the person includes the possibility of sharing. In short, society protects the sphere of individuality and urges it into existential activity. The individual, in turn, is encouraged to transform that freedom into reasoned participation which helps the shared concerns of the whole. The result is a second level of our analysis of environment as place.

> *In the entwining that characterizes social relations, the dialectic of the closed and the open reveals itself as the mutual emergence of individual freedom and shared reason.*

The remaining way in which we must analyze environment is *as built*. We have already seen the human body as fleshly inherence in otherness. Through its structure – gestures of posture, orientation, feel and comprehension – the body articulates the value of its environment. In addition, nature has been seen as a 'rounded' oneness that gives forth multiplicity. The human body feels this generosity when it senses through comprehension the environing fecundity of nature. In terms of the social environment, freedom and reason seek to engage each other on a level higher than that of brute force and compulsion. All these modes of interaction share a common goal: the effort to experience unity and identity through difference. In one respect, as we have already seen, this is a metaphysical quest that has ancient origins. Place, however, is concrete and never just a mere theoretical entity. All these elements – the human body, nature and the social environment – find their highest concrete resolution at the level of the built environment and human dwelling.

There is a phrase that captures all these relations: *city and nature.* I choose it because both terms envelop the grand themes that have been the subject of debate since the 1960s: natural versus artificial; organic versus mechanical; free versus constrained; good versus bad. One could draw up a list of contrasting qualities associated with both terms – a kind of inventory of the American psyche. My concern, however, is not with 'city,' nor with 'nature,' but with why they belong together. Place *as human flesh* showed itself to be the emergence of the value of nearness by reason of the postural fact of distance. Place *as nature* showed itself as an environment whose roundedness provided space for the birth of difference. Place *as social environment* showed itself as the sphere of civility where the otherness of individual freedom is made communal through rational engagement.

With these findings in mind we ask: why do city and nature belong together? Consider three great cities: New York, London and Paris. Without analyzing their specific sources of greatness, we can identify a shared element – the place reserved for nature in the midst of the city. Central Park, Hyde Park, the *Tuileries* are neither city in the sense of built environment nor nature in the sense of virgin wilderness. These tracts of land are spaces of the open. Without the city, these natural spots would be submerged parcels of an unending landscape. Without these regions of the open, the city would be a dense mass of arranged matter. The city transforms nature, and nature transforms the city so that openness can be felt.

The open is not dead, abstract space. In the built environment, the open is that sphere of freedom within which space can be experienced as lived. Unlike Newtonian space, the open is an active potential that lets meanings emerge. It is the cultivated counterpart of nature's generosity, for it encourages the urban person to gather together the strands of existence and attempt their integration. The human body in such a place is fleshed thought seeking the identity of the difference between city and nature. We sense that city and nature belong together and are allowed to experience that possibility. What, for example, is the difference between a cobblestoned street and the grass that asserts itself in the street's cracks? In the presence of such openness, the person begins to wonder about the wild and the tame, the natural and the built. The open lets such contrasts emerge, and our body through its generosity is prompted to respond.

A person sits in a park. He sees and feels the contrast between city and nature. In experiencing this contrast, he does not so much understand the differences as sense in a relaxed, dim way the fundamental unity of all reality. It is not a question of causal explanation or, for that matter, rational effort. His body recognizes the organic rhythms of nature and at the same time the powerful thrust towards order and symmetry which characterizes human building. These dimensions of human experience are different; the natural is not the urban, but the two connect because the body is able to inhere in both regions of value. What unifies these experiences is the active presence of the body. By being there in a fleshly way, the human body is *one* in the presence of a soaring skyscraper glimpsed through the leafy vista of summer foliage. This unification of experience is achieved through the somatic act of being in place. That is why city and nature are not opposed entities warring for our allegiance. The human body in its generosity can experience both contexts as real and laden with value.

We can say, then, that the openness inviting the participation of our being is matched by the openness of our bodies. The experienced contrast of city and nature calls forth the articulated response of our somatic being. This response, in the first place, is *wonder* – wonder about nature, wonder about our human powers of construction, wonder about place itself. To wonder about place through fleshly thought is to seek our home. In the end, city and nature is a question in the most radical sense. When we ask this question, we begin the quest towards home. This is as it should be, for to examine place is to ask for the roots of our being.

In the city – the most civilized and developed level of place – we encounter in a kind of final coda the wondrous thematics of the mystery of place. Engagement was the term used to qualify environment in this exploration of place. Also situation and human were employed. What do city and nature tell us about environment as engaged human situation? Every human being is already situated *in a body*. This personal environment receives what is outside and echoes its qualities. Through posture, orientation, feel and comprehension, human beings record the significance of this world. The hollowness of human flesh amplifies the aroundness of its situation and inheres in it. In nature, this amplification is experienced first of all as a kind of wonder that, when radical enough, witnesses the sheltering openness of the 'ten thousand things.' What seems closed shocks us by its fecundity. Attuned to this openness, the hollow human body echoes it and calls nature 'natural.' In the entwined lives of the social environment, engagement takes on the form of a dialogue of, for and about freedom and its use. When practiced as the habit of civility, reason emerges as the counterpart of natural witness. Through the coaxing of reason, we are led to see the personal body as part of the social body. Engagement becomes more and more education in its original sense – a leading out and away from the bondage of solipsistic concern. Finally, on the level of the built environment understood as city and nature, engagement is seen as building and dwelling in both the natural and the social situation because through the mystery of place they belong together.

What is to be kept in mind is the ground and foundation of these achievements of place – the human body as flesh. The environment as situation, both natural and social, engages this human body and calls forth the emergence of reason. Once this mode of place is experienced, human dwelling and building can literally 'take place.' The "where" of this fully human place must make room for both the natural and the built. This building must not arise out of any weak sense of compromise or empty notion of 'having the best of both worlds.' Such thought is what Hegel called 'ratiocination' – the vague generalization that mocks concrete thinking. Just as our bodies have come to feel the sterility of Bauhaus architecture and reject its lack of tactile depth, so our bodies have come to feel the phoniness of green-belt planning schemes. This kind of thinking, albeit negative, is incarnate in the truest sense. Its force springs from the shudder of emptiness that echoes through our flesh. The human body, in the final analysis, cannot lie. Perception is our conscience. Place, while not our body, arises as a felt phenomenon through our body's participation in it. When we act through our body's posture, orientation, feel and comprehension, we begin the human effort towards founding, celebrating, and building place. All civilization is the enactment of this initial bodily gesture. Through a caring and circumspect attitude, we can see and feel the presence of the open. Beauty, justice and truth can then be made and experienced in a concrete way, for the human body will respond in a spiritual manner to the open that offers itself to our active embrace.

Notes

1. Martin Heidegger, *Being and Time*, John MacQuarrie and Edward Robinson, trans. (New York: Harper and Row, 1962), p. 58.
2. Erwin Straus, "The Upright Posture," in *Phenomenological Psychology,* Erling Eng, trans. (New York: Basic Books, 1966), pp. 144–147.
3. Heidegger, *Being and Time*, pp. 385–391.

4. Samuel Mallin, *Merleau-Ponty's Philosophy* (New Haven: Yale University Press, 1979).

5. Martin Heidegger, *An Introduction to Metaphysics*, Ralph Mannheim, trans. (New Haven: Yale University Press, 1959), pp. 14–16.

6. Abraham Maslow, *Towards a Psychology of Being* (Princeton, New Jersey: Van Nostrand, 1962); Gordon, Allport, *Becoming* (New Haven: Yale University Press, 1955); Carl Rogers, *On Becoming a Person* (Oberlin, Ohio: Oberlin College Press, 1954).

7. A. North Whitehead, *Process and Reality* (New York: Macmillan, 1929), p. 120.

Part II

Environment and place

6. Acoustic space

R. MURRAY SCHAFER

As far as I know, the first scholars to use the term "acoustic space" were Marshall McLuhan and Edmund Carpenter in their magazine *Explorations*, which appeared between 1953 and 1959. There, McLuhan wrote:

> Until writing was invented, we lived in acoustic space, where the Eskimo now lives: boundless, directionless, horizonless, the dark of the mind, the world of emotion, primordial intuition, terror. Speech is a social chart of this dark bog.

> Speech structures the abyss of mental and acoustic space, shrouding the voice; it is a cosmic, invisible architecture of the human dark. Speak that I may see you.

> Writing turned the spotlight on the high, dim Sierras of speech; writing was the visualization of acoustic space. It lit up the dark.[1]

This statement permeates all McLuhan's writings from the *The Gutenberg Galaxy* onwards. For McLuhan, the electric world was aural; it moved us back into the acoustic space of preliterate culture. Carpenter developed the theme in *Eskimo Realities*, where "auditory space" is employed as an interchangeable term:

> Auditory space has no favoured focus. It's a sphere without fixed boundaries, space made by the thing itself, not space containing the thing. It is not pictorial space, boxed-in, but dynamic, always in flux, creating its own dimensions moment by moment. It has no fixed boundaries; it is indifferent to background. The eye focuses, pinpoints, abstracts, locating each object in physical space, against a background; the ear,

however, favours sound from any direction . . . . I know of no example
of an Eskimo describing space primarily in visual terms.[2]

Despite McLuhan and Carpenter's infatuation with the concept, acoustic
space did not attract critical attention until the World Soundscape Project
was established at Simon Fraser University in 1970. The project's intention
was to study all aspects of the changing soundscape to determine how
these changes might affect people's thinking and social activities. The project's ultimate aim was to create a new art and science of soundscape
design complementary to those in other disciplines dealing with aspects of
the visual environment.[3]

Anyone who has tried to hone a new concept for delivery to the public
knows how essential it is to find the right tag words to describe it.[4] Acoustic
space is too awkward a term to have conferred fame on its inventor. Perhaps
one reason is its hybridity, marking it as transitional, caught between two
cultures. The fixity of the noun space needs something more than the application of such a restless and vaguely understood modifier as "acoustic"
to suggest the transition from visual into aural culture as McLuhan perceived it. Nor is it easy to subject aural culture to the same systematic
analysis that has characterized visual thinking. The world of sound is
primarily one of sensation rather than reflection. It is a world of activities
rather than artifacts, and whenever one writes about sound or tries to graph
it, he departs from its essential reality, often in absurd ways. I recall once
attending a conference of acoustical engineers where for several days I saw
slides and heard papers on various aspects of aircraft noise without ever
once hearing the sonic boom which was the object of the conference. This
lack of contact is characteristic of much of the research on sound still, and
one aim of this essay is to show the extent to which considerations with
space, the static element in the title of this essay, have affected the active
element, sound.

When one first tries to conceptualize what acoustic space might consist
of, the geometrical figure that most easily comes to mind is the sphere, as
Carpenter evoked it above. One would then argue that a sound propagated
with equal intensity in all directions simultaneously would more or less fill
a volume of this description, weakening towards the perimeter until it disappeared altogether at a point that might be called the acoustic horizon. It is
clear at once how many spatial metaphors we must use to fulfill this notion.
In every sense it is a hypothetical model. In reality what happens is that
sound, being more mysterious than scientists would like to believe, inhabits
space rather erratically and enigmatically. First of all, most sounds are not

sent travelling omnidirectionally but unidirectionally, the spill away from the projected direction being more accidental than intentional. Then, since there is normally less concern with the transmission of sounds in solids than with their transmission through air, the model should be corrected to be something more like the hemisphere above ground level. Experience shows that this hemisphere is distorted in numerous ways as a result of refraction, diffraction, drift and other environmental conditions. Obstructions such as buildings, mountains, trees, cause reverberations, echoes and "shadows." In fact, the profile of any sound under consideration will be quite unique, and a knowledge of the laws of acoustics is probably less effective in explaining its behaviour than in confounding it. Finally, and most importantly, the sphere described is assumed to be filled by *one sound only*. That is to say, a sound-sphere filled is a dominated space.

The sphere concept may have originated in religion. It is in religions, particularly those stressing a harmonious universe ruled by a benevolent deity, that the circle and the sphere were venerated above all figures. This is evident in Boethius' *Harmony of the Spheres*, in Dante's circles of paradise, and in the mandalas which serve as visual *yantras* in numerous Eastern religions. I will not dwell on this symbolism which, as Jung explained, seems to suggest completion, unity or perfection. The sounding devices used in religious ceremonies such as the Keisu or Keeyzee of Japan and Burma, the temple gongs of India and Tibet, and the church bell of the Western World all retain something of the circle in their physical forms, and by extension their sound may seem to evoke a similar shape.[5]

This circling is quite literally true of the church bell, which defines the parish by its acoustic profile. The advantage of the bell over visual signs such as clockfaces and towers is that it is not restricted by geographical hindrances and can announce itself during both day and darkness. In one of the studies of the Soundscape Project, it was determined that a village church bell in Sweden could be heard across a diameter of fifteen kilometers and there can be little doubt that in past times, given a much quieter ambient environment in the countryside, this kind of outreach was general throughout Christendom.[6] A similar study of a German country parish determined how the profile of the church bells had shrunk since the building of an autobahn, which leads to the supposition that Christianity as a social force has diminished in recent years in part because of the rise in conflicting environmental noise.[7] But in the late Middle Ages, the intersecting and circumjacent arcs of parish bells quite literally gripped the entire community by the ears, so that when Martin Luther wrote that every European was born into Christendom, he was merely endorsing a circumstance that was in his time unavoidable. Those who could hear the bells were in the parish; those who could not were in the wilderness.

The same thing happened in Islam, which centered on the minaret, from which the voice of the muezzin, often blind, could be heard giving the call to prayer. To increase the sounding area, or to maintain it against increasing disturbance, Islam eventually adopted the loudspeaker, which can be seen throughout the Middle East today, hanging incongruously from mosaic-studded towers, booming out over perpetual traffic jams. Like Islam, Christianity was a militant religion and as it grew in strength, its bells became larger and more dominating (the largest of those in Salzburg Cathedral weighs 14,000 kilograms), responding to its imperialistic aspirations for social power. There can be no doubt that bells were the loudest sounds to be heard in European and North-American cities until the factory whistles of the Industrial Revolution rose to challenge them. Then a new profile was incised over the community, ringing the workers' cottages with a grimier sound.

Returning to Carpenter's definition of acoustic space as "a sphere without fixed boundaries, space made by the thing itself, not space containing the thing," one notes that the acoustic space here (which may or may not resemble a sphere) does have fixed boundaries and does indeed contain something. It contains a proprietor who maintains authority by insistent high-profile sound. That space could be controlled by sound and enlarged by increasing the intensity of the sound seems to be an exclusively Western notion, for I can think of almost no examples of it in other cultures or in antiquity. Lest it be objected that Buddhist temple bells produce a similar effect, I might point out that the Buddhist bell is struck by a muted wooden log rather than a metal clapper, which deepens the sound, perhaps giving the effect of "coming from a well," which is how Sei Shonagon describes it in The Pillow Book.[8] This muting is also evident in language. In Sinhalese, for example, the Buddhist bell is called gahatáwa while the sharper Christian bell is called sínāwa.

It is true that in practically all cultures, religious exercises tend to be soundful, and in many they are the noisiest exhibitions the society experiences. Whatever the means − sacred bones, rattles, bells or voices − it is almost as if man is trying to catch the ear of God, to make God listen. But it is the two most proselytistic religions, Christianity and Islam, that have shown the greatest desire to increase the sound output of their acoustic signals, enforcing the idea that there is no private space in God's world. This point introduces a notion I call the Sacred Noise, which is special in that, unlike other noises which may be subject to prosecution, its proprietor is licensed to make *the loudest noise without censure.*[9] The Sacred Noise originated in religion at a time when the profane world was much quieter than it is now. In Christian communities, bell ringing was augmented inside the church with voices raised in song, often accompanied by instruments (the organ being the loudest machine produced anywhere prior to the Industrial Revolution). Both inside and out, the church produced the highest sound levels the citizenry experienced short of warfare. Yet no one ever laid a charge against a church for disturbing the peace.

With the outbreak of the Industrial Revolution, the Sacred Noise passed into the hands of new custodians. Then it was the turn of factory owners to establish their social authority by deafening society. It is ony after the diminution of its power as a social force that the Sacred Noise becomes an ordinary noise and subject to criticism like any other. Today, the church is weak; therefore, it is possible to criticize church bells, and many communities throughout Europe and North America have recently enacted anti-noise legislation to restrict bell ringing. Similarly, as industrialists come under fire, aural hygienists march into the factories, though the deleterious effects of boilermaker's disease were known from the outbreak of the Industrial Revolution. Today's pluralistic society has thrown up numerous recent contenders for the Sacred Noise, among them the aviation industry, the pop music industry and the police. Here, at least, are three nuclei of social power, all of whom are permitted to celebrate their uncensored presence with deafening weaponry.

Contenders for the Sacred Noise are never interested in dialogue. They want only to hector the whole of society into acknowledging their territorial authority. Another example from contemporary times will make this point clear. The sequel to the parish in modern life is the sound profile of the community radio station. Since not only the frequency but also the wattage and transmission direction of a radio station is established by regulation, one can witness in charts prepared by broadcasting authorities the most recent model of the unification of a community by sound.[10] One tends to think of radio as an international medium reaching out to gather information from around the world. Of course, this is exactly the potential that it has, but in practice it is scarcely realized. To prove this, I had students monitor radio stations and then draw maps on which they fixed dots for every toponym in the programming – the names of all towns, counties, business establishments, the location of all events, everything identified that could be tied to a place. What emerged were networks of dots clustered around the community itself, with a vague sprinkling over the rest of the world. Looking at these maps, one could not avoid the conclusion that radio is intensely regionalist, mildly nationalistic, and totally uninterested in the rest of the world except when it meant trouble. The whole globe may be transmitting, and satellites may be moving these transmissions around with fantastic precision, but the most healthy form of broadcasting is community-intensive and resists invasion. Despite the expectation that electronic technology would introduce the unrestricted flow of information, broadcasting remains ethnocentric, while proprietors dispute territories, buy up franchises as if they were parking lots or grocery stores, and reaffirm the territoriality of the whole system in the ground grid of cable linkage.

The territorial conquest of space by sound is the expression of visual rather than aural thinking. Sound is then used to demark property like a fence or a wall. It stems from the bounded shape of visual perception. For the eye, most objects are bounded, either on the outside like a chair or a tree; or on the inside, like a room or a tunnel. Not only does the notion of bounded shape give us our physical sciences (which are concerned with weights and measures), but it also contributes to the establishment of private property and by extension to the private diary and the private bank account. Once the bounding line becomes a strong perceptual distinction, the whole world begins to take on the appearance of a succession of spaces waiting to be filled with subjects or shattered by vectors. Obviously, this pattern works best where the subject can be fenced off physically (like the king's hunting grounds) or mentally (like university departments). Where it cannot be divided into visual components, sound is driven to assist in demarcation, which is why the parish can be regarded as a steeple plus bells or a factory as a slum and a whistle.

The only place where sound can be naturally bounded is the interior space, in the cave, which was extended by deliberate design to the crypt, the vault, the temple and the cathedral. The magical sensation of unbroken, sound-filled space is only possible after man moves indoors and begins deliberately to shape his buildings to achieve that sensation. Then, resonant frequencies are used as natural amplifiers to strengthen fundamental tones, and highly reflective materials are sought to extend reverberation time, giving sound a numinosity and amplification quite unlike anything possible *en plein air*. Spoken rhetoric seeks the long vowel, giving rise, for example, to Gregorian chant. In the uniform and continuous spaces of the reverberant hall or stone church, everyone falls into line as performer or listener. One sounding event is made to follow another in resonant sequence and without interruption. All contradictory sounds can finally be pushed out the door into obscurity. When Giedion says, "this is what one breathes in medieval chambers, quietude and contemplation," he neglects the astounding resonance of the thriftily-furnished cloister or state-room, totally unobtainable in the cluttered and cushioned modern interior; and how the echo of these ancient chambers fortified the voice while reading aloud, singing or issuing orders.[11] What Giedion overlooked, McLuhan overheard and sensed how "a medieval space was furnished even when empty, because of its acoustical properties."[12] When architectural historians begin to realize that most ancient buildings were constructed not so much to enclose space as to enshrine sound, a new era in the subject will open out. This pattern is true of Byzantine and Islamic architecture as well as European.

Nourished indoors, the notion of unbroken sound-filled space was later returned to the outdoor soundscape in the form of the church bell, which attempted to stencil its profile in regular and originally nearly unbroken pealing over the entire community by sound. I do not think I need stress that the other examples I have given – the factory whistle and the broadcasting signal – are equally swivel-moored to inner space, from which they transmit uniform and continuous commands to the outside world.

If indoor space waits silently to be filled with its destined and uncontradicted sound events, outdoor space is a plenum which can never be emptied or stilled. In nature, something is always sounding. Moreover, the rhythms and counterpoints of these soundings interact in dialogue; they never monologue. Who will have the next speech? The frogs may begin, the swallows arrive, geese may fly over, distant dogs may bark at the moon or at wolves. This is the soundscape of my farm, where the orchestration changes every season and every hour. All I can do is listen and try to read the patterns, which is exactly what outdoor people have done for centuries. The influence of sounds on the agrarian calendar has been recorded as far back as Hesiod.

What is true of people living outdoors today was even more true in the primitive societies of the past. In totemic society, the sounds of nature acquired an enlarged meaning as the voices of good and evil spirits whose continued interaction plotted the course of the world. All nature resounded with these spirits and everything in nature had its real or implied voice, put there for some purpose by the totemic gods. In fact, the voice of each object was its ultimate indestructible force. Just as the soul of a man was often reckoned as his voice, which escaped him at death in the form of a death rattle, so the sounds of natural objects came and departed mysteriously from the soundscape. But when they were silent, they were still reckoned to be present. They were merely listening to the sounds of other spirits in order to learn their secrets.

"Terror is the normal state of any oral society, for in it everything affects everything all the time.''[13] Like an animal, with ears bristling, man found himself in a world of strange and sudden voices. Which were his friends? Which were his enemies? And how could be exorcise those which possess evil power over him? He listened and he imitated. By the homeopathic reasoning that anyone who can imitate the specific sound of an object is in possession of the magic energy with which that object is charged, primitive man cultivated his vocalizing and his music to influence nature for his own benefit. Marius Schneider writes:

> By sound-imitation, the magician can therefore make himself master of the energies of growth, of purification or of music without himself being plant, water, or melody. His art consists first of all in localizing the object in sound and then in coordinating himself with it by trying to hit the right note, that is, the note peculiar to the object concerned.[14]

Much has been written about how the dancer, donning the mask, becomes the thing he represents, taking on its spirit or allowing it to possess him. This fact is equally true for possession by sound, and in an aural society probably even more so. Today, this possession survives faintly in the onomatopoeia of our speech, but more strongly in our creation of music, which is the ultimate transcendence of space by sound. For music, freeing itself from objects entirely, moves us quite beyond ourselves and the ordinary, Euclidean geometry of streets and highrises, walls and maps. It is the last kind of sound we really listen to, the last we have allowed to possess us, though most of it today is coalescent with uniformity and imperialism. The heavy amplification of rock music has more in common with the noise profiles of heavy technology in sustaining the grip of Western imperialism than it does with the subtle musical diversions practiced by aural cultures. The ethnomusicologist could provide many useful examples to support that distinction. Steven Feld, for instance, tells how Kaluli tribesmen imitating birds, quite deliberately refrain from synchronizing their drumming because birds never sing in unison.[15] The *aperçu* that the sound world possesses a million unsynchronized centers is illustrative of the consciousness I am trying to describe.

The phenomenologist Don Ihde reminds us that auditory space is very different from visual space.[16] We are always at the edge of visual space looking into it with the eye. But we are always at the center of auditory space listening out with the ear. Thus, visual awareness is not the same as aural awareness. Visual awareness is unidirectionally forward; aural awareness is omnidirectionally centered. This difference is one reason why aural societies are "unprogressive" – they don't look ahead; their world is not streamlined, as the "visionary" would make it. Carpenter points out that the Eskimos "have no formal units of spatial measurement."[17] Aside from the area inhabited at the moment, spatial apprehension by non-literate peoples everywhere is vague, for everything over the hill or beyond the forest is hidden. Here, sound becomes light, making the hidden visible. The cataract on the river is heard before it is seen.[18] The horn is the only straight road in the forest. News of the distant world is received by messenger, who often announces his approach by means of special sounds, for instance, the horns of the old postal coaches or the bells worn by the runners of Kublai Khan.[19] Where geography was impassable or extra speed was required, messages were sent over long distances in code. One thinks of the talking drums of Africa; trumpet communications between armies (the Oliphant of Roland); the alp horns of the Carpathian Mountains; or the great copper drums of the Middle East, sounded by the *chaouches*. The Aborigines practised the art of listening to the ground to pick up the arrival of invaders, just as we used to listen to the rails to learn if a train was coming.[20] The aural man learns that the world beyond his vision is crisscrossed with information tracks. Where I live, for instance, a hunter on the runway can tell by tracing the bark of his dog whether he is in pursuit of a deer or a rabbit: it is the difference between a straight line and a circle.

In aural cultures, the right position for settlement is often influenced by whether warning signals can be properly heard. When the Indians of Canada were numerous and threatening, the fields laid out by the first white settlers along the St. Lawrence were narrow, with habitations at one end. Families could shout warnings across to one another and congregate to defend themselves. We may compare this pattern to the larger and squarer fields of Upper Canada and the North American West, surveyed after the Indians had become peaceable. A book on Charlemagne tells how the ninth-century Huns constructed their habitations in rings so that news could be voiced quickly from farm to farm, with the distance between the rings being determined by the outreach of a warning trumpet.[21] And from Marco Polo, one learns that in the city of Kin-sai, great wooden drums on mounds of earth were beaten by guards and watchmen to telegraph emergencies.[22]

I have given these numerous examples to show how space enters the consciousness of aural society. Here, sound may transpierce space, animate space, evoke space or transcend space but never to the exclusion of contradictory transients. Defining space *by* sound is very different from dominating space *with* sound. When sound articulates and denotes space (as it does for the blind person, or as it does at night, or as it did and does for any group of people in a forest or jungle) the perceptual emphasis is subtly shifted into the aural modality, so that we discover we are discussing something that might be better be called "spatial acoustics" – as if distant sounds, close sounds, sounds up and sounds down were merely a few of the demonstratives which could be used to describe how the sound world imparts its many meanings to us.

When the forests of eastern North America were dense – and they are in places still dense enough to sense the accuracy of what I am about to say – anyone living in them relied essentially on the ear and the nose for information beyond the six-foot range their eyes would carry them. The ear remained continually alert, just as one observes it today among animals. To survive in such a world, people have to learn to respect silence, or at least have to know how to participate in the pattern of give and take, sounding when it is safe or unsafe and listening between times to know when to do so.

"Speak that I may see you," said blind Isaac to Jacob. But the unblind Eskimo says the same today.[23] It is in the sounds one hears that the world becomes palpable and complete. Without the treasury of the soundscape, the world is barren and its objects remain "hidden." Then the post horn or the train whistle is the sound that comes from far away (that is to say, it carries the symbolism of distance and travel wherever or whenever it is heard), just as the storyteller's voice is the sound that comes from long ago. And the lover's voice kisses the air near one, and the child's laughter echoes into the future. Extension and duration acquire an immediacy that visual experience can neither emulate nor even suggest.

Seeing and sounding are different. Seeing is analytical and reflective. Sounding is active and generative. God spoke first and saw that it was good second. Among creators sounding always precedes seeing, just as among the created hearing precedes vision.[24] It was that way with the first creatures on earth and still is with each new-born baby. For a projected publication (which never materialized), I once asked McLuhan to write an article on acoustic space. The manuscript I received was "Changing Concepts of Space in an Electronic Age," where acoustic space was characterized as "a simultaneous field of relations . . . its centre is everywhere and its horizon nowhere." In a letter he embellished this point, which is synonymous with the earlier cultures I have detailed, and which may be a fair comment on the culture we are today retrieving:

> We are living in a acoustic age for the first time in centuries, and by that I mean that the electric environment is simultaneous. Hearing is structured by the experience of picking up information from all directions at

once. For this reason, even the telegraph gave to news the simultaneous character which created the "mosaic" press of disconnected events under a single dateline. At this moment, the entire planet exists in that form of instant but discontinuous co-presence of everything.[25]

At the outset, I called acoustic space a transitional term, touching on two cultures, but in a sense unnatural to each. In the one, everything sounds and has its sound presence, but like a spirit, incorporeal, without precise extension or shape. In the other, this resonating life is beaten down, first in the inner spaces of the church, the concert hall and the factory; then, by extension, through the external soundscape. In the past, it was the parish, today it is broadcasting that conquers space with sound. The first form will be more difficult for indoor man to comprehend, as he hides today behind glass windows listening to the radio and peering out at the silent cacophony of the streets. Glass shattered the human sensorium. It divided the visually perceived world from its aural, tactile and olfactory accompaniments. Or rather, it substituted new accompaniments to the accentuated habit of looking. Until this situation is corrected, all our thinking about the phenomenal world will remain speculative in the literal sense of the word. But fortunately, nature has ways of reinstating the neglected. The fact that we have a noise-pollution problem in the world today is largely a result of having ignored the soundscape. But the fact that we *recognize* that we have a noise-pollution problem is the best sign we have for the rehabilitation and improvement of the soundscape.

Notes

1. Marshall McLuhan and Edmund Carpenter, eds., *Explorations in Communication* (Boston: Beacon Press, 1960), p. 207.
2. Edmund Carpenter, *Eskimo Realities* (New York: Holt, Rinehart and Winston, 1973), pp. 35–37.
3. Publications of the World Soundscape Project include R. Murray Schafer, *The Tuning of the World* (New York: Alfred A. Knopf, 1977); R. Murray Schafer, ed., *The Vancouver Soundscape* (Vancouver: A.R.C. Publications, 1978; book and two cassettes); R. Murray Schafer, ed., *Five Village Soundscapes* (Vancouver: A.R.C. Publications, 1977; book and five cassettes); R. Murray Schafer, ed., *European Sound Diary* (Vancouver: A.R.C. Publications, 1977); Barry Truax, ed., *Handbook for Acoustic Ecology* (Vancouver A.R.C. Publications, 1978). See, also, *Sound Heritage*, vol. III, no. 4, (Victoria: Provincial Archives of British Columbia, 1974), which is devoted to a discussion of the World Soundscape Project; *The Unesco Courier*, November, 1976, which is given over to soundscape articles; and Keiko Torigoe, "A Study of the World Soundscape Project," (Master's thesis, York University, Toronto, 1982).

4. Translation of the word "soundscape" is a good case in point. The French translation, *le paysage sonore*, has caused little difficulty and is now widely employed. The Poles translated it as *sonosphere* and understood at once what it meant. But when the word was rendered into German originally as *Schwallwelt*, it had little impact. *Klanglandschaft* has also been employed. *Klangschaft*, which would be most accurate, seems unacceptable to the German mind and as a result there is little interest in the subject in the German-speaking countries.

5. Proust wrote of the sound of the bell as "oval." A few years ago, when I had a group of students draw spontaneously to sounds played on tape, the bell was one of the sounds evoking the greatest circularity. The other sound was that of the air conditioner. See R. Murray Schafer, *The Music of the Environment* (Vienna: Universal Edition, 1973), p. 21.

6. See *European Sound Diary*, p. 16.

7. See *Five Village Soundscapes*, p. 15.

8. Sei Shonagan, *The Pillow Book*, Ivan Morris, trans. (New York: Columbia University Press, 1967).

9. See *The Tuning of the World*, pp. 51–52, 76, 114–115, 179, 183.

10. For the sound profile of Vancouver radio stations, see *The Vancouver Soundscape*, p. 40.

11. S. Giedion, *Mechanization Takes Command* (New York: Oxford University Press, 1970), p. 302.

12. Personal communication, December 16, 1974.

13. Marshall McLuhan, *The Gutenberg Galaxy* (Toronto: University of Toronto Press, 1962), p. 32.

14. Marius Schneider, *"Primitive Music,"* *The Oxford History of Music* (London: Oxford University Press, 1957), p. 44.

15. Personal communication. For an amplification of this subject, see Steven Feld *Sound and Sentiment: Birds Weeping, Poetics and Song in Kaluli Expression* (Philadelphia: University of Pennsylvania Press, 1982).

16. Don Ihde, *Listening and Voice: A Phenomenology of Sound* (Athens, Ohio: Ohio University Press, 1976).

17. Carpenter, *Eskimo Realities*, p. 37.

18. There are numerous instances of this experience in the Leatherstocking novels of James Fenimore Cooper.

19. Marco Polo, *The Travels* (Atlanta: Communication and Studies Inc., 1948), p. 154.

20. There is a striking instance of this long-distance hearing recorded in C.C. Bombaugh, *Oddities and Curiosities* (New York: Dover Publications, 1961), p. 280. On June 17, 1776, a slave heard the battle of Bunker Hill at a distance of 129 miles by putting his ear to the ground. The same source records that the human voice has been heard a distance of ten miles across the Strait of Gibraltar.

21. Notker the Stammerer, *Life of Charlemagne*, Lewis Thorpe, trans. (Harmondsworth, Middlesex: Penguin Books, 1969), p. 136.

22. Marco Polo, p. 232.

23. Carpenter, *Eskimo Realities*, p. 33.

24. Cosmogonic mythology is full of examples and they occur in Egyptian, Indian, Mayan, Maori and other creation stories as well as in the Bible. See "Ursound," in *R. Murray Schafer: A Collection*, B.P. Nichol and Steve McCaffery, eds. (Bancroft, Ontario: Arcana Editions, 1979), pp. 79–92.

25. Personal communication, December 16, 1974.

7. Bound to the environment: Towards a phenomenology of sightlessness

MIRIAM HELEN HILL

Human experience abounds in unifying conditions and forces which are disguised by an aura of obviousness and implicitness. This situation of normal unawareness is called by the phenomenologist the *natural attitude* – a pre-philosophic dimension of consciousness which conceals the world and prevents close scrutiny.[1] The phenomenologist works to circumvent the natural attitude and to undertake a fresh, exhaustive examination of consciousness and experience. One result of this exercise is a clear sighting of the communion between body and world.

This essay explores the body–world communion as it is revealed through the experience of the blind person. Such explication not only provides an empathetic understanding of blindness, but also provides a situation of contrast for assisting sighted people in realizing taken-for-granted aspects of their own visual world. Vision is only one of the many automatically assumed dimensions of most people's worlds. Although optical illusions indicate that what one sees is not always what is, people tend to think that sight shows them a world which is real and true. By exploring phenomenologically the experience of sightlessness, one establishes a way to separate from vision's crucial role in the natural attitude and to move toward a clearer understanding of what essential "seeing" really is.

In conducting a phenomenology of sightlessness practically, the major method used in this study is called, after Spiegelberg, a "phenomenology of vicarious experience."[2] In this approach, the phenomenologist assembles a set of experiential descriptions which establish an empathetic understanding of the experience of another person or persons – in this case blind individuals. Two techniques are valuable in conducting a phenomenology of vicarious experience: first, the imaginative self-transposal; second, the cooperative encounter.[3] In the former technique, the investigator imagines himself or herself to be in the place of other people so as to critically analyze their situations and experiences. Additional insight may be gained through observation of these people in new encounters or through imagined experiences. The cooperative encounter involves the researcher directly with his or her subjects, who communicate their experiences in firsthand fashion to the investigator. From the cooperative encounter, the investigator may gain enough insight to perform the imaginative self-transposal so that the two techniques may be used together.

The present study employed a combination of these two techniques. Ten totally blind participants ranging in age from sixteen to sixty provided experiential descriptions which served as the basis for cooperative encounter and imaginative self-transposal. In addition, as a complementary ground for the experiential reports, the study uses the descriptive accounts of blindness provided by the French writer and World War II freedom-fighter, Jacques Lusseyran, who lost his vision in a school accident at the age of eight.[4]

The study focuses on acutely visually handicapped persons because they are not burdened by the many blinders which vision ironically entails. Their experiences may offer a lucid starting point from which to bracket the prejudices produced by visual perspectives of examination. In that they are able to solve spatially-based, environmental problems without visual cues, blind individuals demonstrate that sight is not absolutely necessary for orientation and way-finding. Viewing the human situation in such a way provides a "seeing of the world" based on non-visual bonds.[5] Without sight, the other senses reach out to a world and draw closer to it, thereby coming to know these other dimensions of the world more intimately. The result is that those individuals born totally blind may serve as invaluable aids in the investigation of the non-visual ties to the environment because their experience affords a vantage point otherwise obscured by the despotism of the eyes.[6]

Comparing and analyzing the common features of shared environmental interactions reveals what thus far has been hidden as the taken-for-granted. Greater understanding can benefit both the general and visually handicapped populations. For blind persons, increased knowledge of the exchanges between people and their environment enhances the effectiveness of orientation and mobility training; increases the proficiency and confidence of the blind traveler; and yields improved safety and better adjustment to life, which thereby becomes more satisfying.[7] Facilities prepared for the blind population may be better designed and constructed so as to improve utilization. Expanded appreciation of the non-visual attachment to the environment can, likewise, improve adjustment and foster a more satisfying existence for all persons, blind or sighted. Such understanding may aid in the development of better techniques of environmental education and guide planners and designers in creating places which promote human interaction and pleasant, stimulating experiences. By examining the taken-for-granted dimensions of these interactions, insight into the essential core of people's involvement with the everyday world is gained and the nature of body–world interrelatedness is made clearer. Humankind, being intimately bound to the environment, has many resources upon which it fails to draw. The main aim of this essay is to reveal some of these resources with the hope that in the future they may be better developed.

Vision and blindness

Vision deals with shapes and distances; it extends the body to lengths the limbs can not reach.[8] "If someone says 'see,' I reach," said Irene, one blind participant in the study.[9] This brief description points to a crucial insight: seeing is touching with the eyes, and, like touch, the eyes reach only to the surface of things.[10] The eyes are capable of perceiving only lighted objects, the surfaces of which do not necessarily indicate the true nature of the things by their first appearance.[11] An upside-down crepe pan must be demonstrated to the novice cook, who will otherwise place the cooking surface on the burner. The Saarinen Gateway Arch in St. Louis appears vague and ambiguous from a distance but, likewise, if viewed too closely, loses its identity and appears as only a piece of steel.[12]

At the same time, vision more than any other sense enlarges the world. Starlight is seen in the sky, and heat lightning is observed but not heard. One may see light from surfaces far removed from the body – for example, a mountain across a plain. Glances around make one part of his or her surroundings. It is in part a visual grasping of the world which brings us closer to things. Being closer, one is in relationship to them and recognizes familiar objects, sees signs, and surveys the resulting scene for a sense of orientation. Optical scanning more than any other sense allows one to move through the world and find one's way. Rarely does one experience a fog so thick or a night so dark that visual tools can not give some assistance. When such obstacles do occur, one suddenly realizes in a direct way that sight is the dominating sense.

While one generally recognizes the inability to explain sight to a person born blind, communication totally devoid of visual perspective becomes vague and illusive.[13] The vocabulary which totally blind persons have may inadequately name or define their experience, leading to uncertainty, inexactness, and frustration. In regard to environmental knowing, the participants offered replies often emphasizing an inability to describe clearly their way of dealing with and understanding the world. Articulate accounts generally withdraw to conventional and definable terminology at the expense of precise communication, as for example, in this description offered by Susan of her approach to a staircase:

> It's difficult to explain. You can feel that the railing is coming up. You know where you are in relationship to the stairs. You can tell where you are. You can tell. You can just really tell by hearing.

As other accounts substantiate, however, hearing does not adequately convey the perception which yields the knowing. Nor is it feeling. Our language, so bound in words emphasizing vision, is incapable of succinctly defining the blind person's style of environmental knowing. "When I'm walking" remarked Susan, "I can tell when I'm going to run into a wall." Another time, she explained: "I'd listen for the steps and I can just feel that they are there." As this description suggests, the distinction among senses is sometimes unclear. Hearing is immensely informative and as Susan stated, "We do a lot of listening." For example, she mentioned listening to people on steps and using sound from the practice rooms to guide herself in the music building at the college she attended.

Besides giving attention to human sounds, participants also frequently described the experience of listening to more unusual elements in the environment, such as mailboxes, signs, openings, doors, posts, poles and trees. As Neala explained, "We listen for sounds that bounce off buildings." Here it appears that one's footsteps and other sounds echo off physical elements in the environment and indicate the position of each. Or as Lincoln attempted to clarify this style of attention: "Telephone poles are not saying anything, but if everything is quiet, I hear that pole sitting there." Sound also differentiates between objects and movements.[14] Pedestrian or automobile movement can be important. Neala described street-crossing at a busy intersection with a traffic light by "weighing the traffic," listening for the vehicles and going in the same direction. Irene explained that she used sound to tell a person's size, reactions, and characteristics. Neala reported that an alley sounds different than a street even when there is no traffic. Too much movement or activity, however, can drown out sounds necessary to "read" a situation, or cause distortion, for example the trucks which Lincoln described as "barking in your ear." A more common concern was the distortion by wind. "Windy days are terrible, awful!" Jody declared, "I can't hear anything. Nothing sounds the same." Renee added, "You can't tell what direction the sound might be coming from as easily."

Besides sound, touch plays a major role in blind peoples' mastering and understanding their environment. Often, reference to touch relates to direct contact with physical objects, for example, the shape of a faucet or doorknob, the texture of a sidewalk, the unevenness of a curb, the presence of an incline, or changes in floor coverings. At other times, however, the link of touch to the environment involves a more ambiguous description of contact with the environment: a kind of invisible net of awareness that reaches out from the blind person and senses the thing there. Irene and Laura both expressed their abilities to "feel" room dimensions, while Susan spoke of "sensing" a door. Similarly, Irene mentioned that when walking by a fence, it could be "felt." Jody captured the way this sensing facility worked best by describing her awareness of a mailbox:

> I feel it's there. If I didn't know it was a mailbox, I wouldn't know it was a mailbox. I would know something was there, but I wouldn't necessarily know what it was unless I had been told that was there.

In the participants' abilities to "touch" their environment, openings had special significance. The size of openings like doors, windows, stairwells, and corridors were distinguishable by feel and used for orientation. Some businesses were described as being small openings, others had larger openings for display, while grocery stores were repeatedly located and identified by their big openings. Open spaces were occasionally used in this way also; often, however, they were an obstacle to movement and sometimes generated an emotional reaction. Sally commented, "I'm not too comfortable in an open place or a big wide area." Neala stated, "I hate walking in places where it's big open areas because it's hard to tell where you are going." Susan continued, "The sound is strange." Jody declared, "Open spaces are horrible!" She illustrated by referring to the trip from her backyard to a shopping center diagonally across two vacant lots which lacked a "shoreline" – i.e., an edge that could be followed with a cane: "You could almost throw a rock over to that place, but there's no exact way to get there. That empty lot is huge!"[15] Another time, Susan explained, "I got totally lost because there were no buildings or anything surrounding an area I had to go to."

In dealing with open spaces, several kinds of environmental contact can be important. Lincoln mentioned the importance of the sun's position as a means of orientation, while other participants spoke of the importance of smell, at least in some situations. Laura, for example, mentioned the use of odors emanating from the grocery store, doughnut shop, shoe store, and nut shop as a means for locating them. Both she and Susan mentioned that they had been trained to use this skill. On the other hand, Jody failed to comment on the odors of the fish and chip restaurant at a corner which she described.

In retrospect, when one reviews the way in which the blind participants speak about their environment, one realizes that their style of knowing is multimodal, with repeated descriptions of a situation sometimes involving different sensual verbs. While one account may refer to feeling a post, a later description of the same instance may mention hearing it. Locating a stairs may be done by hearing, by feeling, or even by smelling the freshness of the air from the door to which the stairs might lead. The tendency to grasp one verb over another appears to be more from habit than from the actual encounter. Earlier, Susan was twice quoted describing her approach to a staircase. Other times she explained: "You can hear the steps;" or, "You can just sense them;" or, again, "I could tell that the steps were coming up because it kind of echoed when you walked in that direction." No convention verbal description can easily provide a picture of the style of knowing emanating from a synthesis of two or more senses. Yet this multimodal way of understanding the world is crucial to the blind person, and its dimensions can be better identified phenomenologically by examining participant accounts in more detail and turning to other accounts by blind persons.

A holistic environmental knowing

In the absence of sight, no *new* sense develops to compensate for the loss.[16] Through necessity, use, and practice, the remaining senses become more acute and their potential is more adequately utilized.[17] Lincoln explained:

> You make allowances for the sense that's been dulled. You learn to use the ones you've got. We don't have anything that anybody else don't have. We've developed it, that's all. You'd do the same thing.

In addition, the loss of vision automatically leads to a decrease in sensory noise. Environmental information, otherwise obscured by ocular data, becomes exploitable. The visually handicapped utilize their combined remaining senses to learn and know the environment. Through emphasis and expansion, capabilities grow into a style of holistic knowing which the participants referred to as *object perception* – the innate but often unfulfilled ability of the body to know of nearby objects, obstacles, and dangers.[18] As in "feeling" a mailbox, the perception here is neither touch, nor echo, nor movement, but a synergistic blending of all of these awareness.

For the blind person, the achievement of object perception is not always easy. Yet in everyday life, instances of it constantly occur, as above participant descriptions indicate. Often object perception combines with what the French phenomenologist Merleau-Ponty calls *body-subject* – the innate ability of the body to perform movements with neither conscious awareness nor effort, thus leading to the completion of routine activities.[19] The hand knows how to grasp a pencil or the feet know how to climb the typical stairway. As Lincoln commented in relation to eating, which some sighted people conceive of as difficult for blind persons:

I've had people ask how do you find your mouth with your fork. I don't know. When your elbow bends and your mouth flies open, it finds the way. It just goes there. It don't miss.

The simplest level of body-subject involves only bodily movements such as reaching a hand to the mouth or taking a step. The capacity for a greater complexity in the levels of body-subject activities permits an extension of the body into its environment. For instance, walking across an empty room is less complex as a bodily activity than walking through a crowd, even though both behaviors are grounded in the body-subject ability. Body-subject is basic to everyday activities, allowing tasks to proceed with speed and ease while freeing the mind for other more complex operations.[20] Laura described such behavior:

I don't think about what I'm doing. I just do it. If it's something new, I think about it. Most of the time if it's something routine, I don't think about it. It just happens.

Irene demonstrated that blindness does not interfere with the function of body-subject in more complex activities by describing her ease of orientation at home: "People ask, 'Can you get around in your own house?' I should hope so. 'Can you find everything?' Well, I put it away." Such routine, spatial actions depend upon a subliminal communion between body and world. *Basic contact*, the taken-for-granted awareness of the world which grounds body-subject, enables the person to direct taken-for-granted activities easily. Basic contact is "the preconscious perceptual ability of body-subject which keeps the generalized patterns of habit in harmony with the specific world at hand."[21] As basic contact becomes more extensive, the activities of body-subject may become more complex. The basic contact necessary for walking includes most basically the muscles of the body and a sense of the surface; for more complex behaviors, like avoiding puddles on a rainy day, a higher level of basic contact is necessary. Walking through a crowded room requires additional body awareness and cognizance of the people and obstacles within it. It may be said here that basic contact involves various levels of prereflective awareness, which in turn ground object perception. The combination of body-subject and object perception aids the hand in reaching for the pencil on the desk or helps the feet find the first and last step. The spaces in which body-subject and object perception are enacted may be either familiar or unfamiliar because of their foundation on a comprehensive basic contact. Through this precognitive link in the world, object perception ties the body's movements to the environment, making the body inseparable from it experientially. An exchange between the two entities is practically constant. The extent of this exchange, however, is variable.

Object perception can be perfected and amplified into a union and enhancement of the senses through comprehensive contact. The blind actor-musician Tom Sullivan considered his particular sensitivity to be like radar. He described it as "facial vision," a refined object perception centered on the facial muscles which register the different degree and intensity of the waves of air pushed away from the body during movement that are returned from an angle by an obstacle.[22] Even this sensitivity appears to be only a fraction of its full potential. Continued cultivation of the body's ability to utilize the wealth of sensory data available to it and heightened absorption and unity of its entire volume may yield even closer bonds between the body and its environs. Yet to achieve this enhanced object perception, awareness must be coupled with acute attention.

The focusing of attention, in fact, appears to be the key to the development of object perception. "Being attentive," says Lusseyran, "unlocks a sphere of reality that no one suspects."[23] He goes on to argue that all humankind has the ability to experience this ordinarily unsuspected sphere of reality, though in practice, most people forget or have no desire to use it.[24] The ease with which sight supplies environmental information and persistently floods the mind with a multitude of inconsequential or irrelevant sensory input is one reason for the disinterest. For blind persons, the attention which would ordinarily be directed toward the visual panorama may be directed to alternate senses, even yet supplying a plethora of stimulation. Thus, blind persons are distracted by the superficial chaos of the world, although not as thoroughly.[25] They are more capable of seeing what those not handicapped in like manner can not see. In this, they can be more attentive:

> A really attentive person could understand everything. . . . he would need nothing that is tied to the senses. . . . every object would reveal itself to him in all its possible facets. In other words, he would enter completely into its inner world.[26]

In this potential mode of attention, the senses "would no longer work independently"[27] but rather all would merge, a situation described in Sullivan's statement that "sight paints a picture of life, but sound, touch, taste and smell are actually life itself."[28] The body is capable of contacting and truly understanding this life, this reality, through a synergism of the senses, for the body is always actively reacting and collecting non-visually. One need only learn to attentively listen, feel, and experience. Lusseyran attempted a description of the product of such comprehensive contact with the world:

> What the blind person experiences in the presence of an object is pressure. When he stands before a wall he has never touched and does not now touch, he feels a physical presence. The wall bears down on him . . .
>
> Perception, then, would mean entering into an equilibrium of pressure . . .[29]

This pressure touches the body through the sense organs as commonly known, but likewise involves the concentrated attention to the "exchange that takes place between the inner and outer world," with a result that "encompasses the whole being."[30] This exchange may be likened to a current[31] and in one sense corresponds to the empathetic communion with phenomena which the phenomenologists seek: "As soon as we pay attention to this phenomenon, the world comes to life in a surprisingly different manner."[32] Through concerted effort, according to Lusseyran, all senses can join into one and build toward the enhanced object perception.[33] If this combination of awareness could be united in its extreme entirety with the "psychological form of this fundamental contact," Lusseyran argues further, the resulting attention would remove the shrouds which conceal all objects.[34] In one sense, it can be said that such directed attention results in a bracketing of the natural attitude. Lusseyran believes that the consequent unified awareness can supply strength, wisdom, and courage and is intimately bound with love, freedom, faith, fate, and life.[35] Experience, practice and unrelenting effort must be exerted for the maintenance of this perceptive force, or its presence fades and disappears. Lusseyran refers to it as light and reports, ". . . I quickly learned that I knocked against things only when I forgot the light. When I paid constant attention to the light, I ran a much smaller risk."[36] This light or force sometimes draws the world closer and reveals a pervasive peace where all parts work together in a whole. The force destroys the barriers which have been created from habit and may permit the body to be totally in tune with the world beyond.[37] The body may know of its surroundings and maneuver through familiar or unfamiliar obstacles. Beyond the material plane, Lusseyran suggests, this awareness may touch a deeper reality, a communion between the essences of existence, but only if one strives to utilize and achieve its full potential and his or her full power. Habitually, the effort and practice are deficient and the necessary heightened levels of concentration may only be sustained for brief intervals rarely approaching the supreme omniscience. Resultant insight flows like seismic waves, vibrant, sporadic, and, most frequently, minimal. Nevertheless, the potential for deeper contact does exist, Lusseyran argues, and humankind would benefit by mastering the controls.

Who possesses the handicap?

Humankind is intimately bound to the world by a combination of senses. Vision often serves to dull a person's sight to a totally integrated knowing, thus the blind person may be more aware of and more atuned to the dimensions of the world and better able to recognize the full potential of his or her being. Visual interpretations of reality are neither inferior nor superior to that of persons who are visually handicapped but, rather, an alternative means.[38] Both blind and sighted people are in contact with reality, but in different ways. The worlds in which both groups live are the same; only the perspectives differ.[39] The foundations of each, the taken-for-granted dimensions of both worlds, deserve to be excavated and explored. The blind are forced to see the world from another standpoint, but that perspective is not a world of darkness as the seeing prejudicially choose to believe.[40] Rather, that world is free of the deception of physical appearances, where what and how something is said reveals the true purpose.[41] The common space between minds is more easily reached if one's focus is not far off and on the surface of things.[42] People who happen to be blind are not inferior beings or "monsters of strangeness."[43] Sighted people, however, too often do not understand blind persons. Every member of humankind is handicapped in *many* ways. The visually handicapped have advantages that the sighted do not have. They are less distracted by the world and through necessity have refined memory faculties.[44] "No blindness" writes Lusseyran, "exists when it is a question of reflecting, intending, planning something, or even of helping men to live."[45] They may develop and use their skills and abilities just as any other person, often to the considerable benefit of larger society:

> under modern conditions [the] obstacles [of the blind] are hardly noticeable. What lawyer, what engineer, even, could manage today without the help of a few competent assistants? Blindness is a state of perception which – when taken in all seriousness, accepted, and used – is capable of increasing many faculties sorely needed in every intellectual and organizational activity.[46]

Humankind, then, should not shun blind persons but listen, learn, research, investigate, experience, and imagine. As Lusseyran explains,

> . . . if all people were attentive, if they would undertake to be attentive every moment of their lives, they would discover the world anew. They would suddenly see that the world is entirely different from what they believed it to be.[47]

People must not let their eyes blind them to the world. They need to elevate their level of consciousness to bring them closer to the world and more clearly reveal its essence while building towards the revelation of fundamental truths and greater understanding of the human condition. Furthermore, they must share and compare their discoveries to reveal the mutual wealth of experience and to communicate the knowledge gained through the necessity of heightened experience.[48] The loss of vision does not make the individual any less of a person, but rather opens his or her life to a new dimension, one generally ignored and unfortunately undeveloped by the ordinary population. Humankind should listen to the visually handicapped and learn. There is yet far to go, but the results could be invaluable. As Lusseyran explains, when "we regard blindness as another state of perception, another realm of experience, everything becomes possible."[49]

Notes

1. The natural attitude is a commonly discussed phenomenological theme; see Joseph J. Kockelmans, *Phenomenology and Physical Science: An Introduction to the Philosophy of Physical Science*, Philosophical Series 21 (Pittsburgh, Pennsylvania: Duquesne University Press, 1966), pp. 32–42; Amedeo Giorgi, *Psychology as a Human Science: A Phenomenologically Based Approach* (New York: Harper and Row, 1970), pp. 146–154; Marvin Farber, *Phenomenology and Existence: Toward a Philosophy within Nature* (New York: Harper and Row, 1967), pp. 522–524.
2. See Herbert Spiegelberg, "Phenomenology through Vicarious Experience," in Herbert Spiegelberg, *Doing Phenomenology: Essays on and in Phenomenology* (The Hague: Martinus Nijhoff, 1975), pp. 46–53.
3. Ibid.
4. Jacques Luseyran, *And There Was Light*, Elizabeth R. Cameron, trans. (Boston: Little, Brown and Company, 1963); Jacques Lusseyran, *The Blind in Society and Blindness: A New Seeing of the World*, Proceedings no. 27 (New York: The Myrin Institute, 1973).
5. Lusseyran, *The Blind*.
6. Ibid., p. 28.
7. Orientation involves establishing one's position relative to objects in the environment; mobility is the ability to navigate from one position to another desired point. See Herbert D. Angus, Bob Howell, and Jacqueline Lynch, "Twenty Questions about Mobility," *The New Outlook for the Blind* 63 (1969): 214–218; and Jesse Manley, "Orientation and Foot Travel for the Blind Child," *International Journal for the Education of the Blind* 12 (1962): 8–13. As the blind person speaks of it, a "traveler" is one who possesses sufficient orientation and mobility skills coupled with confidence and motivation to enable himself or herself to find his or her own way around without the aid of another person.
8. Lusseyran, *The Blind*, p. 22.
9. Irene is one of the ten blind participants providing descriptive accounts. From youngest to oldest, their pseudonyms are William, Marianne, Jody, Susan, Laura, Neala, Renee, Sally, Irene, and Lincoln.
10. Lusseyran, *The Blind*, p. 22.
11. Ibid., p. 23, p. 22.
12. See Edward G. Ballard, "The Visual Perception of Distance," in F.J. Smith, ed., *Phenomenology in Perspective* (The Hague: Martinus Nijhoff, 1970), pp. 187–201.
13. Our language is grounded in the visual perspective. One watches television although the ears assist, and to see is to understand. Stuart Chase wrote, "No human is free to describe nature with strict objectivity, for he is a prisoner of his language." See Stuart Chase, *The Power of Words* (New York: Harcourt, Brace, and World, 1954), p. 104. The visual perspective so prejudices the vocabulary and thought patterns of language that it can not concisely describe contrary elements.
14. For a phenomenological discussion of this aspect of hearing, see Don Ihde, "On Hearing Shapes, Surfaces and Interiors," in Ronald Bruzina and Bruce Wilshire, eds., *Phenomenology: Dialogues and Bridges: Selected Studies in Phenomenology and Existen-*

tial Philosophy 8 (Albany, New York: State University of New York Press, 1982), pp. 241–251.

15. On a sidewalk, most blind people use one of the edges as a guide to follow rather than attempt to walk straight along the undistinguishable middle.
16. See Lusseyran, *The Blind*, pp. 28–29.
17. See Tom Sullivan and Derek Gill, *If You Could See What I Hear* (New York: Harper and Row, 1975).
18. Other terms used for object perception are "obstacle detection" and "facial perception." See Ann Middleton Kidwell and Peter Swartz Greer, *Sites, Perception, and the Nonvisual Experience: Designing and Manufacturing Mobility Maps* (New York: American Foundation for the Blind, 1973).
19. Maurice Merleau-Ponty, *Phenomenology of Perception*, Coin Smith, trans. (New York: Humanities Press, 1962); Mary Rose Barral, *Merleau-Ponty: The Role of Body–Subject in Interpersonal Relations* (Pittsburgh: Duquesne University Press, 1965). The significance of this bodily ability and its role in everyday activities is explored in David Seamon, *A Geography of the Lifeworld* (New York: St. Martin's Press, 1979).
20. See Seamon, *Lifeworld*, for more detailed accounts and examples.
21. David Seamon, personal correspondence, May 21, 1980; also, see Seamon, *Lifeworld*, p. 115.
22. Sullivan and Gill, *If You Could See*, p. 10, p. 68.
23. Lusseyran, *The Blind*, p. 12.
24. Ibid.
25. See ibid., p. 18, p. 29.
26. Ibid., p. 29.
27. Ibid.
28. Sullivan and Gill, *If You Could See*, p. 181.
29. Lusseyran, *The Blind*, p. 31.
30. Ibid., p. 25, p. 26.
31. Lusseyran, *And There Was Light*, p. 28.
32. Lusseyran, *The Blind*, p. 31.
33. Ibid., p. 30. Lusseyran considers the senses successive stages of a single perception, touch.
34. Ibid.
35. See Ibid., p. 10, p. 14, p. 16, p. 17.
36. Ibid., p. 10.
37. Ibid., p. 26.
38. See Lusseyran, *The Blind*, p. 20.
39. See David Lowenthal, "Geography, Experience, and Imagination: Towards a Geographical Epistemology," *Annals of the Association of American Geographers* 51 (1961): 241–260.
40. Lusseyran, *The Blind*, p. 32, p. 25.
41. Ibid., p. 23, p. 15. This statement applies first to that which is said by a person, but also refers equally to objects.
42. Lusseyran uses these phrases. See *The Blind*, p. 19; and *There Was Light*, p. 16.
43. Ibid., p. 36.
44. See Lusseyran, *The Blind*, p. 18.
45. Ibid., p. 15.
46. Ibid., p. 18.
47. Ibid., p. 13.
48. Ibid., p. 28, p. 30.
49. Ibid., p. 20.

8. Towards revealing the sense of place: An intuitive "reading" of four Dalmatian towns

FRANCIS VIOLICH

Places and people are inseparable.[1] Places exist only with reference to people, and the meaning of place can be revealed only in terms of human responses to the particular environment used as a framework for daily living. In their behavior in places, people reveal, but do not necessarily articulate, their preferences. Whether creating environments as "insiders" or becoming familiar with these environments as "outsiders," people identify with or feel alienated from places.[2] The key question is how in a practical way one recognizes "sense of place," which in many ways is intangible. How can one clarify and interpret the essential qualities underlying the uniqueness of place and consequently understand a basis for identity?

This essay attempts an answer to this question by summarizing results of a field study in selected towns and villages on the Dalmatian Coast of Yugoslavia.[3] My method draws on the creative power of intuitive responses, sharpened by firsthand experience in places of contrasting physical form. Through direct involvement and reflection, I immersed myself in each place for several days and "read" each as a whole.[4] "Mental maps" evolved that served as frames of reference for the images of places and people that emerged.[5]

By identifying environmental qualities which underlie a sense of place, I developed a qualitative style of inquiry that may have important practical value for urban design and planning, which too often today emphasizes a quantitative, aggregate approach to environments. Qualitative criteria for identifying a sense of place are also crucial in the design process and can contribute to protecting and enhancing existing environments or designing new places with greater human significance. Such qualitative criteria may help establish what Norberg-Schulz calls *creative participation* – a concept of design and planning that harmonizes a people's cultural and social needs with natural environment.[6] In this way, people record their particular cultural history and meaning in the built environment and breathe into their urban settlement a "sense of place."

Regional variations and local identity

The four Dalmatian towns examined here were selected for their contrasting spatial layouts. The aim of this contrasting selection was to pinpoint and intensify the towns' varying senses of place. Diverse historical forces have shaped Dalmatian coastal settlements and range from earlier Roman, Slavic and Venetian influences to the later impacts of Napoleon, the Austrian Empire, and the current socialist system.[7] Though threatened by modernization, especially tourism, the off-shore islands of the Dalmatian coast have many well-preserved settlements patterned incrementally by successive historical forces around varying water–land relationships. These towns and villages carry meanings which, in Heidegger's terms, have been "gathered" throughout history. They convey a clear image of a cultural heritage valued by residents. Fortunately, the modern socialist system of Yugoslavia with its belief in non-speculative and decentralized self-management supports this local sense of identity.[8]

At first glance, these shoreline settlements of Dalmatia look very much alike: creamy-white stone houses with slate or red tile roofs stand shoulder to shoulder; dark green pines rise against brilliant blue sky above matching blue sea dotted with ships; marinas, or *obalas*, as they are called, give shape to the town harbors, the focal points of community life. In all of the villages, pedestrian movement still prevails, since planning policies sensitive to human qualities keep cars and buses at the periphery.

When examined more closely, however, the coastal towns of Dalmatia reveal important differences, which in turn reflect marked regional variations and strong traits of local identity, which are all diverse sources of a sense of place. For example, on the island of Brač, across from Split, Dalmatia's largest city, the gentle slopes, upland plateaus, and accessible shores facilitate contact among settlements, fostering a sense of belonging for the residents of each of Brač's twenty-two villages and towns (Figure 1). The result is that participation and economic life are extended more evenly over Brač than on other Dalmatian islands.[9] Two of these towns explored in this essay – Pučišé and Bol – demonstrate well this local identity.

In contrast, a sharp ridge runs the main length of the nearby island of Hvar and settlement concentrates heavily on the northwest, where level land and

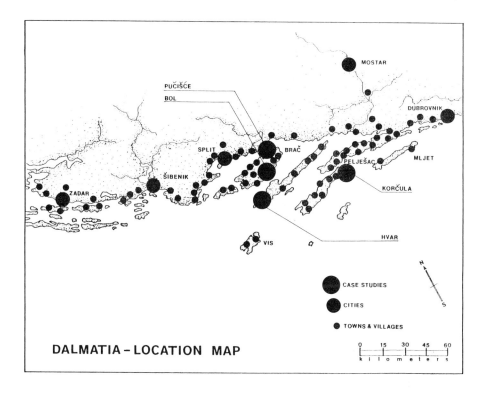

Figure 1. Dalmatia: Location map

large natural harbors meet (Figure 1). There, through their patrician classes, the towns of Hvar and Starigrad have managed the island's affairs throughout history. Hvar is the third Dalmatian town examined in this essay. To the south, the island of Korčula presents topography somewhat similar to Hvar's, though with numerous, less divisive ridges, thus permitting scattered settlements. Furthermore, places suitable as harbors occur generously at both ends of the island; the result is two large towns widely separated, each with a strong sense of regional leadership. One of these, Korčula – the fourth town studied here – is located directly across from the peninsula of Pelješac and has thus been able to dominate the sea channel and to wrest control of the upper end of the peninsula from the powerful city-state of Dubrovnik to the south.

In the process of "reading" the four towns of Pučišće, Bol, Hvar, and Korčula, I came to understand that a major dimension of these settlements' sense of place was the particular way in which water and land meet (Figure 2). Both Pučišće and Hvar "wrap around" their harbors, but in different

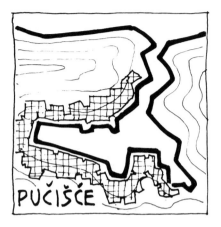
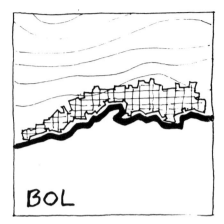
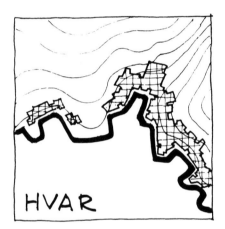

Figure 2. The four Dalmatian towns: The water–land interphase

ways. Pučišće tightly encloses its harbor and town activity reflects an "urban area." Hvar, in contrast, splays into the water and projects an image of "arms open to the sea." In Korčula, land boldly indents water as the town thrusts itself into the sea – a pattern recalling an "urban ship." Finally, in Bol, water and land lie side by side; the town is parallel to the sea, and one is reminded of yet another configuration: the "ladder pattern."

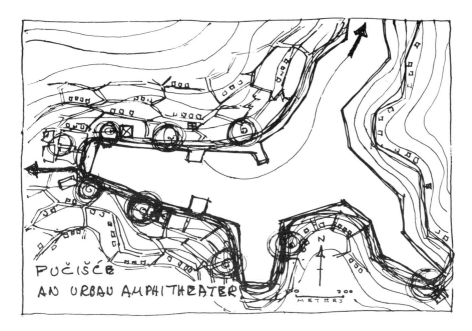

Figure 3. Pučišće: The urban amphitheater

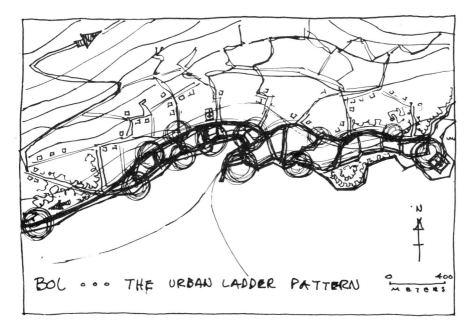

Figure 4. Bol: The Urban ladder pattern

Pučišće and Bol: Arena versus ladder

Both on the island of Brač, Pučišće and Bol have a common history and share similar social and economic traditions. The different land–water interfaces and contrasting local topography, however, have led to differences in qualities of living in the two villages and important differences in the sense of place. The steepness of Pučišće's site and the firm enclosure of its harbor, or *luka*, have affected patterns of class distribution and intensified a sense of belonging for residents and a sense of outsideness for visitors. On the other hand, Bol's linear townsite has a role in promoting greater social equality and sense of openness for the outsider (see Figures 3 and 4).

First, consider Pučišće (Figure 3). This tightly built village of some fifteen-hundred people rises on steep slopes facing the deep, watery cleavage of Brač's north coast (Figures 5 and 6). The path of this inlet zigzags for about a mile from its mouth at the sea to Pučišće's harbor, cutting off visual contact between the town and open shoreline. From its steep slopes, Pučišće looks inward on itself, and for the outsider, the town can seem a private world within which he or she is an intruder. Visible to all from the town's hillside dwellings, the newcomer on the *obala* feels conspicuous in a vast urban arena. The houses step up the steep terrain one above the other like seats in a theater balcony; the windows seem like watching eyes. The broad *obala* following the undulating seawall around the harbor serves as an endless stage with no exist. To walk around the bending waterfront and to see the shifting patterns of dwellings stacked on the hillside leads one to feel that Pučišće's sense of place revolves around this experience. Community facilities – shops, cafes, post office, school, and church – form no strong nodes and are too far apart to work as effective points of sociability. Across the *luka*, one sees these separated places as potential destinations, but distance and lack of common proximity brings on a sense of frustration in reaching them. It is not only food, drink or postage stamps that one might need; one's desire for casual interpersonal encounter is denied by the uncomfortable spacing and lack of gathering places. Pučišće, though forming a dramatic oval of populated land around a centralized body of water, has no clear human center of gravity.[10]

This lack of functional cohesion arose in part from the presence of the larger homes of upper-class families who centuries ago became economically advantaged due to direct access to the harbor – an arrangement which established these families in shipping. Poorer families were relegated to the slopes above the sea and did farming nearby. At the same time, however, the physical containment of the town and its economic independence

Figure 5. Pučišće's tightly enclosed *luka*

because of a large, nearby marble quarry fostered a strong sense of belonging and togetherness at the wider town level.

To leave Pučišće and to walk out to the wild headlands of the open sea along a shore thick and fragrant with pines offers a clue to the town's quality of togetherness. The contrast between this timeless regional setting and Pučišće itself brings to mind the centuries of struggle for possession of the townsite and reinforces a sense of collective rootedness. Pučišće's inwardly oriented sense of place is a powerful identifying force for residents and even for emigrants and their progeny from such far-removed places as Chile or California. On the other hand, this sheltering quality becomes almost menacing for the newcomer with no family ties. This fact may help explain why Pučišće attracts few tourists in spite of a unique natural and human landscape.[11]

To return at dusk along the winding waterfront from the open headlands and sea to the closed-in town is to participate in a grand urban choreography. Fresh perceptions of place follow one on another with shifting views of the town and changing light on the tiered dwellings. At twilight, the windows soften as the sun leaves and the water darkens. Night comes and the

Figure 6. Pučišće's hillside dwellings

lights in the "eyes" of the somber stone houses reflect in the blackened waters, dappling like swaying lanterns. In the darkness, one is relieved of the sense of being watched from the houses above, and Pučišće gives way to a different sense of place than by day.

With a population of about one thousand, the town of Bol on the southern side of Brač sharply contrasts with Pučišće (Figure 4). The town stretches side by side with the sea along low hills at the foot of some of the most rugged limestone terrain on Brač (Figure 7). Across the open channel lies the sharp ridge of the island of Hvar. One senses tranquility and repose in a setting of vast marine space. A "reading" of Bol's architecture clearly indicates less class distinction than in Pučišće. The absence of any natural harbor and the readily accessible shoreline gave rise to a lineal pattern with all dwellings having direct and equal access to the sea and its economic benefits.

A three-mile stretch of road between a Dominican monastery on the east and vineyards on the west established the basic route along which Bol's lineal townsite evolved. A second parallel route on filled land in front of the

Figure 7. Bol's linear form

seafront dwellings was built in the late nineteenth century when a wine boom required port facilities in common. Over time, links between these two roadways formed a ladder-like street pattern with scattered shops and services located at the "rungs" of intersections (Figure 8).

In contrast to the ready "readability" of Pučišće, Bol was more difficult to "read," especially recording the town mentally in coherent map form. In time, I realized that Bol's overall structure could be perceived in its entirety only through experiencing each of the seemingly unrelated parts and incrementally fitting them together into a multifaced image. I had a sense of continual discovery while exploring the connecting points of the town's two main routes and identifying differences among social functions at the nodes. These nodes take many forms, located as they are above and below retaining walls that divide sea level from the higher street above. The evenly spaced breaks in the tightly walled "corridor" of stone dwellings on the upper road open views across planted terraces to the sea and thus provide a sense of rhythm. These breaks often take the form of small plazas and each becomes a place of particular activity – for example, old people sitting, or children playing. At the same time, the linear "ladder" pattern works against

regular contact among larger numbers of Bol residents, since there is no single "stage" in the town common to everyone. Meetings must be deliberate and arranged. The "ladder" pattern encourages privacy of the residents and challenges visitors to explore, discover and develop their own means for integrating themselves with Bol.

Overall, Bol's sense of place arises very much from the linear character of the site and the opportunity it offers to experience a continual back-and-forth movement stopped at one end by the Dominican monastery; at the other, by *Zlatni Rat*, or "Golden Point," a spit of sand unique in all Dalmatia. Reaching out along the water, Bol's townsite generates a sense of involvement coupled with openness and freedom considerably different from the intimacy and closure of Pučišće.

Hvar and Korčula: Open arms versus urban ship

Hvar and Korčula stand as opposites in urban form and offer strong contrasting images rich in meaning for an intuitive "reading" of place (see Figures 9 and 10). At Hvar, the water indents the land and the town becomes a symbol of receptivity, built tightly around a protective harbor made by "arms" of coastline that beckon out toward the open sea as if to welcome the world. At Korčula, the land with the historic "Old Town" pushes out into the water; entering this area offers the experience of boarding an "urban ship," surrounded by water on three sides and thrusting aggressively out to sea.

The symbolic image of Hvar's "arms open to the sea" speaks directly for its historic role in international maritime life. Centrally located between Venice and its Mediterranean Empire, the harbor first served the Greeks and Romans; later, in the early Middle Ages, the inland Slavic newcomers learned the ways of the sea there. Venice's use of Hvar as a port of trade with the Orient established over many centuries the town's sense of hospitality and comfort. Austria's domination up to World War I paved the way for the international tourist who today comes to Hvar seeking an earlier culture grounded in untouched nature.

Serving a year-round population of some two-thousand people, Hvar's central core forms a giant "U" of building facades facing the broad *obala* along the edge of its large *luka* (Figure 11). The result is one vast "pizza of water" furnished with boats. At its innermost end, the "piazza of water" turns at right angles to become a "piazza of stone," terminated by the cathedral and its dominating campanile. Shops and other activities cluster

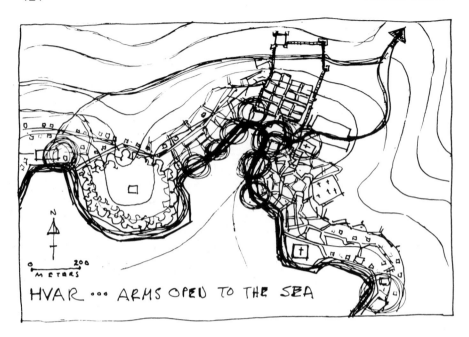

Figure 9. Hvar: Arms open to the sea

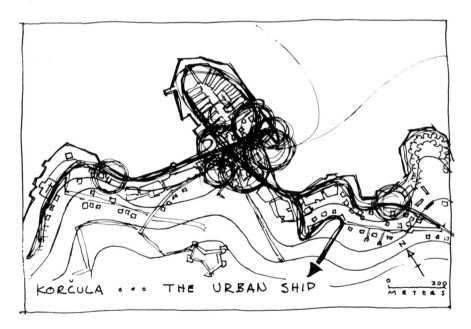

Figure 10. Korčula: The urban ship

Figure 11. Hvar's *luka* open to the sea

around the "U"-shaped core, which sparks both visual interest and informal social contacts (Figure 12). One senses that the power of Hvar to capture and enliven has much to do with these "arms open to the sea" and their rocky outer reaches of shoreline contrasting sharply with the compact urban character of the central harbor.

This contrast between a confined and open experience is true especially of the Old Town, the heart of Hvar's history and huddled within ancient walls just off the piazza of stone. Through a stone gateway, one enters a grid of narrow streets that slice through the three-story stone buildings. Streets and walls together, built of the same cleanly cut stone, form a monolithic geometrical grid that today imposes the will of its sixteenth-century planners over the movement of the visitor and dominates the "reading." Dwellings face each other only a few yards apart and the confined space requires an unaccustomed intimacy: facades must be scanned slowly, since they are too high to be taken in at a glance; an old woman in black kerchief passing but a few feet away revives a sense of earlier town life; a weed in a crack high above flowers in the sun demonstrates the insistence of vegetative life in this urban world of stone.

Figure 12. Hvar's central harbor and plaza

   To immerse oneself all morning in the claustrophobic confines of the Old Town and then, suddenly, to walk into the open world of the piazza, harbor and sea evokes a strong, insightful response. Passing through the stone gateway, one's mood takes a sharp turn: as the unrestricted movement of people in the larger space appears, one feels a sense of freedom to choose directions and intentions; the heart leaps with an exhilarating sense of opening out to the world again. A fresh meaning of three-dimensional space becomes clear as pigeons define the height and breadth of the piazza with their flights back and forth between children below and roof tops above.

   The introspective quality of this shifting sequence of experience parallels movement through a succession of interrelated environments in Hvar. First come the individual rooms within dwellings identified by their windows that often connote specific uses. Put together, rooms form a house with all its social implications; and dwellings, in turn, collectively form the stone blocks separated by streets; their geometric network together makes up the Old Town encased in its ancient wall. Beyond is the larger environment of the piazza, which is but part of another large whole – the town of Hvar itself. From the *obala*, the openness of the harbor tells of yet another environment

Figure 13. Korčula's Old Town and its link with the "crossroads"

— the island of Hvar as a whole and its many towns and villages. The island becomes but a part of the larger maritime region with its ties and linkages continuously reaching out to the world at large. Thus, Hvar's sense of place is perceived as rooted in the wholeness of each of its separate parts and their interrelatedness to larger spatial systems. Just as important to the sense of place is the way Hvar embraces the sea and thus serves to communicate the role of water as a forceful element connecting the town to the world at large. The result is a sense of place for Hvar that is broad and out-reaching, with the power to generate emotional responses from urban form particularly rich in insights.

In sharp contrast to Hvar's sense of place, Korčula's is revealed not by focus on the sea, but rather on the way the sea sets forth the town and calls attention to its human-made character (Figures 13 and 14). One becomes aware of man's ability to collaborate with geography and thrust his work and ships out upon the sea from a built environment designed for that purpose. To understand this concept, it is first necessary to distinguish between the Old Town and the larger townsite with its twenty-five hundred residents. Because of the oval, convex shape of the Old Town, its spatial system can be

Figure 14. Korčula's Old Town seen from the "mainland"

"read" as a whole quickly and requires none of the extended exploration called for by the "environments within environments" of Hvar. The commanding presence of the Old Town built on a rocky promontory is like a ship docked and ready for departure; a "mental map" can be drawn almost a first sight.

The Old Town is attached to an undulating, receding shoreline along which, since the turn of the century, Korčula has grown in linear fashion, forced by steep topography and increased vehicular routes over the island as a whole. Two principal routes converge at the base of the "docked ship" and loop around it, forming a concentrated regional "crossroads" at the very gate of the Old Town. Here, facilities needed for modern living such as markets, shops, services, banks and civic activities are located, as well as a bus terminal and dock for coastal ships, and the ferry to Orebić. A main theme contributing to a sense of place here is the "gathering" at a single center of so many elements and activities. One is drawn to this center and rewarded by the variety of levels of experiences offered, especially in contrast to the all-pervading sense of history expressed by the adjacent Old Town.

Unlike Hvar's, which is hidden in the larger townscape, Korčula's Old Town dominates its surroundings and provides the basis for a lasting imagery. Enclosed by the remnants of medieval embattlements, the Old Town

Readability
The first phase in "reading" a place is orientation to the basic spatial system. While the use of a map may be more efficient, a deeper sense of relationship will come from discovering the spatial structure through the actual experience of finding and mentally recording one's way. In Bol, there were feelings of frustration, inconvenience and even a sense of insecurity in developing a "mental map." The ultimate result, however, was a much firmer sense of possession of the town and richer insights into its sense of place. In Pučišće, on the other hand, the system was so legible that there were few opportunities for exploration and discovery, which was also the case for Korčula.

Freedom of choice
The number of options for routes to follow in "reading" urban places can become an emotional issue. In attempting to experience an entire spatial system, one comes to rest having to follow the same pattern as in the old portions of Hvar and Korčula. On the other hand, the meandering hillside districts of Pucisce and Hvar (not described here) reflect the freedom of individuality of the rural peasantry who built them, intuitively following the topography. In perspective, this response, strongest in Hvar and Korčula, raises the question of the sterile quality of totally planned environments devoid of citizen participation so common in today's metropolitan areas.

Privacy and sociability
Both visitors and residents in places of small scale like the four towns described here can no doubt feel the need at times to retreat into settings of privacy for reassurance of a sense of belonging to the place. This is particularly true of areas devoted to pedestrian use, like these towns are, or to the increasing number of non-vehicular streets in larger cities. The total exposure of onself in Pučišće could be as alienating for the visitor as is the overly private quality of linear Bol. On the other hand, Hvar and Korčula both have high degrees of friendliness and sociability because of a balance between places for casual assembly as a part of daily routine and places intended for less public social interchange.[19]

The impact of contrasting urban forms
Contrasting physical forms among the spatial elements of a single town evoke contrasting emotional responses and thus provide the basis for a deeper experience. The claustrophobic quality of Hvar's Old Town served

to give greater significance to the open quality of the piazza and harbor, and the passage from one to the other enriched Hvar's overall sense of place. In Korčula, the contrast between the disciplined, compact form of the Old Town and the open sea around its three sides offered quite a different experience than viewing the "Urban Ship" from higher ground above. On the other hand, Pučišće and Bol were devoid of this kind of striking contrast among their parts. Rather, it was the contrast between going from one town to the other that brought forth the qualities of each.

Reading the cultural heritage
An experience high in emotional content uses the wholeness of the environmental pattern of each place as a vehicle to sense the "collective subconscious" of the generations of people who built a town and lived there.[20] I felt a sympathetic feeling grow toward the mass of humanity that stands behind the creating of each environment. The revealing of the chronology of spatial sequences of development lent perspective to our own "instant" city-building and tearing down of the past, often leaving us rootless. In gaining this kind of awareness of sense of place, one develops the capacity to see previous periods of history in rich unison.

The awareness of regional ties
Finally, those places having some visible ties or links to the regions of which they were a part offered the most complete experience and therefore a higher level of sense of place. To enjoy the quiet of Hvar's waterfront and the relatively simple day-to-day life taking place there, then to see a majestic white steamer from some outside port arrive silently at the sea wall, reminds one that cities are but elements in larger networks covering the globe.

Urban planning and design should take sense of place into account in creating a built environment that reinforces it against alien forces. An intuitive, comparative style of "urban reading" helps reveal how the spatial and environmental context plays a major role in generating a sense of place. By developing a greater sensitivity to the meaning of our environments through intuitive awareness of this kind, we might overcome some of the problems of conflict between the mechanized environmental processes of today and the human and participatory process of urban growth in the past. Working with users of cities, we might discover ways to build into new areas more authentic qualities of uniqueness and thus assure greater feelings of identity with the places where we spend our daily lives.

Notes

1. This paper was originally presented at the annual meetings of the Society for Phenom-enology and the Human Sciences, University Park, Pennsylvania, October, 1982, for a special session, "Phenomenologies of Place," organized by David Seamon. A fuller ac-count of the work presented here is provided in Francis Violich, "An Experiment in Reveal-ing the Sense of Place: A Subjective Reading of Six Dalmatian Towns – A Working Paper" (Berkeley: Center for Environmental Design Research, University of California, 1983). The field research was made possible by a Yugoslav-American Fulbright Award in 1979; a grant from the Beatrix Farrand Fund in the Department of Landscape Architec-ture, University of California at Berkeley in 1981; and collaboration from the Faculty of Ar-chitecture and Urbanism at the University of Zagreb, Yugoslavia, and its branch in Split. In interpreting the findings here, I wish to thank Anne Buttimer, David Seamon, and the late Donald Appleyard for valuable stimulus.
2. Donald Appleyard, "Inside vs. Outside: The Distortion of Distance," Working Paper no. 307 (Berkeley: Institute for Urban and Regional Development, University of California, 1979).
3. The distinction between towns and villages in Dalmatia is not easily drawn and depends on size and rural or urban character. Typically, villages involve a population ranging from several hundred to a thousand people, while towns incorporate a population of several thousand or more. Furthermore, the coastal settlements – even when small – are quite urban socially due to close sea ties with larger cities like Split and Dubrovnik. Accordingly, the terms "town" and "village" are used more or less interchangeably in this essay.
4. Particularly useful in developing this method was Paola Coppola Pignatelli, *Roma: Esperienze di Lettura Urbana [Experience in Urban Reading]* (Rome: New University Press, 1973), especially pp. 8–9.
5. See Thomas Sharp, *The Anatomy of the Village* (London: Penguin, 1946), for drawings of widely differing spatial systems.
6. Christian Norberg-Schulz, *Genius Loci: Towards a Phenomenology of Architecture* (New York: Rizzoli, 1980).
7. Francis Violich, "An Urban Development Policy for Dalmatia" – Part I: The Urban Heritage up to the Time of Napoleon," *Town Planning Review* 43 (1972): 151–165; Francis Violich, "An Urban Development Policy for Dalmatia – Part II: Urban Dalmatia in the Nineteenth Century and Prospects for the Future," *Town Planning Review* 43 (1972): 243–255.
8. Tomislav Marasović, "The Methodology Used in the Revitalization of Split," in Donald Ap-pleyard, ed., *The Conservation of European Cities* (Cambridge, Massachusetts: MIT Press, 1979).
9. Marijean Eichel, "Dalmatia in Microcosm: An Historical Geography of the Changing Land Use of Brač, Yugoslavia," (Ph.D. dissertation, University of California at Berkeley, 1975).
10. For a portrait of a Dalmatian town where the centralizing qualities of the physical environ-ment *do* generate sociability, see Francis Violich, "'Urban' Reading and the Design of Small Urban Places: The Village of Sutivan," *Town Planning Review* 54 (1983): 41–62.
11. My own family ties with Pučišće have enabled me to explore this aspect of identity with places and the role it plays in cultural continuity and change. See Francis Violich, "Three Houses: Three Grandmothers," in *Zajednicar* (Pittsburgh, Pennsylvania: Croatian Frater-nal Union, August 1981).

12. See, for example, Kevin Lynch, *The Image of the City* (Cambridge, Massachusetts: MIT Press, 1960).
13. See Rene Dubos, *A God Within* (New York: Scribners, 1972).
14. See, especially, Martin Heidegger, "Origins of a Work of Art," in *Poetry, Language, Thought*, Albert Hofstadter, trans. (New York: Harper and Row, 1971), pp. 17–87.
15. David Seamon, "Sense of Place and Phenomenological Structures," paper given at the annual meeting of the Society for Phenomenology and the Human Sciences, University Park, Pennsylvania, October, 1982, for a special session, "Phenomenologies of Place," organized by David Seamon.
16. Norberg-Schulz, *Genius Loci*.
17. Ibid., p. 185.
18. See Francis Violich, "Vernacular Urban Places: The Search for Cultural Identity Through Urban Design," paper presented at the annual meeting of the Environmental Design Research Association (EDRA 15), San Luis Obispo, June, 1984.
19. Violich, "'Urban' Reading."
20. Pignatelli, *Roma*.

9. The circle and the cross:
Loric and sacred space in the holy wells of Ireland

WALTER L. BRENNEMAN, JR.

Early texts on Ireland often refer to the sacrality of Ireland as a place. Rufus Festus Avienus, a Roman author of the early third century, refers to Ireland as "Insula Sacra" and writes: "This Isle is Sacred named by all the ancients, from times remotest in the womb of Chronos ..."[1] Ireland contains within herself intrinsically a mystery and power which are manifested specifically in her geographical features.[2] Rivers such as the Boyne and Shannon, hills such as Tara and Uisnech, caves such as the Cave of Cruachan and St. Patrick's Purgatory – all are bearers of particular powers inherent in their geography.

I was unaware of Ireland's sacred topography prior to a trip to Ireland with my wife some years ago. Driving down a country road, we noticed a sign at a picturesque intersection that read, "St. Farnan's Shrine." Out of curiosity, we followed and came to an enclosure containing a statue of the Irish saint and in the rear a gate leading by a path to a wooded ravine through which a small brook flowed. We again followed, crossed the brook and on the far bank were startled when we saw a picture of the Virgin Mary beside a small spring.[3] A cup, some coins, and several rosaries were nearby. Beside the cup was a sign reading, "Drink Me For Eyes." We had heard stories of fairies, but we knew nothing of holy wells and their lore. Ten yards downstream we came upon another spring with similar sanctions and beside it a sign, "Drink Me For Feet" (Figure 1).

We were impressed by this experience and later came to realize that the peculiar power we felt at that place derived from the subtle melding of the natural setting and the sanctions of the Catholic tradition – an experience of sacred space one ordinarily associates with the elaborate architecture of human-made, albeit divinely inspired, structures.[4] If such formed, synthetic building was sacred, then what was the nature of the space in which we

Figure 1. Well obscured by underbrush with small statue of Virgin Mary, St. John's Well, the Burren, County Clare

found ourselves that afternoon in the Irish countryside? Was it, too, sacred, or was there a different form of power that imbued that place and entwined itself with the sacrality of sanctions so familiar in a more refined setting?

Our chance experience in Ireland set off a study that focuses ostensibly on the holy wells of Ireland. At the same time, the study seeks to probe beneath the form and structure of the wells to the peculiar natural power which combines with the power of the sacred manifest in the myths and

Figure 2. Well complex including stone wall and large tree upon which is a shrine box, Well of the Blessed Tree, Corofin, County Clare

rituals of the Catholic tradition attached to these wells. It soon became clear that the power of the wells was of a different genre than that of the sacred, though intimately connected as one side of a coin to the other.

The sacred is a form of power that is world-creating. It transforms whatever lies in its path to its mode of being as it extends out from the "center" seeking to define the boundaries of its domain. It is an explosive power, whether in cosmic or historical form, and goes about establishing structures

Figure 3. Well opening with white cross, St. Patrick's Well, Ballyshannon, County Donegal

which are universal and equally applicable to all within the "world." One of the crucial dimensions of sacred myths and rituals is that they be repeated in the same way at the same times throughout the totality of the sacred world. The Catholic Mass, for example, follows the same liturgical pattern in all Catholic Churches. Eliade has shown that the structures established by the sacred are themselves universal and can be studied fruitfully from a cross-cultural perspective.[5] This universalizing aspect in large measure gives the sacred its peculiar being.

Figure 4. Well complex including stone table with round stone upon it, St. Laiser's Well, County Rescommon

As my wife and I reflected upon our experience at St. Farnan's well, we felt that its distinctiveness resulted from the conjunction of two forms of power. One was clearly that of the sacred as manifest in the sanctions of the Catholic church, known throughout Christendom. The other was a power that was by function, at least, the opposite of the sacred, and what I call here, *loric*. What we felt when we were surrounded by the wooded grove nestled in the watery bowl was a power that was drawing us *inward* toward a center. It was a power that was implosive rather than explosive and was connected exclusively to that place. This centering was the most outstanding sensation, an impression of being truly there within that place and responding to its power and its uniqueness. It was like no other place on earth, and it was precisely because of this uniqueness that it was powerful. The spring, the trees, the stone manifested something that was nothing more than it was. It was its own self in its own uniqueness that invited us within it; that absorbed and, in a sense, intoxicated us with its presence.

This form of power is present in all lore, by which I mean the unique particulars attached to a person or thing which set it apart. For example, the power of storytelling lies in the event of the telling and in the unique way that the particular teller tells it. The story is not meant to be repeated in a uniform way from teller to teller as is a myth in the sacred tradition. Rather, the idiosyncrasies of the event and the teller afford the power to draw listeners into the experience. These characteristics are common knowledge to folklorists, but what is overlooked is the otherness of the loric power – an element shared with the sacred. An element of mystery was present in that grove as we drank from the cup marked, "Drink Me For Eyes." The loric and the sacred share a participation in the archetypal, repeating timeless and powerful themes. The difference is that the sacred derives its primary power from the eternal, identical repetition of the archetype, whereas the loric derives its primary power from the differences manifested from repetition to repetition. Each storyteller, each singer, each place gains its power from the uniqueness, the differences, the imperfections (Figures 2, 3 and 4).

The notion of *place* is one of the most important forms of loric power. In Ireland, this power is expressed in her geography – her rivers, caves, and hills. An understanding of the sense of intimacy that resides in such places provides a key to the understanding of loric power. As a power, intimacy is so self-contained that it is completely hidden to those who possess it. Intimacy is revealed only to those who chance to enter a place in which the possessors dwell. When the stranger enters, he is immediately aware of the otherness and intimate nature of the "place." He senses the odors unique to the place – its sounds and artifacts. He may feel extremely uncomfortable and wish to flee, or he may be fascinated and wish to participate in the power. It is this quality of intimacy based upon uniqueness that provides the possibility for placehood, which in turn is the ground of the loric.

Some years ago, my wife and I were members of a tomato-picking crew in southern Pennsylvania. We were the only white members on the crew, and when we had occasion to enter the home of another member, we were struck by a rush of sensations that conveyed the intimacy of the place and its inhabitants. It was strangely other to us as whites, and we were both afraid and drawn to what we experienced in that place. Based upon these insights, our experience at St. Farnan's presented us with the conjunction at the well of two forms of power – the sacred and the loric. The well itself was a powerful symbol capable of uniting opposites, of joining levels of reality that are ordinarily incompatable.[6]

Irish cosmology and the establishment of sacred power

Cosmology provides the clue to the distinctive nature of sacred power as it establishes a world in early Ireland. The notion of a sacred world – that is, Ireland as a consolidated group of provinces held together by a fundamental group of myths and rituals – did not emerge in Ireland until perhaps the fourth or fifth century A.D. It was the cosmology brought to Ireland by the Celts that formed the mythic and symbolic foundation of the Irish sacred world.

From the perspective of Western and even most Eastern cosmologies and the world views deriving from them, the Celts have an inverted cosmos in that the source of all power is not found in the sky but in the otherworld beneath the earth. The result is that power and wisdom radiate upward from below rather than downward from the sky. Although the sky contains some powerful forces such as the sun, it is understood by the Celts as a secondary or complementary power to the forces found in the otherworld and the earth.[7]

The otherworld in Ireland is located in various places, as a means of providing several complementary shades of meaning. The most common location of the otherworld is beneath the surface of the earth, and access to that world for the living is possible only at particular places on the earth's surface which are containers of loric power. The most common of these access points takes the form of a hill or mound and is called in Irish a *sid*. The *sid* is hollow and opens of its own accord at certain critical times to allow movement both from the surface downward and vice versa. Upon the *sid*, various rituals of kingship in Ireland took place, such as inauguration and periodic festivals and banquets of symbolic import. Access to the otherworld can also be gained through a lake, cave, or well.[8] As these examples indicate, the emphasis on geographical entrances provides a clue as to the importance and power of the holy well.

Another location for the otherworld is an island to the far west. In general, the direction of west at its extremity is understood as the otherworld. Originally in Celtic lore, Ireland herself was seen as the otherworld and a holy place because of her westerly location vis-à-vis the then-known world.[9] Another place in which the otherworld is found is beneath a lake or sea. This theme is present in several Celtic traditions, including the French, where the otherworld is depicted as a submerged city presided over by a magico-divine princess.[10] In Ireland, the sea theme is present in a tale from the *Leabhar na hUidre*, where another magical princess escapes the flooding of a well to live beneath Lough Neagh.[11] Three hundred years later, she is transformed into a salmon and returns in human form to the surface world. Her divine nature is confirmed when she is baptized as the goddess Murigen, or "born of the Sea."[12]

The otherworld in Irish myth is understood as the first form or archetype of all life and wisdom. The surface world is a reflection of that archetype and contains the same structural components but is lacking the power present in the otherworld except at critical times and in particular places. The two worlds are like two electric circuits, one (the otherworld) alive and the other (the surface world) dead until a contact wire links the two. This connection occurs at particular times and places when access is established between the two worlds.

The otherworld itself is generally described as a pleasant place, though there are some descriptions of certain otherworld islands which contain tormenting or horrible forms. Many descriptions suggest a feminine identity to the otherworld, thus one of its names is *Tir na mBan* – the Isle of Women. In "The Adventures of Conle" and "The Adventures of Bran," one finds the otherworld described as a land of women ruled by a seductive queen. It is this queen who *is* the otherworld, possessing the occult or hidden wisdom of which the otherworld is the source.[13] The theme of most adventure tales in Irish literature and myth is that of the young warrior journeying to the otherworld to gain the affection of its irresistible queen and thus attain the hidden wisdom necessary to rule on the surface world.[14] Still another theme is the queen as guardian of a sacred spring which is the true source of wisdom. The queen is actually identified with the spring or well, and her marriage to the young warrior constitutes the archetype of the marriage of the king to Ireland, which is the world.[15]

The otherworld was also understood as a site of cosmic ritual whose center was a *bruiden* or a banquet hall in which the perpetual feast of the otherworld queen and her consort, the Lord of the Otherworld, was held. There were five *bruidne* in the otherworld, and these *bruidne* were reflected in the inauguration sites of each of the five provinces of Ireland.[16] The in-auguration sites were a complex of the following elements: a *síd*, on which was a *bruiden* where the king lived; a sacred tree or *bile* under which he was crowned; a holy well; and a sacred stone which functioned as a throne.

These same elements were present in the otherworld, which contained the archetypes of these power-bearing forms as well as several other magico-religious objects that were, in turn, reflected in the inauguration sites of the surface world. Taken together, these sacred objects were identified with Ireland as they convey sovereignty. They were managed by the Lord of the otherworld who is the sun of the otherworld, the divine smithy and the husband of the goddess, Ireland.

The otherworld, then, is the pre-barren–birth state. She is the Great Mother, the voluptuous, mysterious, forbidden container of secrets. She is the Original Mother, and most essentially, the well of Segais whose water creates the world and imbues it with wisdom. It is she who provides the power and models for the actualization of the surface world, and it is she who through her power sacralizes this world. Within this feminine "place" were located the five *bruidne*, with their host, the Lord of the Otherworld, and the magical weapons forged by him. He was the husband of the hidden woman, and through his mating with her the world was born. When the Lady at the Well is raped by the Lord of the *bruiden*, the well overflows and the world is reborn.[17] It is this well that forms the model for the present holy wells of Ireland.

The otherworld well of Segais and its symbolism

The archetypal well of Segais is located in the otherworld and is associated with a magical, beautiful woman, often guardian or keeper of the well.[18] It is frequently visited by warrior chieftains seeking her "favor," which takes the form of sexual intercourse symbolically identical with drinking from the well and achieving wisdom. Around the well are nine hazel trees, all in the tradition of the aforementioned *bile*, whose red berries drop into the well. These berries are magical and cause a mist to arise from the water, which is called in Irish *na bolcca immaiss*, or "bubbles of mystic inspiration."[19] Further, there are five salmon, also divine beings, who live in the well and consume the berries and are thus known as *eó fis*[20] – the salmon of wisdom.[21] As the well is the source of the holy rivers Shannon and Boyne on the surface world, the berries and salmon periodically flow into these rivers. Whoever eats the berries or is fortunate enough to catch and eat a salmon is endowed with wisdom and becomes an accomplished bard, or *file*.[22]

The symbolic meaning of the well of Segais is contained primarily in its identification with the Great Goddess, the central fecundator and power of Irish spirituality. More precisely, the well is the vagina of the goddess which consumes the offering of the Lord of the Otherworld, who is finally transformed into the sacred salmon who lives within the "belly" or *yoni* of Ireland. Through the offering of the male to the female, the goddess overflows with power thereby revivifying the world. Here, we see that power is manifest primarily in the feminine mode, and, as such, is ambivalent. The goddess is both devouring mother in her consumption of her husband/son, and also nurturing mother in her instrumental role as recreator of the world.

The salmon symbolize the offered son, lover and husband now full of divine wisdom through his death to the Goddess, within whom he dwells. Here again, however, one encounters ambivalence, for the salmon is a fish of two waters, the salt and the fresh, the feminine and the masculine. In his boundary crossing, the salmon, like the mercurial Hermes of Alchemy, brings the power of the hidden Goddess to the surface and thus encourages transformation in ordinary humans. The salmon symbolizes the male Lord who has, like Jona, been swallowed by the watery feminine and through this intimate relationship has absorbed the healing quality associated with Her. This meaning accounts for the male Lord's ambivalence and for the fact that the salmon is sometimes understood in this role as "anima," as a woman or girl.

The nine sacred hazel trees, or *bile*, stand by the well of Segais. The berries of these trees fecundate the well, producing the mist of wisdom or feeding the salmon of wisdom. The sacred tree in Irish myth plays a masculine role, symbolizing the ancient timeless ancestors, the Lords of the Otherworld who are sacrificed to the Goddess/well and cause her to overflow, bringing about the wisdom of a new creation or transformation. The wisdom is always a hidden wisdom and so it manifests itself as a mist or a cloud through which the world is seen in a shadowy form.

One final component of the well of the otherworld is the *lia fál*, the sacred stone and one of the five primary power bearers of the otherworld. This stone was most probably situated near the well of Segais, although it is not perfectly clear in the text.[23] My interpretation is based upon the fact that sacred stones are commonly present in association with holy wells on the surface world prior to Christian times, and these surface wells are understood as reflections of the Well of Segais. One of the best known of these Sacred stones was the one located at Tara, primary inauguration site of the high kings of Ireland. Here, the stone played a role in the ritual of inauguration. The stone itself was commonly understood to be in the form of a pillar and interpreted, therefore, to symbolize the power of the king as fecundater.[24] O'Rahilly amplifies this interpretation by his association of the stone with the sun god and, consequently, the Lord of the Otherworld. The connection with the sun is made through the Otherworld God's role as divine smithy. It is the smithy who manifests the lightning stroke of the sun in his forge and the voice of thunder on his anvil.[25] As the sun of the otherworld, the stone possesses the voice associated with it on the surface world but is often in the shape of a circle and understood as a "circle of light," identified with the sun.[26] These linkages are further indication that the stone of *Fal* did, in fact, lay by the well of Segais in the otherworld.

Wells as establishing sacred space in pre-Christian Ireland

Keeping in mind the mythological significance of the well of Segais, one finds fresh meaning in the ritual activities that occurred at the holy wells in pagan Ireland. The primary and, thus, archetypal ritual of the otherworld was the great banquet that occurred in the five *bruidne*, or banqueting halls. There, the Lord of the Otherworld, host of the banquet and husband, lover and son of the Great Goddess Ireland, mates with her at the well near the *bruiden*, thereby recreating the world through the consequent flooding of the waters of the well. This same ritual was imitated in the kingship rituals and inaugurations of the provincial kings of Ireland.

The earliest rituals relating to what would now be called holy wells are centered around votive deposits found by archaeologists in sacred pools, lakes and rivers. These deposits were related to Celtic peoples and indicate the sacred power of water within the Celtic world. This power applied particularly to springs and pools because they offer access to the otherworld beneath and thus become a channel for power originating there. These deposits were referred to by the classical scholar, Posidonius, who quotes an earlier work by Strabo dating from the second century B.C.[27] It appears that water particularly in the form of springs and pools, has reflected sacred power within the Celtic world from earliest times.

Turning to Ireland, one recognizes that the success of kingship depended on the fecundity of the land, and the success of the king depended upon his virility and his ability to mate with "sovereignty" who was identified with the great goddess, Ireland. She guarded the well and handed the goblet of ale to the king − lover and son as a symbol of their marriage. The king's drinking of the ale symbolically united him with the goddess and he became sovereign and sage. For example, it was said of King Cormac that until he slept with Queen Medb of Connaught he was not rightly king of Ireland. Queen Medb was originally identified with the great goddess and with sovereignty; her name means intoxication,[28] and thus the link between the queen, ale and wisdom (intoxication) is established. "The Phantom's Frenzy" is another tale establishing the relationship of the earthly king with the lady of the well and with ale. In this tale, King Conn one misty night is wisked away to a *sid* where he encounters the 'Lady' who is seated on a crystal throne. She prophesies the future kings of Ireland and with each prophecy she pours out a goblet of ale.

As the virility of the king waned with age, so too did the fecundity of the land due to the king's reduced ability to unite with her and maintain sovereignty. This change was reflected in the imagery of the goddess gradually transformed from lovely virigin to ugly hag. To recreate the "world," it was necessary for the present king to die and for a new, younger man to take his place.[29] There are several tales which emphasize this theme, a motif common also to many fairytales. Perhaps the most typical one is "The Five Sons of Eochaidh," related in the *Temair Breg* and *Echtra mac Echdach Mugmedoin*. The old king is waning and five brothers go in turn to a sacred well (presumably located at the inauguration site) to drink of the water and thus to gain wisdom, sovereignty and kingship over Ireland. The well is guarded by a hideous hag who demands from each a kiss before she will grant the draught of sacred water, here equal to the ale. Each of the brothers refuses until the last and youngest, Niall, arrives. When she makes the request of him, he throws his arms about her "as if she were forever his wife."[30] At this moment she is transformed into a beautiful young maiden and foretells his rule at Tara.

The central importance of the holy well at kingship rituals becomes clear from these tales: there is a symbolic homology between the maiden at the well, the goddess sovereignty, the great goddess of fertility, the ugly hag, the goblet, ale and the well itself. The inauguration took place at the well around which the prospective king, having been identified as the sun/son by the scream of *lia fál*, circumambulates sun-wise. He is then granted the goblet of "ale" – i.e., water from the sacred well. Upon drinking, he is simultaneously united with the goddess, becomes sovereign through his marriage, and is intoxicated and thus wise through the appearance of the salmon in the well at that moment. The goblet remains with the king as a symbol of goddess, well, wisdom and sovereignty.[31] The new king is now granted a white wooden wand under the sacred tree, usually located by the well.[32] This rite confirms his kingship by linking him to the great ancestral god, Lord of the Otherworld, whose roots are under the earth (as otherworld sun) and whose branches are in heaven (as celestial sun).

This symbolic ritual constitutes the fundamental ground of all rituals connected with the holy well. It is connected, as all rituals, to the myths of *illo tempore*, here located in the otherworld; and is reflected at various levels in the ritual life of the surface world. This ritual was the heart of the inauguration rite held periodically at the ascension of a new king, and kingship was reflected on several levels. Each *tuath* (a small collection of several nobles and land-holding farmers) had a king, or *rí*, who in turn was bound to a *ruiri* – a superior king who ruled over several *tuatha*. The *ruiri* owed allegiance to a "king of superior kings," or *rí ruirech*. This was the provincial and highest king known to Ireland until the tenth century, when the high king at Tara was established. Each of these kings had his inauguration site and holy well.

The holy well also played a significant role in the annual seasonal festivals. These festivals, called *oenach* in Irish, were structurally patterned after the inauguration rituals in that they involved the mating of the kings to the goddess, thus involving the ritual complex of stone, tree, and well. The rituals held at *Samain* (November 1), *Imbolc* (February 1), *Beltain* (May 1), and *Lugnasa* (August 1) were all primarily focused upon the continued fecundity of the goddess and the king. They also provided a time for games, poetry, the selling of wares, paying of rents to the king, the settling of lawsuits, the discussion of new laws, and fights between rival factions of various families. Horse racing also played a major role in the *oenach* and must be understood, especially in the province of Ulster, as a sacred event. In general, the *oenach* was what we would call a fair. These fairs were held not only at seasonal transitions but also at all ascensions of new kings. The holy well was involved at all rituals on all levels. For example, the *Instructions of a Prince* states that at the festival of *Lugnasa*, the high king was to be given of "the fish of the Boyne, the venison of Luibnech . . ., the heather harvest of Bri Leith . . ., the crosses of the Brosna . . ., the water of the well of Tlachta, and the *milrad* . . ., of Uas . . . ."[33]

Finally, the holy well played a part in the kingship ritual known as "hosting," or the taking of hostages. In this ritual, the king would rise before dawn, bathe and drink from the sacred well attached to the inauguration mound, ritually don his sword and lance, then at dawn, depart for the center of each of the chiefs of the *tuatha* under his dominion. There, he would be hosted and would take a hostage, usually a powerful personage, and continue on to the next *tuath* until he had circumambulated his "world." The direction of the trek was always "with his left hand to the sea," or sunwise. The intention of the ritual was to bind the king to each of his holdings through the actual presence of a part of the holding – the hostage – in his *bruiden*.

Practically, this rite provided security for the king: if there were a challenge from a particular *tuath*, he would sacrifice the hostage of that *tuath* to the goddess, thus the ritual insured and maintained "sovereignty." Further, the ritual occurred on all levels of kingship, so that one might imagine a series of concentric circles all enclosed by the great circle made by the high king of Ireland.

Contemporary lore of wells and its symbolism

Contemporary lore surrounding the wells provides a transition from the power of the pagan well to that of the Christian holy well. The lore and ritual surrounding the present-day wells are a mixture of survivals from the Irish mythological tradition and the present attitudes and traditions of the Catholic Church in Ireland. One can examine some of the lore and ritual that bear a resemblance to motifs in the material presented earlier concerning Irish traditions at the wells. My wife and I have gathered many stories of wells both in the present and the past which harbor magical fish. In every case, the fish is either a trout or a salmon and very often is speckled with red spots. Sometimes the trout is white, sometimes golden, and sometimes the fish is described as a white eel. In essence, the fish in the well of today patterns itself after the salmon of wisdom of the well of Segais. The present belief is that whoever sees the fish will be granted a prayer – i.e., the granting of grace or wisdom – thus the sighting of the fish is identical symbolically with the transformation of the hag at the well into the beautiful maiden. In both cases, the fish is a symbol of the transformation of the visitor to the well and reflects that transformation.

Consider, for example, the case of a woman my wife and I interviewed in Astee West, County Kerry. On the eve of her wedding, she went to meditate at St. Eoin's well. She sat on the grass before the well, and from out of a nearby bush there sprang a golden trout moving on its tail as a salmon skims across the surface of the water. The trout leapt into the water and disappeared. From the spot where he disappeared, there arose a continuous stream of bubbles. These are considered to be full of power and no doubt they refer back to the *na bolcca immaiss*, or mystic bubbles of inspiration of the Well of Segais.

Another common motif in contemporary lore about wells is that the water of the sacred well will not boil. This theme suggests a surviving connection between the water of the well on the surface to that of the eternal well in the otherworld. The water of the otherworld well is changeless, immutable and perfectly stable in the same sense as that of the philosopher's stone or alchemical gold. The water of the surface well, through its identity with the water of the Otherworld well, is seen to be as immutable as alchemical gold and thus becomes the water of life, the *aqua vita*.

This same symbolic reasoning applies to the wood from the sacred tree standing by the well. Eternal and immutable, the wood will not burn. In both cases, the transformatory agent of the water and wood is that of fire – i.e., boiling and burning. It is fire and drought which are the antithesis to the creative principle of pagan Ireland in which creation is brought about by a watery flood flowing out of the body of the goddess. That which resists fire resists death.

The holy wells for many local people, therefore, are healing centers par excellence. Healing is derived primarily from the water itself, but often from items that are associated with the water, such as moss or cress in the well or "blessed clay" in or near the well. Healing is also connected to the tree and stone present at the well and completes the archetypal complex of rock–tree–water. One may implant a coin in the blessed tree, or hang a rag or rosary or piece of clothing upon it. The stone can be rubbed, or one may circumambulate it, crawl under it or slide through a crevice. The tree as ancestor/king takes upon itself the burden of one's illness as deposited through the "clootie" – i.e., cloth and coin. The stone as Lord of the Otherworld and sun straightens that which is crooked through its law and thus is related to healings of the limbs and arthritis.

Most cures at the wells and many wells themselves are related to the eyes. *Tobar na súil*, or "well of the eyes," appears on well after well in the Irish countryside today. A cure for the eyes is a cure for sight, but it is difficult to imagine that so many Irishmen have sore eyes, thus the symbolic meaning arises: not sight but insight and wisdom, the primary benefit of the well of Segais. Beyond these practices, the central ritual associated with the well today involves the circumambulation of the well and very often the sacred tree and stone. This ritual is always performed clockwise – a pattern paralleling the motion and meaning of the sun. There is no basis for this ritual in Christian tradition, and one must look again to the pre-Christian custom of the king circumambulating the well "sunwise" prior to his drinking from the well. Here, the king takes on the role of the sun and thus the Lord of the Otherworld as it circles the goddess, the earth. He is the consort and servant of the goddess, and this same symbolism is maintained in today's circumambulation ritual at the well, though the meaning is long forgotten.

What has taken the place of these forgotten meanings is the connection of the holy well with a particular saint of the Christian tradition. When my wife and I asked the woman who had seen the golden trout what she thought it was, for example, she replied that it was a form of St. Eoin. Holy wells today are encouraged by the church because they are catalysts for prayer, not because they are thought to have any power of their own. Christian symbolism has overshadowed the ancient memories.

Loric space at pre-Christian wells

Having considered the primary sacred motifs of holy wells, one next can ask what their relation is to the power of the loric in pre-Christian Ireland. There are tens of thousands of springs, or wells, in Ireland. Why is it that some are holy and others not? The distinction lies partially in the location of the well upon the body of the goddess, Ireland. It is the uniqueness of the location – the *locos* – that makes one well powerful and another just a spring. In examining hundreds of holy wells, we noted three primary configurations of the terrestrial surface which emerged over and over again: first, wells emerging from a shaft in a rock; second, wells located in a bowl-like area; third, wells near the sea. These topographic configurations contain abundant power simply because of their shape and their location. Let me cite an analogy to clarify what I mean. In traditional polytheistic cultures, tools are bearers of power and therefore sacred. A basis for their sacrality is shape, thus a hammer is powerful because its form gives it the particular power to do what it does. The power of the hammer is within its shape and is not derived from some external being or force. This same principle applies to the power of the earth. Particular shapes or configurations of the earth are powerful because they are what they are, not because they gain their power from another source such as a god. Because these shapes or configurations are "other," they possess the force of place and thus are examples of loric power. In addition, the three topographic configurations point to the three types of water set forth in Irish myth, namely, the water of the heavens, of the earth, and of the sea.[34]

Yet even among these configurations, not all are loric. There may be a well in a bowl or near the sea that is not regarded as holy. One way of understanding why there is a distinction between sacred and non-sacred wells of the same terrestrial configuration involves systems of energy beneath the earth's surface, usually called *ley lines*. These veins of power are said to penetrate the crust of the earth like a grid, converging at particular spots. The suggestion is that when these lines converge at the location of one of the three types of surface configurations, a well at that place acts as a link or axis allowing the two forms of energy to meet.[35] Indeed, there appears to be considerable evidence that Irish wells recognized as sacred are located at such points.[36] On the other hand, we need not take this information literally, but it does serve us as a metaphor or even a myth, telling us the nature of particular power of a particular place.

Another way in which loric power relates to the holy wells involves the regional nature of the wells vis-à-vis the *tuath* and the royal family connected to the well. Each well is identified with not only a place because of the configuration of the earth at that place, but also because of the people who live there. The well is thus limited in its influence to a particular group of people – members of a certain *tuath* or even of a certain family. Such a well exists today on the tip of Kerry Head, County Kerry, on the Corodin family compound, a small group of houses and farms along the seashore. The well, located by the sea, is dedicated to St. Erc, and is used only by the Corodin family. The healing power of the well is only effective on Corodins, and only on blood members of the family, thus no daughter or son-in-law could gain a cure from the well. Michael Corodin, eighty-six years old, is presently the chief of the family and in his possession is a sacred rock known as the bouly stone (Figure 5). This stone is always cool and moist, even on the hottest day in July, and is kept in the house of Michael in a bag. When the well is used, the stone is removed from the bag, carried to the well and placed in the water. Then the rounds are made and the prayers said. Only with the stone in the water would the well be effective, and then only on blood members of the Corodin family. Here one sees the power of intimacy, region, and place converging to present a strong manifestation of the loric.

But what of the sacred? do the holy wells of pagan Ireland point beyond themselves to a "world," to some archetypal referent? Insofar as there is a consciousness of Ireland as a whole, there is a consciousness of the sacred. For Ireland is the world, she is the goddess, sovereignty, and therefore sacred. After the tenth century and the establishment of the high king at Tara, the possibility of a sacred world creating power presented itself. The wells located at Tara gained their power now primarily because they were instrumental in recreating the "world" each *Samain* and at each inauguration. Originally, their power was derived from the place. This power was still retained, but with the coming of the High King was covered over by the lofty and explosive power of the sacred. Great world-creating and world-encompassing rituals were held at Tara and the provincial sites, and focused on the well, seeking Her sanction. Further, each well in each bowl, mountain cleft or seaside pointed beyond itself to the archetypal well of Segais located in the otherworld. Each well is thus a sacred symbol; although each well

Figure 5. Family chief Michael Corodin holding a bouly stone, Kerry Head, County Kerry.

gains its primary power from the 'place', it also participates through resemblance in the sacred world-creating well of Segais. Through this con-sciousness of cosmogonic themes on the part of the families using the well, it is sacralized. The closer Ireland came to nationhood, the more open the well was to the power of the sacred.

The Christian influence on sacred and loric power

With the coming of the Christian hermits in the late third century and, later, of St. Patrick in 432 A.D., Ireland became more and more influenced by the sky god *Yaweh* and by the world-creating power of the sacred. To be sure,

10. Many dwellings: Views of a Pueblo world

DAVID G. SAILE

The forms of Pueblo Indian villages in the southwestern United States have fascinated anthropologists, architects, and travellers for more than a century. These forms are intricately interwoven with the semi-arid climate; the dramatic canyon, mesa and mountain landscape; and the social, ceremonial and symbolic fabric of Pueblo life. The main villages and their houses constitute both domestic and ritual residences possessing ties with a complex everyday and mythical world. Study of these house–world relationships offers valuable insights into the nature of Pueblo dwelling and touches upon broader attributes of dwelling described in a number of phenomenological enquiries.[1]

 This essay discusses the world of one Pueblo group, the Tewa, and the dwellings within that world. A sketch of the broader pan–Pueblo universe is also presented to provide an environmental and cultural context for viewing the Tewa world. Both aspects of this study grow from and utilize materials gathered for earlier studies of the role of architecture in the Pueblo world.[2] These materials include photographs from the past one hundred years; archeological and ethnographic reports; written observations of surveyors, traders, travellers and others; and my personal experiences of the villages. Especially useful for the research were the meticulous records of early scholars in the Southwest and the more recent investigations of native Pueblo scholars.[3] The resultant picture of the Pueblo world is based upon accounts of both insiders and outsiders to that world. In Edward Relph's terms, my own observations in this essay are a blend of the 'vicarious' and 'empathetic' insider.[4] I have been affected deeply by the landscapes and dimensions of life in the Pueblo world, and in this sense I share in its richness. Because, however, I am a foreigner to both the United States and Pueblo culture, I experience that sharing against my own cultural background and through the literature of various authors. I attempt to describe ideas of dwelling inside the Pueblo world, but I also compare this inside view with the accounts of travellers and governmental agents.

These insider and outsider accounts, focusing upon the same place and environment physically, raise significant questions about the many dimensions of Pueblo dwellings. These accounts also raise questions about commonalities between Pueblo dwellings and more widespread notions of dwelling. As an architect, I believe these questions are extremely important. First, ways to understand dwelling are vital because architects design houses and other residential environments which comprise the fabric and spaces associated with dwelling. Second, deeper understanding of environmental experience is important because designers need to share in others' experiences of their designs. To a greater or lesser degree, architects are always outsiders relative to the places and communities for which they design. Ways of understanding the insider's perspective and experience are crucial if architects are to foster appropriate and significant places in which other people may dwell.

The Pueblo setting

The communities of the Tewa Indians in New Mexico are one of six Pueblo linguistic and cultural groups. The other Pueblo groups are the Hopi and Hopi-Tewa in Arizona; and the Jemez, the western and eastern Keres, the Tiwa, and the Zuni – all in New Mexico. The locations and layouts of the thirty existing Pueblo villages vary considerably. The six Tewa villages – San Juan, Santa Clara, San Ildefonso, Pojuaque, Nambe and Tesuque – are situated in and to the east of the Rio Grande valley north of Santa Fe (Figure 1). Their traditional layouts involve rows of houses organized around one or two courtyards. Figure 2 shows the court of San Ildefonso in 1975. The Spanish mission church lies just outside to the west, and the Jemez Mountains across the Rio Grande are in the background. Traditional Hopi village sites are on high mesas with bare-rock surfaces. Villages are arranged in both parallel house-row and small courtyard layouts. Figure 3 shows a view of the Hopi village of Walpi in 1897. Narrow parallel streets and small exterior spaces are formed by the irregular terraces of house structures.

Village linguistic roots have been traced to three widely separated geographical origins, and dialects often vary from village to village. Social organization in the western villages differs markedly from that in the eastern ones, as do many aspects of ceremonial. The agriculture of corn, beans and

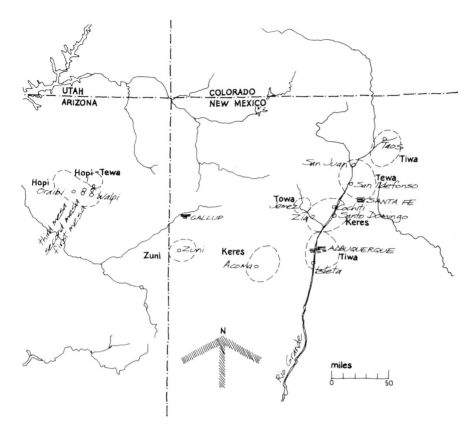

Figure 1. Sketch map of the locations of Pueblo linguistic and cultural groups in the south-western United States.

squash was more dependent upon the unreliable rainfall in the west, whereas more irrigation was utilized along the Rio Grande than those for the Hopi and Zuni in the west. As a result of these many variations, each village has a unique history within the broadly shared outline since the first Spanish explorations in the early sixteenth century.

Despite the many linguistic, social and environmental differences, however, there are many similarities among the settlements. All Pueblo groups live in permanent villages, built until recently of stone, adobe and un-squared timber beams. Most have farm houses or settlements in the surrounding areas, and some villages are seasonally occupied. Subsistence was until the mid-twentieth century based upon a balance between agriculture undertaken in stable traditional locations and hunting and gathering within traditional territories. All the main villages possess ceremonial and

Figure 2. The court of San Ildefonso looking west.

communal chambers, termed *kivas*, which vary in number, in shape and in particular villagers associated with them. A kiva is a special room for certain religious and social activities of a village or village group. The word, now Anglicized, comes from the Hopi term for house and can also be an entrance to the underworld and a place of emergence. The eastern Keres village of Cochiti on the Rio Grande, for example, has two circular kivas built of adobe at ground level. All villagers belong to one of the two groups, or *moieties*, associated with them. In contrast, the Hopi village of Walpi has five rectangular kivas, built of stone below ground and associated with clan groups and certain ceremonies. Despite such variations, all villages share the outline of a common world view and knowledge of similar mythical origins.

Dwelling in the Tewa world

Because of the work of anthropologist Alfonso Ortiz, himself a Tewa, more is known about the relationships among spatial ideas, myth, human and supernatural categories in the Tewa world than in the world of other Pueblo groups. In *The Tewa World*, Ortiz attempted "to understand how the Tewa perceive human and spiritual experience, and how they organize time and

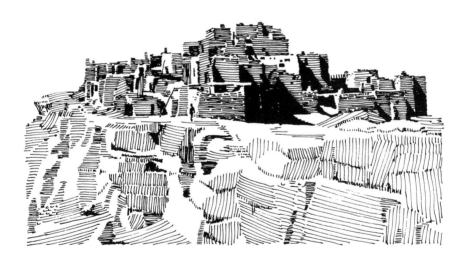

Figure 3. Walpi from the northeast.

space within the geographical area they consider their world, utilizing their own categories, concepts and distinctions."[5] Although Ortiz would probably not describe himself as a phenomenologist, his desire to understand how the Tewa experience their world in their own terms is a desire shared by many in the field of phenomenological enquiry. He also noted the similarity between his uncovering of Tewa experiential structures and those in other cultures: "When I read the sizable comparative record compiled by the phenomenologist and historian of religions, Mircea Eliade .... I get the distinct impression that by simply altering the terminology a bit for ancient Near Eastern religions the statements could apply just as well to the Pueblos."[6]

Ortiz based his synthesis in part upon the observations and findings of earlier studies, but he also uncovered and developed a more inclusive and coherent framework for understanding the experiential complexities of the Tewa world.[7] He includes village location, layout and architectural form as part of this world, and also sheds light on the significance of the Tewa dwelling places. As a Tewa from the village of San Juan, perhaps Ortiz's insights most significantly stem from his own participation in the Pueblo world.

As with other Pueblo groups, the origin myths of the Tewa provided the key to Ortiz's understanding. Ortiz used a summary of his own records of the myths and noted that most particulars had appeared in earlier reports. The first Tewa were said to have lived beneath a lake far to the north. Supernaturals, animals, and people shared this home. Two of the supernaturals were the first mothers of the Tewa: 'Blue Corn Woman' (Summer Mother) and 'White Corn Maiden' (Winter Mother). These Mothers sent one of the men to each of the cardinal directions and to the world above. He returned as the Hunt Chief, Mountain Lion, and was thereafter considered the first 'Made Person'. He appointed Winter and Summer chiefs, also 'Made People', to look after the Tewa in the respective season. Later, these two chiefs sent six pairs of brothers, *Towa e* ('persons'), to the cardinal directions to investigate the world above. The first pair, who were blue, saw only a mountain to the north, and the second pair, yellow, saw a mountain to the west. A red pair went south, a white to the east, and dark ones went to the zenith. The first four pairs also made flat-topped hills by throwing mud toward their directions. During this period, before finally leaving the lake, other groups and societes of Made People were instituted by the first chiefs to take care of particular activities in the world above. When the last pair of *Towa e*, the all-colored of the nadir, saw a rainbow and returned, the people prepared to emerge from the lake to the world above. The earth was soft and could not be walked on until it was hardened, frozen by the Winter chief.

The common people and the Made People were divided into two groups under the leadership of the Winter and Summer chiefs and travelled south. The *Towa e* went to their cardinal mountains to stand watch over the travel-

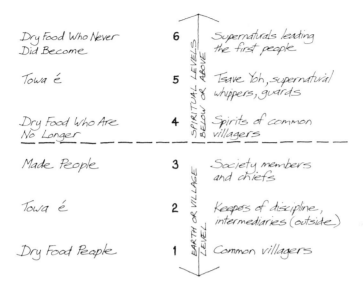

Figure 4. Tewa levels or categories of being.

lers. The Winter people journeyed down the east side of the Rio Grande and lived by hunting. The Summer people moved down the west side of the river and lived by gathering plants and by agriculture. After resting at various separate places, the two groups of people came together and built a village, which was eventually abandoned. Later, they again divided and six groups founded the six present Tewa villages, each with their complement of Winter and Summer people. Their resting places and the six village sites were felt to be secure, guarded by the *Towa e* and connected through subsistence skills and spiritual power with the landscape. The people became settled again and the sites fostered identity and dwelling.[8] Because they were founded in mythic times, the sites are still considered to be auspicious.

To understand better the relationship between the mythic and spatial worlds within which the villages are located, it is useful to examine six levels or "categories of being" which Ortiz identified and defined (Figure 4). Ortiz stressed that these six categories "divide and classify *all* of Tewa social and supernatural existence."[9] In the first or lowest category are the common villagers, 'Dry Food People,' with no official ceremonial or political position. The title 'Dry Food' comes from the terms *seh t' a*, which in the context of ritual before emergence was 'moist', 'green', and 'unripe'. The second category refers to the village representatives of the six pairs of *Towa e* who were instituted before the emergence. These brothers are not considered totally Made People because they emerged but did not travel with the Tewa people on the journey south. They made the flat-topped hills before emergence of the common Tewa and stood guard on the cardinal mountains. In the third category are the representatives of the Made People. They are members of the Winter and Summer societies and various other powerful groups and societies all formed before emergence, including Hunt, Medicine, Scalp, and Women's Societies and the two ritual clown groups, the *Kwirana* and *Kossa*.

The remaining three categories constitute the "supernatural counterparts of the first three."[10] The 'Dry Food Who Are No Longer' make a fourth group and are the spirits of the 'Dry Food People', the ordinary villagers who have died. In the fifth category are the supernatural *Towa e*, the six pairs of 'sibling deities' who explored the directions before emergence. The sixth category, termed 'Dry Food Who Never Did Become', includes the spirits of the Made People and all the other supernaturals acknowledged to have been with the Tewa *prior* to emergence.

Ortiz recognized how these categories of being and their substratum of myths were associated with the physical order of the landscape and the village within it. Ortiz used the village of San Juan as it was in the 1960s for his example, but there is sufficient evidence from other villages in the late nineteenth and early twentieth centuries to conclude that the framework was Tewa-wide and had been relatively stable for at least one hundred years.[11] In the south plaza at San Juan, the town court, was a place called 'Earth Mother, Earth Navel, Middle Place' – a loose stone circle regarded as the true center of the village and held to be an extremely sacred place.[12] Medicine men, who were Made People, had the power to reach deeply into the ground here to deposit seeds to reawaken nature each year in late winter while the *Towa e* stood guard. At the village of Nambe a similar place was in the middle of the plaza; it was said to contain stone spirits and to have an underground connection with a lake.[13] At the other extreme, marking the boundaries of this Tewa world, were four sacred mountains which had at their peaks earth navels where the *Towa e* stood guard as their supernatural counterparts had first stood after emergence. The mountains were associated with a lake where the supernatural 'Dry Food Who Never Did Become' of the respective directional colors dwelt.

These recurrent centers in the six villages indicate a sacred channel of connection and communication between the village middle place and the mountains and their lakes. This communication was a link between the Made People and the 'Dry Food Who Never Did Become'. The *Towa e* guarded the Made People at the middle place and the supernaturals at the mountain navels. The earth navels on the mountains were like satellites

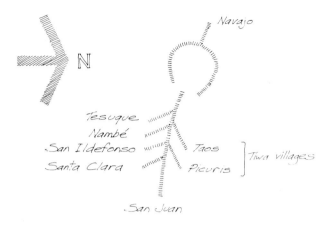

Figure 5. Shrine at Mt. Tsikomo, Mountain of the West.

focused on the village and each had a specific 'ritual path' as part of its design which led to the village (Figure 5). These sites comprised a horseshoe arrangement of stones on the ground and were visited ritually at times appropriate to the powers of that direction.

This pattern of places formed the center of the Tewa world and the focus of their existence. This center was a place of profound connectedness and power and echoes the insights of Heidegger when he says that dwelling gathers the 'Fourfold' – the earth, the sky, divinities and mortals.[14] These 'earth-mother-earth-navel-middle-places' gathered the Tewa world toward its center in a seemingly precise and geometrical manner. There were further powerful reinforcements to this centering. Earth navels were open to the sky and the underworld, a network of communication clarified by Figure 6. The lower part of the figure shows an outline plan of San Juan with overlaid coordinates of the cardinal mountains. The upper part is a cross-section through the earth's surface in one cardinal direction. Spirits and supernaturals were associated with the levels above and below the earth level. Other smaller earth navels were located on other hills or lower elevations; these also opened toward the village, and Ortiz identified them with spirits of specific species of game animals.[15]

Another set of channels of communication associated with the *Towa e* was focused on the flat-topped hills created by the first pairs of brothers. These hills were considered to be sacred and dangerous. Their caves and tunnels were said to be the dwellings of the *Tsave Yoh*, supernaturals associated with discipline and curing, who were represented by masked *Towa e* in the village. The *Towa e* of these hills, associated with colors of

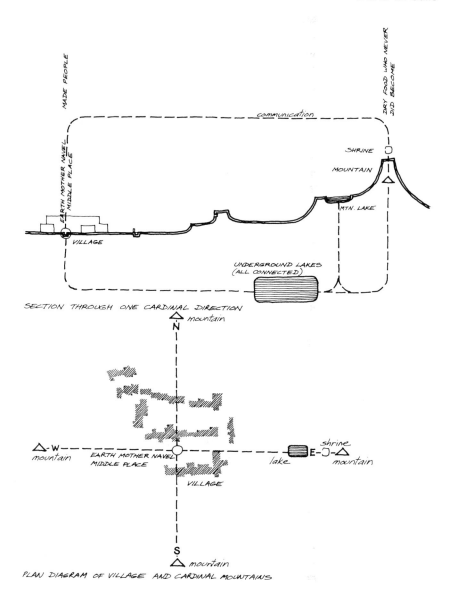

Figure 6. Communication between made people and the dry food who never did become.

the cardinal directions, were said to watch over the village. These spirits were believed to dwell in the flat-topped hills and to guard the navels at the middle place and the mountains. The anthropologist Elsie Clews Parsons recorded a description of the village representatives of the *Towa e* as 'outside chiefs', acting as intermediaries between the Made People and the Dry Food People, for whom mutual contact was dangerous.[16] The flat-topped hills were also at intermediate locations between the village and the mountains. In the village, the *Towa e* were also responsible for the maintenance of the 'old' and traditional ways; they stood guard for sacred ceremonies and were present for the installation of both sacred and secular officers. In addition, they guarded and were responsible for the upkeep of kivas and the Made People Society houses.

This physical fabric may also have been regarded as taking an intermediate position between the very sacred earth-navel-middle-place and the normally more secular and less powerful houses of the common people. It mirrors the intermediate role of the *Towa e* in the social fabric. The network of communication between the *Towa e* of the second and fifth categories identified by Ortiz may now be added to the diagram (Figure 7). 'Outside chiefs' reappear in other pueblo groups. They are not like ordinary villagers nor are they like pre-emergence powers. They dwell in the interstices and function as intermediaries at dangerous supernatural-human boundaries. Things, events, and people in this intermediate state are considered 'outside'. 'Inside' or 'houses chiefs' also occur in other Pueblo groups and this inside/outside duality is expressed concentrically in each Pueblo world. It is possible to think of the inside, village leaders as 'dwelling' chiefs. They brought power and fruitfulness from the outside world to the home place of the village. They sought harmony between the actions of villagers and the cycles of nature. They were guarded by outside chiefs from dangerous contacts. The outside chiefs were associated with warfare, bunting and journeys out to the hills and mountains.[17] This pattern was also manifested in the tendency to consider the main village as home, as a residence for the winter and for ceremonies; and to live and work in the farms away from the village in summer. In recent years, many Pueblos who live and work in the outside urban world still return to the home village for ceremonies important for 'power' and Pueblo identity.

Communication with the spirits of common Tewa who had died focused on shrines just outside the village in the four directions. These spirits of the Dry Food People constituted just a few of the large number of spirits which were associated with a wide range of objects. This larger group of spirits was called *xayeh*.[18] One informant told Ortiz that "long ago we buried the dead there and left a pile of stones. Every pile of stone you see shows where the *xayeh* live, for the dead have become *xayeh*."[19]

These channels of communication can be included on the diagram, which now shows an outline of a complex system of relationships among human

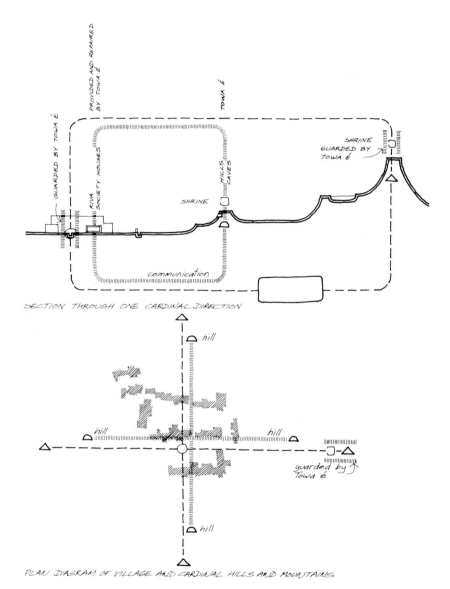

Figure 7. Communication between the village *Towa e* and their supernatural counterparts.

and supernatural levels of being; physical elements of landscape and village; animals, plants, objects, and colors; and the myth of orgin which pervades, supports, and was supported by them all (Figure 8). Although spatial, locational and physical elements have been emphasized here, the system also

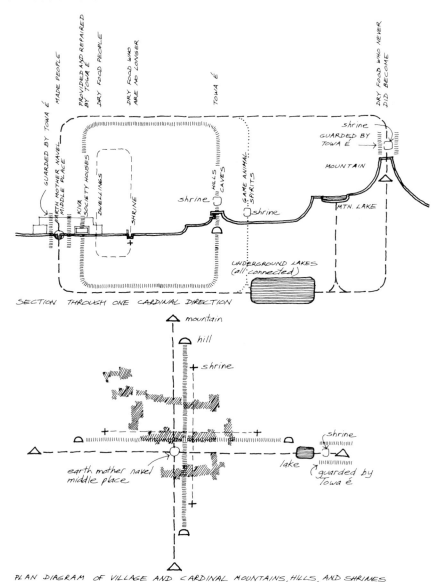

Figure labels in section diagram:

GUARDED BY TOWA É
MADE PEOPLE
PROVIDED AND REPAIRED BY TOWA É
DRY FOOD PEOPLE
DRY FOOD WHO ARE NO LONGER
TOWA É
DRY FOOD WHO NEVER DID BECOME

EARTH MOTHER NAVEL MIDDLE PLACE
KIVA SOCIETY HOUSES
DWELLINGS
SHRINE

shrine
GUARDED BY TOWA É
MOUNTAIN

shrine
HILLS CAVES
GAME ANIMAL SPIRITS
shrine
MTN. LAKE

UNDERGROUND LAKES (all connected)

SECTION THROUGH ONE CARDINAL DIRECTION

mountain
hill
shrine

earth mother navel middle place

lake
shrine
(guarded by Towa é)

PLAN DIAGRAM OF VILLAGE AND CARDINAL MOUNTAINS, HILLS, AND SHRINES

Figure 8. Communication between the dry food people and the dry food who are no longer.

integrated a whole realm of social and ritual responsibilities connected with the spiritual and subsistence activities and well-being of the villages. It incorporated, therefore, all dimensions of human life, but at heart was grounded in *place* – tied to particular landscapes, springs, fields, villages and buildings.

Not all villagers could have contact with the major spirits or use the powerful places. Supported by mythological precedent, certain people were installed to communicate with the upper and lower spiritual worlds, and in this capacity represented the first people or supernaturals who had been present in the first or earlier world. Special groups were responsible for interceding with spirits or powers tied to hunting, medicine, agriculture, weather, plants, and animals. The village chief, or the acting Winter or Summer chief, headed these groups and represented the mythological first being or the person appointed as leader by the first being. His titles were associated with dwelling and with the village settlement, for example, 'houses chief', 'house chief old man', 'people chief', 'house rule chief'.[20]

Other persons in village ceremonial organizations were installed to guard these appointed figures and to act as intermediaries between them and the ordinary villagers. These people were seen as guardians of custom, the earlier ways, and as protectors of sacred places and their roles were spatially significant. They were associated with other dwellings, with intermediate locations between cardinal mountains and sanctity inside the villages. There were also places within the villages which were temporarily or permanently used for activity dealing with external forces and which were occasionally open to a broader village community, for exemple the 'outside' kiva at San Ildefonso.

The Tewa world, therefore, was an integrated series of worlds with somewhat different powers, supernaturals, social models, and mythical sanctions for each of the Tewa societies or groups. This interconnected pattern extends into each Tewa village itself, establishing an integrated series of distinct Tewa dwellings. As Ortiz describes this overall pattern,

> The fact that these beliefs, ideas, and practices are often permuted in seemingly endless combinations from village to village should not obscure the fact that they form general classes and categories which conform, at an abstract but basically meaningful level, to structural principles common to them all. Among the Tewa, awareness of these more general considerations is restricted to only a reflective few, usually Made People, in each village, and no one of these is aware of more than a portion of the entire system . . . .[21]

The wider Pueblo world

My earlier studies were concerned with this building–dwelling–world system and they can serve here to illuminate aspects of the Tewa system which were shared by all Pueblo groups.[22] I examined records of rituals which were associated with stages in the construction and renovation of houses and other buildings. This topic interested me as an architect and such materials had not been gathered together before. Rituals accompanying house and kiva construction reiterated common themes. For example, there was a concern for cardinal directions and their "powers" and a recognition that built structure was 'living'.[23] Those persons directing the rituals or preparing ritual materials often held village positions connected with communication with spirits and supernaturals. Prayers offered during house and kiva construction were for the strength of the building, for long life and health, for the fertility of people and their crops, and for rain. The records also suggest that *any* construction was once accompanied by prescribed procedures. Certain ideas were common to all villages.[24] The world was constituted of three levels: there were upper and lower spiritual levels with the earth lying between them for the residence of people. The upper and lower spiritual levels may also be considered as one combined spiritual category which corresponds to Ortiz's supernatural categories of being in the Tewa scheme (numbered four, five and six in Figure 4). The earth level is similar to the village categories in the Tewa system (numbered one, two and three, Figure 4). Many irregularities in the earth's level acted as places of possible contact with the spiritual levels. Mountains touched the sky and earth; springs and caves were potential passageways to the underworld. The origin myths of all Pueblo villages bore striking resemblances to each other and were related to this conception of world levels. The myths described the emergence from the lower world and the early travels of the first people and their guidance by supernaturals. These myths not only gave significance to cardinal mountains, springs, colors and animals but also to their sequence in ritual and prayer.

This background seemed to offer clues to the understanding of the places and purposes of construction rituals. Each building construction had to be 'located' with respect to cardinal directions and their powers. Each 'house' took its proper place in the world, becoming real, and "endowed with a soul," a pattern which Mircea Eliade has demonstrated common to many cultures.[25] Actions and material things possessed power and strength by following prescription which was effective because it reiterated the actions of first beings and supernaturals. Conversely, this prescription also gave

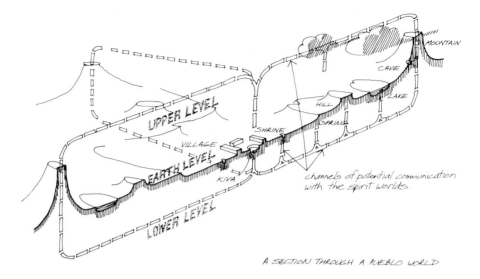

Figure 9. The network of human communication with the levels of the spirit world.

power an embodiment, and made it controllable and safer. It gave power a 'house', which was not only a term for residence, kiva or storehouse. Sun had his house in the sky during the day and in the earth at night. Spirits had their houses in clouds, rain, springs, mountains and hills.[26] Houses in this sense were not just places of habitation. They were also places of potential communication with the spiritual world, places where a connection could be formed between the three cosmic levels. Figure 9 shows an extended cross-section through a generalized Pueblo world. A comparison with the Tewa scheme shows that individual models were more detailed and possessed many variations (Figure 8 and 9). The significance of the general model varied with particular landscape, with the spectrum of deities and super-naturals, and with season in the ceremonial cycle.

Although they might have been humble residences, village enclosures, ponds, or mountain peaks, these places were "profound centres of human experience."[27] These places concentrated powers and meanings for the benefit of those humans who dwelt there. Their attributes resemble those of dwellings and are unified by an arrangement similar to the fundamental structure of "dwelling" described by Christian Norberg-Schulz:

> From the beginning of time man has recognized that nature consists of interrelated elements which express fundamental aspects of being. The landscape where he lives is not a mere flux of phenomena, it has

structures and embodies meanings. These structures and meanings have given rise to mythologies (cosmogonies and cosmologies) which have formed the basis of dwelling.[28]

Outsiders and Pueblo dwelling

The title of this essay refers to the many dwellings inside the Pueblo world, but it also is a reminder of the ways in which others have experienced the same environments. It was partially through records of these other experiences, structured and illuminated by other-world frameworks, that Ortiz was able to undertake his work of synthesis. Outsiders' observations can also often clarify themes which are obscured for insiders. How these worlds interact is a crucial and fascinating question for designers who almost always work in worlds other than their own. When a collector of museum artifacts showed some Zuni Pueblo Indians how to build a 'proper' door in 1884, he acted as a designer and his notion of dwelling belonged to another context.[29]

When Carl and Lillian Eickemeyer made their wagon exploration of Pueblo villages one summer in the early 1890s, their observations of customs, primitive houses, and uncomfortable social communication were genuine but immersed in the Eickemeyers' own taken-for-granted social world.[30] They made their trip from New York, spent two weeks in New Mexico, and published a small volume of their recollections. In many ways they can be accused of what James Duncan called the "celebration of inauthenticity" in that they dressed in 'Western' garb, carried a six-shooter, and partook of "entertainment by glimpses of Indian life."[31] They found the scene of men plowing the fields near the Tewa Pueblo of San Ildefonso to be "most picturesque."[32] As they explored the village further, they implicitly confirmed their connections with homes in the east. They noted "rudely constructed ladders" and observed that Pueblo mothers did not seem to feel the "slightest anxiety" about children playing on them.[33] One evening the Eickemeyers visited the "estufa or council house" where they said the Indians make decisions and practice dances. Dancing, the Eickemeyers claimed, was the Pueblo's major pastime.[34] The building holding the dancing was the kiva or roundhouse and they found it to be bare and dark. They talked with the village governor and were surprised at the complex form of government which was outlined to them. They classified the system as both "monarchial and republican."[35]

Their understanding of the Pueblo world was colored by comparisons with their home in the East and their preconceptions of the West. They valued the things they would have valued back home. They found it difficult to come to terms with what appeared to be rude, bare mud rooms and the untidy spaces of the village layout. They found they could better understand the house of a Mexican family in the nearby Keres village of Cochiti: "This Mexican room was very different from those in the Indian houses, resembling one that might be seen in the poorer quarters of any town. There was a rag carpet on the floor (the rooms in the Indian houses were not even boarded), and, besides several chairs and a table, there was a bedstead . . . ."[36]

In spite of the inability of the Eickemeyers to share the particular ideas of dwelling of the Pueblos, there were some underlying feelings revealed in their report which are related to more deeply felt aspects of dwelling. They visited the school in Cochiti and at "about nine o'clock the little bare-footed, scantily clad children were seated at desks similar to those used in any well-regulated schoolroom . . . ."[37] They perceived a sense of familiar order and described further that on a white wall hung the "Stars and Stripes" and that in spite of the dusky faces and unintelligible language, the experience gave them a "pleasurable home-like feeling."[38] The order of the students in class; their probable conversation with the teacher, a Mrs. Grozier from Boston; and the flag allowed them to make connections with their own world and to feel at home. These comments on the Eickemeyers' trip are not meant to mock. The couple did experience the landscape, climate, and people firsthand. They exposed themselves to richer experiences even though they imagined themselves to be adventurers. Their purpose was not entirely clear, but they took little personal advantage and did not use their experience to markedly alter the world which they had touched.

Other outsiders have not used their knowledge of Pueblo worlds so benignly. The power of the village sites for focusing Pueblo identity was understood by the government Indian Agent responsible for the Hopi Pueblos in the 1890s. These agents and other "representatives of Washington came to realize that preservation of the Hopi way of life lay to a great extent in the social structure of their village communities" and their relationships with their mesa-top sites.[39] The government plan was to allot land below the mesas to individual families and to supply lumber and other materials for house-building to those who moved down. This scheme was deliberately designed to fracture the system which gave traditional responsibility for the land to clans whose ancient claims were supported by myth. It was part of the government policy instituted in the Dawes Act of 1887, which crystallized the interests of Ango-American culture in alloting lands to individual families. According to these interests, if Indians were to ever take on the obligations of citizenship, they "needed to be civilized and the basis of civilization consisted in knowing how to handle individual property."[40] Building houses was also a traditional Pueblo communal undertaking that used local materials and forms and produced climatically appropriate residences. In 1892, materials for twenty-six of the timber and corrugated-iron houses were furnished, but by 1894 they were abandoned or used as summer farmhouses.[41] A report by the Acting Indian Agent that year, First Lieutenant S.H. Plummer, includes an observation that the house and land allotment plans were not as successful as desired. He surmised: "their habits, customs, and general mode of living are so intimately connected with the conditions of life on the mesas that it is doubtful whether anything else than compulsion will cause them to abandon their pueblo dwellings."[42]

Another visitor, Theodore Roosevelt, thought it was a mistake to move the Hopi into tin-roofed houses below the mesas. He judged the thick-roofed Hopi house to be cooler and pleasanter. He compared Hopi houses and villages to those of Mediterranean Europe and saw them as notable and attractive as the castles on the Rhine. Not only did he care about the village environment for its value to Hopi residents. He also felt that there were lessons for other cultures there − that arts and environments connected with the spirit and joy of living should not be altered lightly. He suggested that the Hopi builder should be given "a chance to utilize his own inherent sense of beauty in making over his own village for himself . . . a chance to lead his own life as he ought to, and realize that he has something to teach us as well as to learn from us."[43] Roosevelt decried planting the Hopi "in a brand-new Government-built house, precisely like some ten million other cheap houses. The Hopi architecture is a product of its own environment . . . ."[44] He sensed that the Hopi dwelling was firmly rooted in the places that had nurtured it.

Conclusion

This brief reappraisal of Pueblo dwellings and world allows some comparison of ideas and experiences across cultures and suggests that there can be valuable examination of all kinds of descriptions of places − ethnographic, photographic, popular, literary and personal. The aim of such reappraisal is richer understanding, or as Seamon explains, "the coming to see more thoroughly and respectfully the essential nature of the thing and the context in which it finds itself."[45]

Dwelling is experienced unself-consciously in the everyday world and is renewed more explicitly through ritual. Both processes are crucially significant in the traditional Pueblo world and follow Heidegger's "characterization of person-in-world (as) a sense of immersion and inextricable togetherness rooted in time and space."[46] These generally unself-conscious processes allow dwelling to be natural and meaningful, but make the understanding of our own and other's dwelling more difficult. "Caught up in the natural attitude, . . . we normally do not explore the way we dwell, nor the ways in which place and environment sustain our existence as people."[47] When we explore how each particular group or person dwells, we cannot experience their taken-for-granted world. At best we glimpse regularities and some shared feelings.

By examining the taken-for-granted world of the Pueblo as it is portrayed in accounts by insiders and outsiders, one finds certain fundamental regularities and commonalities. Pueblo dwelling is a structure of relationships involving orientation, order and harmony with the powers of the world. The relationships involve continuity and association and occur through ritually prescribed channels leading to and from the cosmic powers of nature. The dwelling is a center – a safe and protected inner place. There are many centers in a Pueblo world. The village is a center, as are earth navels, shrines, sacred plazas and kivas. All of these places, however, are part of and versions of the structure of relationships of all Pueblo dwelling. These centers are phenomena which gather or conjure powers and significance through a web of connections.

The theme of the dwelling as a place of beginnings and first roots also appears in both insider and outsider descriptions. Theodore Roosevelt talked of the importance of a nurturing environment and the Eickemeyers expressed the connection between their feeling of home and the places of education and mother's supervision. The place of beginning and emergence is consistently evoked during the making and reaffirming of Pueblo dwelling places.

Finally, in many accounts, dwelling appears as both a place and a process through which a person understands and accepts a position in the community and the broader world. Persons are at home when they find an acceptable place in the network of social relations and social order. The Eickemeyers felt these ties when they resumed gossip with the social network of an Anglo feedstore they returned to after their 'native' interlude of two weeks. The social role of house-building was also certainly realized by the Indian Agent during the Hopi land allotment scheme. For the Pueblo Indian, revelation of, and initiation into the network of social and supernatural order brought with it demanding subsistence, domestic and ritual responsibilities. It also brought a sense of harmony and oneness with the world and its powers and enabled the Pueblos to dwell in a landscape which sustained them both materially and spiritually.

Notes

1. For example, Martin Heidegger, "Building Dwelling Thinking," in *Poetry, Language, Thought*, Alfred Hofstadter, trans. (New York: Harper and Row, 1971), pp. 145–161; Christian Norberg-Schulz, *Genius Loci: Towards a Phenomenology of Architecture* (New York: Rizzoli, 1980); Edward Relph, *Place and Placelessness* (London: Pion, 1976); David Seamon, *A Geography of the Lifeworld* (London: Croom Helm, 1979); Yi-Fu Tuan, *Space and Place: The Perspective of Experience* (Minneapolis: University of Minnesota, 1977).

2. David G. Saile, "The Ancient Pueblos: An Introduction to the Village Forms of the Anasai," *Planning Outlook* 16 (1975): 35–54; David G. Saile, " 'Architecture' in Prehispanic Pueblo Archeology: Examples from Chaco Canyon, New Mexico," *World Archeology* 9 (1977): 157–173; David G. Saile, "Making a House: Building Rituals and Spatial Concepts in the Pueblo Indian World," *Architectural Association Quarterly* 9 (1977): 72–81; David G. Saile, "Architecture in the Pueblo World: The Architectural Contexts of Pueblo Culture in the Late Nineteenth Century," (unpublished Doctoral dissertation, University of Newcastle upon Tyne, 1981).

3. Early recorders include Adolf F. Bandelier, "Final Report of Investigations Among the Indians of the Southwestern United States, Carried on Mainly in the Years from 1880 to 1885: Part I," *Papers of the Archaeological Institute of America* 3 (1890); Frank H. Cushing, "Outlines of Zuni Creation Myths," *Bureau of Ethnology 13th Annual Report, 1891–92* (Washington D.C.: Smithsonian Institution, 1896), pp. 321–447; John P. Harrington, "The Ethnogeography of the Tewa Indians," *Bureau of Ethnology 29th Annual Report, 1907–08* (Washington D.C.: Smithsonian Institution, 1916); and Victor Mindeleff, "A Study of Pueblo Architecture: Tusayan and Cibola," *Bureau of Ethnology 8th Annual Report, 1886–7* (Washington D.C.: Smithsonian Institution, 1891), pp. 3–228. Accounts by native scholars include Alfonso Ortiz, *The Tewa World: Space, Time, Being, and Becoming in a Pueblo Society* (Chicago: University of Chicago, 1969); and Edward P. Dozier, *The Pueblo Indians of North America* (New York: Holt, Rinehart and Winston, 1970).

4. Relph, *Place and Placelessness*, pp. 52–54.

5. Ortiz, *The Tewa World*, p. 9; see, also, Alfonso Ortiz, "Dual Organization as an Operational Concept in the Pueblo Southwest," *Ethnology* 4 (1965): 396–398; Alfonso Ortiz, "Ritual Drama and the Pueblo World View," in *New Perspectives on the Pueblos*, Alfonso Ortiz, ed. (Albuquerque: School of American Research, University of New Mexico, 1972); Alfonso Ortiz, "San Juan Pueblo," in *Handbook of North American Indians: Vol. 9*, Alfonso Ortiz, ed. (Washington D.C.: Smithsonian Institution, 1979).

6. Ortiz, "Ritual Drama and the Pueblo World View", p. 141.

7. Ortiz used, for example, Harrington, "The Ethnogeography of the Tewa Indians;" and Elsie Clews Parsons, "The Social Organization of the Tewa of New Mexico," *Memoirs of the American Anthropological Association* 36 (1929).

8. Compare these themes with Yi-Fu Tuan, "Mythical Space and Place," *Space and Place*, pp. 85–100; and David Seamon, *Lifeworld*, pp. 86–93.

9. Ortiz, *The Tewa World*, p. 17.
10. Ibid., p. 18.
11. Bandelier, "Final Report," pp. 302–313; William B. Douglass, " A World Quarter Shrine of the Tewa Indians," *Records of the Past* 11 (1912), pp. 159–173; Harrington, "The Ethnogeography of the Tewa Indians;" Parsons, "The Social Organization of the Tewa."
12. Parsons, "The Social Organization of the Tewa," map 2; Ortiz, *The Tewa World*, p. 21.
13. Parsons, "The Social Organization of the Tewa," pp. 246–247.
14. Heidegger, "Building, Dwelling, Thinking," p. 150.
15. Ortiz, *The Tewa World*, p. 24; one of these navels is illustrated in Parsons, "The Social Organization of the Tewa," plate 42C.
16. Ibid., pp. 102–107.
17. The arrangement is reminiscent of the rest/movement and home/reach dualities explored in Seamon, *Lifeworld*; and Anne Buttimer, "Home, Reach, and the Sense of Place," in *The Human Experience of Space and Place*, Anne Buttimer and David Seamon, eds. (London: Croom Helm, 1980), pp. 166–187.
18. Ortiz, *The Tewa World*, p. 20.
19. Ibid., p. 20.
20. Parsons, *Pueblo Indian Religion*, 2 vols. (Chicago: University of Chicago, 1939) table 1, facing p. 208.
21. Ortiz, *The Tewa World*, p. xvi.
22. David G. Saile, "Pueblo Building Rituals: Religious Aspects of a Productive Activity," unpublished manuscript on deposit, Arizona State Museum Library (1976); Saile, "Making a House."
23. Saile, "Making a House," pp. 72–75.
24. These are summarized by Dozier, *The Pueblo Indians*, pp. 203–209; and in Ortiz, "Ritual Drama and the Pueblo World View," pp. 135–161.
25. Mircea Eliade, *The Myth of the Eternal Return*, Willard R. Trask, trans. (New Jersey: Bollingen Foundation, Columbia University, 1954), p. 20.
26. Elsie Clews Parsons, *Pueblo Indian Religion*, 2 vols. (Chicago: University of Chicago, 1939).
27. Edward Relph, *Place and Placelessness* p. 43.
28. Norberg-Schulz, *Genius Loci*, p. 23.
29. Matilda Coxe Stevenson, "The Zuni Indians: Their Mythology, Esoteric Societies, and Ceremonies," *Bureau of American Ethnology 23rd Annual Report, 1901–02* (Washington D.C.: Smithsonian Institution, 1904), p. 379.
30. Carl and Lillian Eickemeyer, *Among the Pueblo Indians* (New York: Merriam, 1895).
31. Ibid., p. 137. Tourist worlds are discussed by James S. Duncan, "The Social Construction of Unreality" in *Humanistic Geography*, David Ley and Marwyn Samuels, eds. (Chicago: Maaroufa, 1978), pp. 269–282.
32. Eickemeyer, *Among the Pueblo Indians*, p. 21.
33. Ibid., p. 22.
34. Ibid., p. 33.
35. Ibid., p. 29.
36. Ibid., pp. 91–92.
37. Ibid., p. 79.
38. Ibid.
39. Harry C. James, *Pages from Hopi History* (Tucson: University of Arizona, 1974), p. 111.
40. Edward H. Spicer, *Cycles of Conquest: The Impact of Spain, Mexico, and the United States*

on the Indians of the Southwest, 1533–*1960* (Tucson: University of Arizona, 1962), p. 347.

41. James, *Pages from Hopi History*, p. 112.
42. From "History of the Moqui Indian Reservation, Compiled from Annual Reports of Indian Agents at Keams Canyon and Fort Defiance," manuscript at Museum of Northern Arizona, Flagstaff (MS. 135–2–3-), compiled by Leo Crane; excerpt in James, *Pages from Hopi History*, p. 114.
43. Theodore Roosevelt, "The Hopi Snake Dance," *The Outlook* (October 18, 1913), p. 368.
44. Ibid.
45. David Seamon, "The Phenomenological Contribution to Environmental Psychology," *Journal of Environmental Psychology* 2 (1982): 122.
46. From a discussion of Heidegger's notion of dwelling; see David Seamon, "Heidegger's Notion of Dwelling and One Concrete Interpretation as Indicated by Hassan Fathy's *Architecture for the Poor*," in *Geosciences and Man* 24 (1984): 43–53.
47. Seamon, "The Phenomenological Contribution," p. 122.

11. A phenomenological approach to architecture and its teaching in the design studio

BOTOND BOGNAR

As an achievement of the twentieth century, phenomenology is a relatively new branch of philosophy. It is a method of inquiry into people and the world or, more precisely, into their relationship. As opposed to traditional Western understanding based on a sharp distinction between person and the world, phenomenology – highly critical of Cartesian dualism in any form – regards subjects and objects in their unity.[1] Phenomenology understands a world wherein people and their environment mutually include and define each other. It focuses upon nature and reality not as an absolutum existing only outside us, but as subject to human scrutiny, interaction, and creative participation.

The phenomenological approach has been recently introduced to architecture, a discipline which not only interprets but, as a matter of course, guides and creates the person–environment relationship. An early effort toward a more humanistic architecture was research in semiology – i.e., investigations of the meaning of built form.[2] Semiology alone, however, has proved to be insufficient to reach such a goal.[3] Building upon the pioneer works of such phenomenological philosophers as Martin Heidegger, Maurice Merleau-Ponty and Gaston Bachelard, scholars have extended their probe of a visual architectural communication into the more complex field of the synesthetic reality of the natural and human-made environment. This reality involves not only the functions of the eyes and mind, but also the multidimensional capabilities of the human body and intuitions. In this respect, Kevin Lynch's studies of urban images are one important early contribution, though a phenomenological criticism of this work is its overemphasis on the cognitive dimensions of urban experience.[4] More significant is Christian Norberg-Schulz' work, which provides an initial step toward an existential phenomenology of landscape and architecture.[5]

In relation to a phenomenology of architecture, one can ask the question of how a comprehensive understanding of the person–environment relationship can extend the awareness of architectural students who, in their subsequent careers, must make important decisions about the quality of the human environment – that is, decisions relating to planning, designing and building the concrete world in which we live. The question is particularly timely and the answer urgent with regard to the predicament of modern architecture, where the prevailing trend of rationalist design, even with its occasional flirting with formalistic trends and populist post-modernism, is not only inadequate to mitigate, but also frequently contributes to, the worsening human condition in modern mass-societies.[6]

As the philosopher Hannah Arendt has pointed out, one source of the difficulties which the Western World faces today is the growing schism between people and their objects, and further, between people and their built environment.[7] There is a loss of intimacy or, in Heidegger's words, the "loss of nearness" between people and their world as well as between person and person.[8] This tendency, coupled with the escalation of the suburb, results in the gradual disappearance of both the public and private realms of the human-made physical and social environment, while undermining the role of the city as the most important cultural and political nucleus.[9] At the same time, architecture reinforces alienation by a serious disregard of existential qualities such as imageability, memorability, inhabitability, and so forth.

There is, therefore, an urgent need to reinstate the conditions for the development and cultivation of sensitively differentiated, yet commonly shared value systems which in architecture are rooted in and represented by concrete human *places*. It is this human significance of the environment which is what phenomenology investigates, describes, and promotes. A phenomenological perspective within the scope of architecture and environmental design should, as a matter of course, start in the classrooms of architectural schools at the beginning of the curriculum, if not earlier, within primary and secondary education. In the design studio, the introduction of a phenomenological perspective would necessarily mean a return to a design sequence that begins with and runs parallel to students' exploring and understanding their own environmental and architectural experience. This essay is an inquiry into the possibilities and potential values of a phenomenological approach to architectural design.

The studio and architectural design

The majority of recent architectural education and practice is concerned with design as an objective process of producing an objective environment. Designing is approached analytically, programmatically and scientifically – that is, primarily along *rational* principles and theories. Students are provided with a list of objective, well defined goals and methods to achieve such ends as utility, efficiency, economy, structural stability and formal appearance. The problems faced in reaching such ends are regarded as definable, analyzable, measurable, predictable, and solvable. The task is to *reduce* the difficulties of the design process into logical and exact problems which, if well stated, should lead to clear-cut, rational solutions. As Norberg-Schulz says, today "the rationalistic idea of man of the post-medieval epoch is still dominant and the belief that all problems may be solved if we grasp reality as it 'really is' is generally accepted."[10] Even when the relationship of architecture to human responses is considered, if at all, it, too, is usually reduced to measurable effects and results and, therefore, either disregarded or largely misunderstood – a fact which seriously limits architecture's primary grounding in human experience.

This rational approach to architectural education and design teaches the student how to organize and assemble buildings precisely and how to manipulate their appearance logically without illuminating first how architecture, as part of the physical, social and cultural environment, is experienced – how it plays a role in the totality of human experience and understanding. As a result, students come to anticipate and accept that designing is a value-free operation that can be practiced routinely and mechanically. They presume that by acquiring and applying the proper formulae and quantitatively measurable, optimal parameters, their designs will lead to successful buildings and environments. Here, designing the environment is an activity which needs not be related to one's own experience with the environment itself; such meanings are seen as subjective and generally discounted.

Without such experiental awareness of their own relationship with *concrete* natural and built environments, however, students' understanding of architecture remains abstract – a situation which too often leads to facile, insensitive design. Students frequently do not or cannot go beyond the level of 'squaring-out' bubble diagrams or focus only on the efficiency of means. Instead of being concerned with the synesthetic qualities of a multi-dimensional architectural reality, students are preoccupied with the rationalization of such design components as function, technology, construction, and form; and with designing two-dimensional drawings and sheets as "well-packaged," complete projects. In other words, the abstraction of the architectural drawing as a tool for problem-solving plays a major role in the final design.

Even if students seek to extend themselves beyond the rational, abstract level of designing, they usually lack sufficient concrete experience and turn instead to some prescribed formulae or ready-made solutions from books and magazines. "Formulae" and "imitations" as archetypes can surely help the student learn design, but they cannot substitute for the value of rich personal encounters, investigations, and intimate discoveries of actual places, environments and landscapes.

In the rational approach to architecture, there is a serious discrepancy between the methods of design activity and the perpetuation of human values as the ultimate goal of this activity. Until the eighteenth century, this gap did not exist, since architects were both designer and builder, and their everyday construction experience successfully made up for any imprecision in drawings and plans. The division of building process into autonomous invention and fabrication – i.e., into design and production – had not yet occurred, and the aspects of *what* and *how* in architecture were generally identical. Architectural drawing was regarded not as a one-to-one representation of the building or architecture itself, but – in Alberto Perez-Gomez's words – as "the expression of a symbolic intention in the form of architectural ideas."[11] These drawings necessarily had to be interpreted by builders, and their contribution to the whole creative procesess was thereby integral and significant.

With the Industrial Revolution, however, design and construction became two separate, highly specialized professions – a schism which through increasing specialization has continued to grow.[12] To provide communication and collaboration that would close the gap between designer and builder, the procedure of working drawings, based on the elaboration of a scientific, descriptive geometry, developed, paving the way toward turning architectural drawings into unambiguous "pictures" of the building and its smallest details.[13] Working drawings as neutral collections of technical information fit the requirements of exact industrial production and products. Their disavantage, however, was the inability to invite and communicate the designer's experiential understanding of the concrete world of architecture. Most modern architects have accepted the "role of drawing as primary and unquestionable," while gradually turning the design process itself into a method of reduction – that is, progressively eliminating symbolic or poetic intentions and content.[14] Many designers became preoccupied with the instrumentality of means, whereby either the modes of autonomous production or the configuration of autonomous form became ends in themselves. Despite the many differences in these two approaches, they both are equally rooted in Cartesian subject-object dualism and come surprisingly close to each other with regard to misunderstanding human experience in relation to architecture.[15]

The first of these design approaches can be called *productivist rationalism*, which follows the performance principle of positivist science and limits architecture to the aspects of how buildings are constructed and how they work. This approach looks upon human implications and values as totally unpredictable and undefinable by any precise method and, as such, "irrelevant" to design.[16] Toward them, productivist rationalism takes the attitude of absolute neutrality. Buildings which are designed and erected as a result of this attitude assume the form and essence of efficient technological products or *machines*. They feature a "total" non-determination of human events and occupancy in relation to the architectural structure and space, whereby people are converted into objects or, at best, operators of their environment. With regard to this design approach, Kenneth Frampton comments that "increasingly, buildings come to be designed in response to the mechanics of their erection . . . . Processal elements such as tower cranes, elevators, escalators, stairs, refuse chutes, gangways, service cores, and automobiles determine the configuration of built form to a far greater extent than the hierarchic and more public criteria of place."[17]

The second dominant approach in modern architecture can be called *formalistic rationalism*, which restricts architecture primarily to the aspects of how buildings appear visually. Since this approach relies heavily upon the methods of positivist behavioral sciences and the theories of objectivist aesthetics, it sometimes gives attention to people's awareness of architectural form, but only as far as these human aspects are measurable, predictable and controllable – that is, fully designable. As opposed to productivist rationalism, this second approach presumes that human events and experience in relation to the built environment can eventually be predicted completely – as if meaning was the sole property of the building itself. Accordingly, formalistic rationalism works not only to heighten architectural experience but to determine it from every conceivable point of view. This intention comes close to the idea of "total design," which Walter Gropius advocated in his works.[18] As a result of this approach, buildings are shaped as sleek *objects*, the forms and appearance of which are supposedly so transparent and self-evident that they would leave no doubt for anyone as to what their purpose or meaning is, aiming at, in fact, an "ultimate reality."

Much of architecture today follows its own rationale outside of human needs, or else, serves the interest and growing imperatives of consumerism, which frequently propagates superficial and seductive embellishment and the meaningless application of meaningful forms wherein banality or speculative false reality is a substitute for real experience. Buildings dressed in latest formalistic fashion with competitive, skin-deep novelty offer effortless, spurious experience and instant identity which leave people with no choice but to become their mere consumers.

The greatest weakness of both the productivist- and formalistic-rational approaches to design is that they not only look upon architecture and human beings as remote and abstract concepts or things, but eventually *turn them into* such abstract things.[19] Both styles of design produce environments which are deterministic and too infrequently real places for people. These architectures do not understand or generate fundamental meanings of human existence. Instead, people are deprived of the creative use of environments and ultimately become passive onlookers of places for which they feel little belonging.

Undeniably, architectural design has to deal with many problems. Function, utility, technology, construction, form, programming, economics and marketability are all important issues, most of which today can be supposedly solved by scientific procedures and computers. To provide meaningful environments for people, however, these aspects of design must play supportive rather than primary roles in the process of architectural creation. Architectural design has to go beyond the "servile . . . role of only solving already stated problems with buildings."[20] Architecture must create places as the synthesis of its various elements and aspects, where people can find themselves and thereby feel that they are human beings somewhere.

Spirit of place

"Spirit of place," or *genius loci*, arises from the special character or synesthetic quality of a particular locality. The significant aspects in the evocation of this sense are numerous and can include spatial structures, topographical patterns, textures, natural and climatic conditions such as light, wind and sound, in addition to people and the pattern of human events. Spirit of place, however, is not only the numerical summation of its various components, but more so, the complex interplay of these aspects – a largely intangible atmosphere or, in Christopher Alexander's words, a "quality without a name."[21]

People's capacities to relate intimately to their world is a poetic sensitivity which forms the foundation of what Heidegger calls *dwelling*.[22] The quality of human life depends upon how people are able to dwell, wherein dwelling means inevitably more than a rational, utilitarian act such as merely occupying rooms or buildings. A phenomenological perspective interprets dwelling largely as an active human urge, involving a desire to participate creatively in the events of the concrete world around – an act by which people affirm their own existence.

As "the basic character of being," dwelling also involves a wish to belong to the environment, to feel inside a place and to be at home.[23] Home is a place that people inhabit; it is a place capable of providing dwelling for the biological functions of the body, the capacity and comprehension of the intellect, and the needs of emotion and spirit. Home is both a repository and witness of one's life – it is human life itself. Home is where a person finds *identity*, and one's own home is most often the place where the person and environment's identities overlap most. A house is a home, or should be, but a home is not necessarily a house. In other words, besides our house, we can feel at home and find identity with other places. A place is successfully a place to the degree it generates a sense of being at home. In Hannah Arendt's words, "In order to be what the world is always meant to be, a home for men during their life on earth, the human artifice must be a place fit for action and speech . . ."[24]

Heidegger argues that human existence is unquestionably spatial, environmental and architectural and, thus, inseparable from *genius loci*. The answer to Chris Fawcett's paradoxical question, "Do we live to build or build to live?" is inevitably both, since the significance of building goes beyond the erection of only practical and effective shelters, and gains a cosmic dimension.[25] We build to grasp and concretize the universe; we structure the world into some understandable whole. What we build, most especially our own homes, are miniature universes – indeed, microcosms which, in turn, help us understand and remember who we ourselves are. As opposed to the predominantly rational, scientifically determined and objectified world of today, an architecture of dwelling, in Mircea Eliade's words, requires that "the house is not an object, a 'machine to live in;' it is the universe that man constructs for himself."[26] Thus, the ontology of the "sense of place" implies both a macro- and microcosmic dimension, in fact, a transcendental or mythical significance (*mythos*), assigning people always the role of in-between. In other words, this ontology is rooted in the perceivable and perceived unity of the material and the spiritual, or the tangible and the intangible. In this unity — what Bachelard calls the "direct images of matter" — the concrete reality of the physical, through its actual and immediate presence in our human experience, is capable of transcending its materiality and evoking the "form" of metaphysical.[27]

The multiplicity of one's experiences is closely interrelated with the multiplicity of the environment itself. Since human experience and perception are not absolute but circumstantial and frequently coincidental, a successful place promotes a variety of circumstances for human interaction. Such a place cannot be created with an absolute or scientific certainty and objectivity, which reduces place to the meaning of utility only.[28] The need is that human values and qualities be intuited within the design activity. While the rationalist architect intends to create an absolute clarity of 'self-evident' meaning of a univalent environment or proposes meaningless neutrality, the designer sensitive to phenomenological insights aims at a multivalent environment which is poetically ambiguous, with "endless" layers of meaning. It is this "ambiguous reality" which, as catalyst, can generate creative human responses involving imagination, memory, association, differentiation, and where people not only receive meaning from, but also give meaning to their environment, thus, evoking the "spirit of place."

The multiplicity of a place, however, is not equivalent to the multitude of its composing elements. Japanese Zen-Buddhist architecture and gardens, for example, illustrate well that the richness of place is attributable, first of all, to the concerted ability of the constituents to induce a feeling of totality or to signify eternity in the elusive phenomenon of existence, regardless of how few the elements and how "simple" the place may be.[29] Such an environment involves what Aldo van Eyck calls a "labyrinthian clarity," with always another layer of "hidden" meaning or "infinite" depth to discover.[30] Real places have a continual possibility for revision, reinterpretation, reenactment and recreation. The "spirit of place" as a sense of totality and wholeness, therefore, can be only imprecisely precise. It touches the intellectual faculties but eventually eludes the assertive rationality of the mind alone and comes alive through sensitivity, intuition, and empathy.

Real places have another feature in common. They do not sell themselves out easily with clichés, promising experience without personal involvement. The discovery and understanding of place cannot be an instantaneous and once-and-for-all event. Places must be inhabited and cared for, taken into possession through time and learning — a process often requiring considerable effort and involvement. Only in this way can a place make sense and provide a lasting bond between people and their environment. Places, therefore, should have a certain permanent quality – a *permanence with change* – which provides the possibility for both "human limitations . . . and freedom," for action and intimacy in the person–environment relationship.[31]

Design as phenomenological inquiry

Human life is an intricate web of concrete and symbolic relationships. The gist of design is to provide chances for this web to begin, develop and strengthen. The need is to conceive of the environment as a network of potential places capable of inviting and sustaining a complex of physical, emotional, intellectual, and spiritual interactions.

To be able to design such places, the student of architecture should understand the nature and patterns of experiental relationships with the environment. This sensitivity can probably be best achieved if students observe their own environments with regard to human events and then record and reflect on their observations. This style of observation and reflection is necessarily an interpretative activity, since it involves not only the discovery of pre-existing patterns but also the creation of relationships which do not exist in absolute terms. These relationships are hidden or invisible, being closely related to the patterns of activities performed by the experiencers. A taxi driver, for example, structures and understands the city in a way different from the housewife or child. In the same and shared environment, different people have their own percepts and feelings depending on their own particular world of meaning. As Italo Calvino points out, beyond the visible urban environment are endless layers of "Invisible Cities" which make that city real.[32]

Investigations in both observation and design should begin with primary elements of existential space, such as path, edge, domain and place – all of which structure the human environment.[33] The study of these elements is inseparable from the investigations of the patterns of relationships among them. A place is distinguished within its environment by its higher degree of density with regard to gathered events and meanings, and above all, by its capability to provide one with the feeling of being existentially inside and centered. A place can be perceived and understood as such only in relation to its larger surroundings, which are always the "outside." The inside–outside relationship is one of the most important existential phenomenological aspects of place and brings forth the issue of boundaries — that is, how the edges of place are demarcated. Heidegger describes boundary as "not that at which something stops but, . . . that from which something *begins its presencing.*"[34] These demarcations are sometimes concrete and clear but, often, elements overlap, leading to a complex, ambiguous system of in-terrelationships. In such a "discontinuous continuity," every place is a "twin-phenomenon" — that is, it is both a part of its larger environmental context and a totality of its composite sub-place.[35] The result is an "endless" series of transitions, often with "invisible" but, by all means, always recognizable or sensible thresholds among lesser and greater places.

In Japan, for example, the sense of being inside is not necessarily related to the physical boundaries of the house; rather, it is dependent on the actual elevation of the floor area relative to its surroundings. The higher the level, the spiritually cleaner and more inside it is perceived to be. On the lower level of the ante-room (*genkan*), a person is not regarded as being inside the house even if the area, as in all traditional as well as modern homes, is behind the entrance door. To enter in Japan means the "ritual" act of removing one's shoes and stepping up!

The succession of environmental levels from region, city, districts, blocks, buildings and so forth can be interpreted as gradually smaller and inclusive worlds where the larger contains the multiplicity of the smaller which, in turn, in a more condensed and concretized form, refers to and signifies the larger. As Heidegger said, "the single houses, the villages, the towns are works of building which within and around themselves gather the multifarious in-between."[36] Phenomenologically, the issue of scale has to be understood as a sequential pattern of identification with multidimensional "worlds."

In their observations, students should recognize that understanding of place is a sensitive capability for both experiencing and interpreting the en-vironment anew. This "revision" involves the changing circumstances be-tween observers and observed — that is, the changing viewpoints of ob-servers themselves. This style of observation requires the student to be open to things yet purposeful at the same time. Openess is a state of recep-tivity, while purposefulness involves directed intention. In phenomenol-ogical observation, these two opposites must occur simultaneously, resulting in an in-between state where learning and knowing depend on suspending one's preconceptions.[37]

In other words, students must find a way to distance themselves from their taken-for-granted ideas about things around them. As Merleau-Ponty said, "the world is not what I think, but what I live through."[38] Understanding the phenomenon of place involves a sensitively structured, flexibly layered knowledge, acquired within a large variety of both individual and collective experiences − a knowledge which involves the functions of memory, anticipation, imagination, and fantasy. Donald Schon calls this indispensable capacity of the designer "multiple vision," which can be developed through repeated observations and inquiry.[39]

The range and nature of experiences and interpretations of an environment also depend on individuals' previous experiences and memories and may show considerable differences. The patterns of these interpretations, however, are neither arbitrary nor absolute. Beyond the multiformity of their distinctive features, the individual interpretations and preferences are, or should be, guided and structured by a hierarchy of patterns which have been verified intersubjectively. In other words, by regularly sharing and checking their own experiences with descriptions of others, students can both verify and sharpen the accuracy of their observations.

A design studio example

To promote an experiential awareness of environment and design, the author has organized a set of experimental exercises used in second- and third-year architectural design studios at the University of Illinois. The aim is to sensitize students to the experiential qualities of environments and places. The semester starts with students' writing an essay accompanied by sketches and diagrams which focuses on "places in the memory." Students are asked to recall memorable encounters with one place and to consider how memory portrays important properties of environmental experience, enabling individuals to evoke and communicate a "sense of place." In class, students present their recollections to the group, comparing and contrasting the varying experiences associated with different places. In the second project, students explore "imagined versus experienced landscapes" in relation to commonalities and disparities. To begin, each student is provided with a detailed map of a town in the vicinity of Champaign-Urbana where the University of Illinois is located. This map indicates the width of roads, types of institutions, building sizes, land use and so forth. After choosing one site from a list the author has generated, students have to "picture" the character of the place, relying only on the limited information provided on the map, plus their own imaginations. Having established an imagined picture, each student must design something on the site, using as a base the anticipated "spirit of the site." In addition, students make a visit to their respective sites, comparing experiences and observations to previously imagined ones.

The third project investigates "experience versus experience" and focuses on one district in downtown Chicago. Students explore the area through several different activities – e.g., walking, finding places to eat, riding through the area on bus, and so forth. Based on their experiences and observations, students prepare "maps" of the district, identifying boundaries, centers, places, enclosures, zones and connecting links. In addition, they are asked to describe the overall character of the district from the particular point of view gained through their observations. Later, the students present their findings through group presentations and discussion.

The final two projects of the term are related to students' observing and designing in their own local environment, Champaign-Urbana, with an emphasis on areas that they "use" regularly, and thus "know." Students investigate various places and paths in the city from the aspects of what and how they feel about them. They carefully collect observations and then compare places which they feel to be "real" with places seen to be "out of tune" or "out of place." One of the less satisfactory places is then selected as site for a design project. Students consider the failures of the site and then seek ways to strengthen its sense of place, making it, in Louis Kahn's words, what it "wants to be."[40] Students outline intensions and aims for the place and produce an actual design.

In the final project of the semester, students design a "home for the eternal traveler," grounding their work in earlier exercises. Observations and investigations of the urban environment continue, running parallel to students' interpretations of who the "eternal traveler" is and what his or her "home" might be. Students begin this project reflecting on the words of medieval Japanese poet Matsuo Basho, "Traveling is my home;" and those of philosopher Mircea Eliade, ". . . every life, even the least eventful, can be taken as a journey through a labyrinth."[41] Coming to understand these themes is inseparable from the selection of a potential site where this special home can be best imagined and located. After finding the site and the "client," students design the actual "home" without sacrificing symbolic intentions.

Conclusions

Students of architecture could usefully develop an intuitive sensibility toward the world – a holistic view grounded in personal experience and reflection. A cultivated sensibility channelled into design could provide important insights for an architecture reflecting "spirit of place." In this sense, designing is an act through which the architect implants values in the environment, hoping they will be discovered, cultivated and nourished by others as their own, regenerating a sense of human rootedness so often lacking in today's fragmented world. Within the framework of possibilities and limitations provided by modern society, it is the designer who takes an important first step in the direction of the recovery of place – a direction which, in Alexander's words, is "the timeless way of building."[42]

A phenomenological approach to design challenges the recent impasse in architecture and is therefore a *critical* inquiry. Architectural schools must not only serve the too often narrow interests of the profession, but also consistently challenge and lead it. In this regard, a phenomenological approach to design has much to offer.

Notes

1. In oriental cultures, the understanding of the ontological relationship between people and their world developed differently from Western approaches. Though it is not an explicit phenomenology, Japanese Zen-Buddhism, with its implicit existentialism reflected in the traditional arts and architecture, has many similarities to the phenomenological method; see D.T. Suzuki, *Zen Buddhism*, William Barrett, ed. (New York: Anchor Books, 1956); and Botong Bognar, *The Challenge of Japanese Architecture* (New York: Van Nostrand Reinhold, 1984).
2. E.g., Geoffrey Broadbent, Richard Bunt, and Charles Jencks, eds., *Signs, Symbols, and Architecture* (New York: Wiley, 1980). For a critical review of semiotic research in architecture, see Linda Groat, "Meaning in Architecture: New Directions and Sources," *Journal of Environmental Psychology* 1 (1981): 73–85.
3. As Christian Norberg-Schulz points out, "Architecture cannot be satisfactorily described by means of geometrical or semiological concepts." (Christian Norberg-Schulz, *Meaning in Western Architecture*, (New York: Rizzoli, 1974), p. 5; also, see Christian Norberg-Schulz, "Heidegger's Thinking on Architecture," *Perspecta: The Yale Architectural Journal* 20 (1983): 68.
4. Kevin Lynch, *The Image of the City* (Cambridge, Massachusetts: MIT Press, 1960).
5. Christian Norberg-Schulz, *Existence, Space and Architecture* (New York: Praeger, 1971); Christian Norberg-Schulz, *Genius Loci: Towards a Phenomenology of Architecture* (New York: Rizzoli, 1980).
6. This is a reference to the almost total penetration of the market of modern mass-societies today into the field of architecture, which results in the gradual devaluation of the built environment to the level of consumable commodity.
7. Hannah Arendt, *The Human Condition* (Chicago: The University of Chicago Press, 1958).
8. Quoted in Kenneth Frampton, ed., *Modern Architecture and the Critical Present* (New York: St. Martin's Press, 1982), p. 45.

9. Ibid., p. 19.
10. Christian Norberg-Schulz, "Meaning in Architecture," in Charles Jencks and George Baird, eds., *Meaning in Architecture* (New York: George Braziller, 1970), p. 219.
11. Alberto Perez-Gomez, "Architecture as Drawing," *Journal of Architectural Education* 36 (1982): 5.
12. This schism – reflected also in the split between theory and practice – started, in fact, in the Renaissance when Filippo Brunelleschi as the first architect-engineer left the actual construction of buildings to others. This "widening the incipient division between invention and fabrication . . . led to the degradation of the traditional craftsmen into the status of the *animal laborans*." (Frampton, *Modern Architecture*, p. 10).
13. A. Perez-Gomez, "Architecture as Drawing," p. 3; also, see A. Perez-Gomez, *Architecture and the Crisis of Modern Science* (Cambridge, Massachusetts: MIT Press, 1983), pp. 271–291.
14. A. Perez-Gomez, "Architecture as Drawing," p. 3.
15. See George Baird, " 'La Dimension Amoureuse' in Architecture," in Jencks and Baird, eds., *Meaning*, p. 78.
16. George Baird (ibid., p. 79) quotes Cedric Price, a contemporary modern English architect, who recently criticized architects' preoccupation with "the role of architecture as a provider of visually recognizable symbols of identity, place and activity . . . ." Price considered these roles of architecture as "both incomprehensible and irrelevant."
17. K. Frampton, *Modern Architecture*, p. 13.
18. Walter Gropius, *The Scope of Total Architecture* (New York: Harper and Row, 1956).
19. Edward Relph, *Rational Landscapes and Humanistic Geography* (New York: Barnes and Noble, 1981).
20. Rodney Place, "Studio Program, 1981," unpublished paper, School of Architecture, University of Illinois at Urbana-Champaign, p. 1.
21. Christopher Alexander, *The Timeless Way of Building* (New York: Oxford University Press, 1979), p. 19.
22. Martin Heidegger, "Building Dwelling Thinking," in *Poetry, Language, Thought*, Albert Hofstadter, trans. (New York: Harper and Row, 1971), p. 143.
23. Ibid., p. 160.
24. Hannah Arendt, *The Human Condition*, p. 173.
25. Chris Fawcett, "Do We Live to Build or Build to Live? Toward an Ontology of the New Japanese House," *GA Houses*, no. 4 (Tokyo: Global Architecture, 1978), p. 11.
26. Mircea Eliade, *The Sacred and the Profane* (New York: Harcourt Brace Jovanovich, 1959), p. 56.
27. Gaston Bachelard, *The Poetics of Space*, Maria Jolas, trans. (Boston: Beacon Press, 1964), p. 4.
28. Hannah Arendt, *The Human Condition*, p. 154.
29. Zen-Buddhist architectural examples such as the small tea pavilions, *shoin*-type residences, and rock and moss gardens were designed so that, while their composing elements were reduced to the "minimum" materially, their symbolic content and gathered meanings were increased to the "maximum," always suggesting existential totality. See Bognar, *Japanese Architecture*.
30. Aldo van Eyck, in Alison Smithson, ed., *Team 10 Primer* (Cambridge, Massachusetts: MIT Press, 1968), p. 41; Jencks and Baird, eds., *Meaning*, p. 209.
31. Erwin Panofsky, "The History of Art as a Humanistic Discipline," in *Meaning in the Visual Arts* (Garden City, New York: Doubleday Anchor Books, 1955), p. 2.

32. Italo Calvino, *Invisible Cities*, William Weaver, trans. (New York: Harcourt Brace Jovanovich, 1974).
33. C. Norberg-Schulz, *Existence*, pp. 17–24.
34. M. Heidegger, "Building Dwelling Thinking," p. 154.
35. Aldo van Eyck, in Alison Smithson, ed., *Team 10 Primer*, pp. 83, 96.
36. Martin Heidegger, quoted by Norberg-Schulz in *Genius Loci*, p. 10.
37. Gaston Bachelard, *The Poetics of Space*, pp. XXVIII–XXIX.
38. Maurice Merleau-Ponty, *Phenomenology of Perception*, Colin Smith, trans. (London: Routledge and Kegan Paul, 1962), p. xvi.
39. Donald Schon, quoted by Donlyn Lyndon in "Design: Inquiry and Implication," *Journal of Architectural Education* 35 (1982): 2.
40. Louis Kahn, quoted in Charles Jencks, *Modern Movements in Architecture* (New York: Doubleday, 1973), p. 43.
41. Matsuo Basho, *A Haiku Journey – Basho's Narrow Road to a Far Province*, Dorothy Britton, trans. (Tokyo: Kodansha International, 1974); Mircea Eliade, *Patterns in Comparative Religion*, Rosemary Sheed, trans. (1958), New York: The New American Library, 1974), p. 382.
42. Christopher Alexander, *The Timeless Way of Building*.

Part III

Place and dwelling

12. The dwelling door:
Towards a phenomenology of transition

RICHARD LANG

A meditation upon human dwelling reveals our primal embodied existence, our being-in-the-world. The notion of dwelling is the most taken-for-granted aspect of human existence. For this very reason, inhabitation, our familiar though enigmatic circumstance, is the most obscure problem upon which we may reflect. To understand this radically occluded aspect of our being is to ask a dangerous and disruptive question. Contemplating the notion of inhabiting discloses our primitive alliance with the world and thereby unsettles the natural embeddedness and forgetfulness of human existence. Subjective life is embodied existence.[1] Subjectivity is not a dream that passes over reality, nor is it a surveying of thought or a mechanical process. Human subjectivity involves us in a suffering of the inherent limitations and possibilities of the flesh. This subjectivity must be thought as opened up by the very limitation of what Unamuno has called a humanity of "flesh and bone."[2] To think within this context means to arouse the slumber of our dwelling, to reflect on the mysterious alliance between person and world; it means to begin to move toward an understanding of human habitation.

The primary center of human habitation is the home. In the first section of this essay, I articulate how the home is incorporated and assimilated into the fabric of embodied existence; the home is our second body. In the next section, I further elaborate this bodily act of incorporation by focusing on one facet of the home — i.e. the door. Here, the intention is to reanimate the meaning of the door by demonstrating how ordinary doors embody human experience and thus reflect subjective life. To begin, I turn to the French existential-phenomenological psychologist Maurice Merleau-Ponty, whose work can be approached as a profound meditation on human embodied existence, particularly *inhabiting*.

Inhabiting

In *The Structure of Behavior*, Maurice Merleau-Ponty shows how our body
lives space by means of the intriguing example of a soccer player. This soccer player does not encounter the field upon which he plays as an object;
the soccer field is a domain permeated with "lines of force" − articulated
areas and pathways between adversaries which guide and solicit the active
body to move in certain ways in accordance with the unfolding play. The soccer player is not a distant consciousness surveying the field as an object of
thought; the field is given as "the immanent term of his practical intentions,"
and the vectors of force in it are constantly restructuring with his actions during the game: "The player becomes one with [play] and feels the direction
of the 'goal' . . . as immediately as the vertical and horizontal planes of his
body."[3] The player understands where the goal is in a way which is lived
rather than known. The mind does not inhabit the playing field but the field
is inhabited by a "knowing" body.

Inhabiting co-constitutes our primitive situation. Being an initiative of the
active body, inhabiting is an intention and not merely a fact of nature; it is
not just to be somewhere, to find oneself somewhere, but to *inhabit* a place.
With subjectivity, a radical metamorphosis sets in as the world is grasped
in a new way. Inhabiting, the essential feature of subjective life, is an act of
transformation where space becomes place. Inhabiting is an act of incorporation; it is a situation of active, essential acquisition. Incorporation is the
initiative of the active body, embracing and assimulating a certain sphere
of foreign reality to its own body. In this sense, incorporation is essentially
the movement from the strange to the familiar. This commerce of strange
and familiar, which forms a central dialectic of human existence, is instituted
and embodied in our dwelling, our home. The home is the intimate hollow
we have carved out of the anonymous, the alien. Everything has been transmuted in the home; things have truly become annexed to our body, and
incorporated.

This act of transformation is disclosed in one way when I move to a new
residence. Though I may legally possess this abode, it does not belong to
me at first. Somewhat like being a foreign face, the presence of the former
occupant lingers about the house. If I am sensitive to this atmosphere, I am
acutely aware of the alien texture of this reality. This new enclosure − the
walls, the ceiling, the floor − is hard, crisp and foreign to the touch. It seems
to face someone else, resisting me, failing to reveal itself. The labor of my
caretaking turns this place into a home, into a place that addresses me as
familiar, as belonging to me. This act of familiarization is performed as if by

magic by the active body. It is enacted at the most primitive level without the assistance of conscious thought. There eventually comes a time when this house feels familiar. At certain moments as I stand and move about in the house, I catch a sense of my active body communing in it. The atmosphere has become warm and intimate, as though the body has established a sort of uncanny alliance with it, a bodily understanding of it. It has become *of* the body, transmuted to the nature of the active body. My existence as embodied finds a new access to the world in the home. The home becomes my second body.

Alphonso Lingus provides a simple but profound example of how the active body annexes a certain region of alien reality to its own body. Lingus utilizes the most intimate site of the home – our noctural and erotic place, the bed:

> My bed was, the first night, crisp and brittle, foreign; little by little it has become intimate. It has acquired a very decided and very obvious fleshy texture; as I lie enveloped with it I no longer distinguish where my body leaves off and where an alien surface begins. At first I had that very vivid awareness of these sheets *touching* me, an alien surface *in contact* with the frontiers of myself. Little by little, this frontier fades, obliterates itself, and becomes indefinite. The intimacy of the flesh diffuses throughout the whole bedsheet, finally into the bed itself, and the room also by a sort of contagion. They have become incorporated.[4]

In contrast to this experience of incorporation, Lingus speaks of a form of nausea in regard to the bedsheets of another. Because the bedsheets have been assimulated to the body, there is something indecent and repulsive about sleeping in someone else's bedding, something similar to lying with or even sitting too close to a stranger:

> Obviously, this nausea is not aroused by something merely accidental, like their smelling, or being stained perhaps. Because, after all, we are not nauseated in sleeping in our own bedsheets even after they have become quite dirty, and, after all, there is nothing nauseating about sleeping outside, on the bare humus itself. This nausea is the flesh's revolt against what is not of itself; the flesh knows its own. One violates the home of another like one violates a virgin.[5]

The door and embodiment

In this same manner, everything in the home becomes incorporated by the body; the body extends itself through household things. The bodily character of the home is a reality that can be observed through a meditation upon any example, for instance, the front door to a dwelling. If I am outside a stranger's beautiful Victorian house and notice the door and desire to go immediately inside to view the ornate interior, I have a very strong impression of the difficult passage between this outside to that inside. This door is an imposing barrier; it is closed to my coming and going. But I do not experience my own front door as an obstacle; it is the portal, resembling a mouth, through which the outside and inside communicate. The house, via the door portal, is speaking to the outside; likewise, the house is looking out from its windows at the surrounding landscape. Through incorporation, I have the very distinct experience of my home enveloping me as a kind of extended tissue of my own body. The home has been transformed into a region through which courses my life as it courses through my body. Bodily existence pulsates through the home, transforming a sphere of the anonymous in such a way that it becomes part of the self.

The example of the door demonstrates well how a common household object partakes in the domain of bodily existence, and how subjective life is embodied in things. Though a door can be seen purely as a physical object — the functional solution to transition — it also can be viewed as a new access and disclosure of the world. Thinking of the house as embodied, as a kind of second body, means to see it in all its aspects not as thing but as *access* to things.[6] The door is the incarnation of my experience of transition, animating in a visible manner the dialectic of inside and outside, fundamentally presenting either a welcoming or rejecting face. The door is one of the expressive habitations of human experience.

Here, there is a shift from the traditional natural-scientific attitude which understands objects as muted, inanimate, quantifiable things, to a psychological attitude where things speak the language of human experience. This shift in posture is necessary to recover the psychological world and thereby to understand our involvement in situations.[7] Here, I adopt an attitude which understands the door as a mirror of the way in which I comprehend myself: "It is through my relation to 'things' that I know myself."[8] As a physical object, the door has measurable dimensions and is made of certain materials with consistent properties. As a practical object that I meet on my way, it is first of all access to an inside and an outside, it is disclosure and closure, it yields or resists, it beckons or rejects. A person cannot construct a door without in some way designing himself or herself and installing a typical experience of transition.

A question as simple as, "What is a door?" disturbs the familiarity and slumber of things as mere objects of use. When things are seen as merely material they do not *matter* any longer – their existential meanings have been forgotten. A phenomenological inquiry bring this forgetfulness to light, seeking to reanimate the everyday things of our existence. To disclose the meaning of personal doors or the architectural doors of our culture is to comprehend how we live and embody transition in everyday existence – the lifeworld. Again, the intention is to show that from the perspective of phenomenological psychology, human experience is visible and expressive even in a common door. As van den Berg declares, "Who wants to become acquainted with man should listen to the language spoken by the things in his existence."[9]

Existential meanings

Following this provocative suggestion, I attend to the language spoken by doors.[10] Doors close to tell me of my rejections or another's isolation, doors swing wide open like broad smiles to welcome my approach, or doors sternly bar my way, imprisoning me by becoming impenetrable walls. Doors punctuate my tearful farewells or joyfully celebrate my reunion, doors are dramatically slammed during scenes of anger or resemble whispers when tentatively unlatched. Doors call me to an intimate enclosure when life's struggles become too demanding and embrace me in conviviality and familiarity, protecting me from the elements, the dangerous wilds, or the anonymous. Through doors, the world comes to meet me: trusted neighbors, new friends, invited guests, intrusive salesmen, the afternoon breeze, the setting sun and the clockwork regularity of the paper boy. The doorway is between outside and inside, between public and private, between anonymity and familiarity, between foreign and personal; doors frame our precious moments of meeting and parting, and across their thresholds passes our fate. Through doors we move from one world to another; here the first step of our journey commences and the last stride of our homecoming ends. Gaston Bachelard has eloquently summarized the expressive presence of the doors in our life and the stories they tell:

> How concrete everything becomes in the world of the spirit when an object, a mere door, can give images of hesitation, temptation, desire,

security, welcome and respect. If one were to give an account of all the doors one has closed and opened, of all the doors one would like to reopen, one would have to tell the story of one's entire life.[11]

The vital significance of the door is expressed by the numerous religious activities surrounding passageways. In many cultures there are elaborate rituals of transition: doorposts are often inscribed with symbols and other sacred objects, and the threshold is held to be sacred. For example, the opening and closing of the door and the passage of people from their homes into the outside world was a vital transition in Roman society. This critical event was under the power of Janus, the two-faced god of passings: Janus Patulcius opens the door, and Janus Clusivius closes it.[12] Here, the door is simultaneously uniting and separating, it is a bridge of arrival and departure. The tension between the beginning and end, the centripetal and centrifugal, constitutes an essential aspect of the door. The door is a pivotal reality, for life literally swings on its hinges.

Thresholds

The central structure of the door is the threshold. The uniting and separating quality is most clearly visible in the threshold. With the institution and acceptance of the threshold, we install a radical discontinuity in human existence. In a poetic rendering, Martin Heidegger highlights this cardinal structure:

> The threshold is the ground-beam that bears the doorway as a whole. It sustains the middle in which the two, the outside and the inside, penetrate each other. The threshold bears the between. What goes out and goes in, in the between, is joined in the between's dependability. The dependability of the middle must never yield either way.[13]

In a related way, the religious scholar Mircea Eliade speaks of the difference in existential space regarding the sacred threshold:

> For a believer, the church shares in a different space from the street in which it stands. The door that opens on the interior of the church actually signifies a solution of continuity. The threshold that separates the two spaces also indicates the distance between two modes of being, the profane and the religious. The threshold is the limit, the boundary, the frontier that distinguishes and opposes two worlds – and at the same

time the paradoxical place where these worlds communicate, where passage from the profane to the sacred world becomes possible.[14]

In considering this passage, it is useful to examine the cathedral portal because what occurs at this threshold clearly demonstrates a particular experience of transition. At the cathedral threshold, I take pause from my everyday concerns and reflect on the deeper dimensions of existence. It is only after I have performed the proper ritual of transition that I may pass to the other side. The cathedral doorway marks the transformation of my profane path to a sacred journey which eventually leads to the altar itself. The threshold proclaims and embodies a reflective pause between two worlds. As a spiritual gateway, the church portal beckons me to a movement in depth both in the spatial and psychological sense. The passage into this enclosure is also a movement through time because the doorway is a container of memory. At this portal, the historical quality of human existence is remembered in living stone. At the cathedral of Reims, for example, the immense embrasured portals are inscribed with numerous sculptured personages; the gateway reverberates with religious images. The Biblical text appears in stone, and these images preserve the sacred history and tell the divine stories. By standing before the cathedral door, I sense the religious history of the world from creation onwards. I find proclaimed the principles of the church: the examples of the saints; the roles of virtues; the place of science, arts and crafts.

In a similar manner, a temporal dimension is also preserved and manifested at the door of my home. This threshold, where I hospitably receive others into my personal domain, is a place of remembrance. Here, at the site of my reunions and farewells, the persons and events of my past quietly continue to dwell. My history is present at the portal and is preserved in the benign lingering or haunting presence of the people who have passed through this gateway. Long-lost friends, former guests, inquisitive strangers, departed relatives, trusted neighbors – all are marginally present at the door gathered by the enduring quality of remembrance. These intimate others are silent, invisible sentinels, standing as door posts to preserve and indirectly reflect who I have been and am. In a similar way, the cathedral gateway, populated with religious personages, makes explicit what is generally implicit in human experience, revealing the sustaining presence of others at every door. Human dialogue is a crucial aspect of all threshold symbolism.[15]

At the same time, however, the door speaks of a basic rift in my dialogue with others. By honoring the threshold, I accept an essential limit in ex-

istence, marking a division in the homogeneous space, establishing an outside and inside, installing a difference. As a radical discontinuity and a place
of transition, the door is also a reminder to me of my final threshold –
death's door. By accepting the threshold as an undeniable limit in life, I
welcome the tragic dimension of existence. At a doorway there is an inten-
sification of life; I become truly aware of shifts and turns in life, of openings
and closings, of beginnings and ends. Here, I live my transitions concretely.

Modern thresholds

To offer a contrast to the cathedral door, I turn to the sense of threshold in
contemporary architecture. What door best typifies the modern experience
of transition? According to the architect Robert Venturi, "one of the powerful
twentieth-century orthodoxies has been the necessity for continuity between [building and surroundings]: the inside should be expressed on the
outside."[16] The boldest way to achieve this so-called flowing space – the
continuity of inside and outside – is by radically exaggerating glass windows. In modern architecture, we literally have walls of glass; even our
doors, once solid wood borders, are glass constructions. Modern doors
have become windows. How has our *experience* of doorways altered in accordance to this new architectural statement?

Standing before a glass door, I am struck by an undeniable, paradoxical
impression of being at two places at once. While bodily being outside the
building I am, simultaneously, visibly present inside. In contrast, at the
cathedral doorway there is a suggestion of what is inside, but I envision this
in imagination and await in anticipation. While the interior of the cathedral
gradually discloses itself as I enter, before the modern glass door I have the
unmitigated presentation of the interior. The transparent door blurs and
merges the juncture between inside and outside. By subduing the threshold
as a limit, the glass door reflects a modern desire for flowing space. Most
modern architecture – whether skyscraper, office building or shopping mall
– has adopted transparent doors to facilitate free flowing movement. People easily enter and exit. While transparent doors solve a functional problem
of accessibility, they also obscure the significance of transition.

Rather than the strict ritual demarcation of an inviolable domain, there is
in much modern architecture a quest for technological regions – worlds
where any and all desires are effortlessly satisfied, where one may go
anywhere and do anything. Modern technology has provided a previously
unimaginable freedom of movement. How is this distinctly contemporary ex-

perience expressed in modern doors? These doors are mechanically operated as my mere presence trips an electric eye, and the door magically swings open. I move without any hesitation, and there is not the slightest pause or deflection in my stride. As an invisible barrier, the glass door gives the impression that it is always open. This glass transition lulls me in the illusion that the door is always speaking in the affirmative. It appears to be always accessible and open to me. Even with its modern modifications, however, the door is a place of judgment, a yes and no, a disclosure and closure.[17] Though the glass door seems to refuse to say no, it can. I am rudely awakened to this fact when I forget the door, absent-mindedly walk inside and dangerously collide with a glass boundary.

The glass door is the incarnation of a particular experience of transition. It embodies the modern desire for accessible and transparent passageways. The glass door is a radical modification of customary wooden and metal portals. The contemporary transparent door is a reflection and transformation of cultural intentions. In the past, the door as physical entity marked in tangible form the passage from outside to inside and thereby reinforced the psychological shift accompanying bodily transition. Modern entranceways frequently obscure psychological passage and contribute to a built environment which less frequently supports and reflects essential qualities of human experience and meaning.

The hospitable door

How human experience is incarnated in doors is further elaborated in another example. The door is an access and its accessibility is in relation to my attitude towards what lies beyond the threshold. When visiting the house of a friend, I confidently approach this hospitable door, invited by the familiar sounds of domestic life – the murmur of conversation, the laughter of children's voices, the clink of dinner plates and the tempting aroma of the prepared meal. Though outside the house, I am already in contact with the receptive world within. The door is but a convenient screen between me and the friends I am about to visit. My knocking on the door already transports me into their company – the interior changes, the laughter abates, the conversation subsides and someone comes to greet me. Here the door has only partially held me back and I hardly notice its presence. The door effaces itself as a resisting object, while serving as a means through which I meet others. As the active body is my access to things and other people, likewise, the door as my second body resounds to this bodily access; it is the bridge to the world of others.

In this example, the door is not primarily in need of paint or repairs, nor do I notice its ornate designs. The hospitable door stands as benevolent and inviting shadow between me and my friends as the moment of meeting approaches. It is only when the interior of the house and its inhabitants acquires a hidden or ambivalent meaning that the door gradually transforms into a massive object which demands my attention for its own sake. It is at this moment that I no longer can reach beyond the door towards a receptive known interior, welcomed by others that the door materializes as a resisting object. The fully visible door speaks of an interrupted journey – i.e., a disruption of my dialogue with others. When I am refused admittance to the interior, the door takes on the character of a substantial barrier; the door is transformed from an inviting foreshadowing of a pleasant meeting to a massive piece of laminated wood, with ornately carved designs, with metal decorations and cross braces with exactly forty-nine bolts. The door has now become primarily a surface spectacle, and I begin to notice and count the details of its construction. My progress towards others is interrupted at this barrier. To be refused access to the interior and denied access to others is to be *obsessed* with the door.

Kafka's door

The predicament of being before the door is frequently addressed by the Czech writer Franz Kafka. Kafka's stories teem with doors – closed doors, open doors, anonymous doors, concealed doors, fake doors, secret doors. For Kafka, the door is a crucial meeting place of dialogue and encounter. Waiting before a door is one of the central themes of his work.

In the parable, "Before the Law," in the cathedral scene of *The Trial*, such fateful waiting is dramatically presented. Although the protagonist of this story is seeking an encounter with the divine, his dilemma can be interpreted as paradigmatic for all human meeting. After an arduous journey, a man from the country appears before the open door at the gate of the Law. Before this portal stands an ominous doorkeeper, and the provincial man begs him to be admitted to the Law. But the doorkeeper refuses his request, and the man sits on a stool beside the door in the vague hope of being admitted in the future. As his waiting turns from days to years, the countryman makes many requests to be allowed entrance, even attempting to bribe the doorkeeper by giving him valuable gifts. Over time, the man learns to know the insignificant fleas on the doorkeeper's fur collar and even begs the fleas to aid him to persuade the doorkeeper to change his decision. At first bitterly cursing his fate, he later only mumbles to himself and grows more childish. What is the meaning of this inaccessible door, and how can we characterize the attitude of the countryman who sits waiting?

The door interrupts our progress, blocks our access to the interior and thus poses a question. Our practical projects and desires are curtailed at the doorway, and we are no longer allowed to stride in a totally self-determined world. When confronted by the door, the provincial man is unable to draw back from his steadfast quest for admission. He is unwilling to allow the door to become unattainable for a moment and thus interrupt his unrelenting advance. Before this gateway he is unable to disentangle himself from his all-consuming preoccupation with the doorkeeper; consequently, his own existence remains concealed from view. Unaware that the door is a place of reflection, the country fellow fails to turn inward and thereby discover a new sensibility and understanding of himself and his fate.

The man's lack of self-reflection continues to the very end. Drawing near death and with his last breath, he asks the doorkeeper a practical question: "How does it come about, then, that in all these years no one has come seeking admittance but me?"[18] In reply the doorkeeper bellows, "No one but you could gain admittance through this door, since this door was intended only for you. I am going to shut it."[19]

As the door shuts, its resonance moves through the body of the reader. Kafka arouses the basic longing and anxiety contained in all waiting – i.e., when will this closed door be opened? Being obsessed with admittance, the man obstinately sits before the inaccessible door, which emerges here as the gravitating end-point of all his intentions. The door is his predicament. To be denied admittance is to be obsessed with the door. The word "obsession," is, in fact, derived from the Latin *obsidere*, meaning "to sit down before," "besiege," "occupy," "possess." Obsession is the attempt to gain forced entry by sitting before the city gate and waiting the occupants out – a tactic employed by an army besieging a fortress.

Kafka's story says much about the etymology of obsession and, in fact, an entire psychology of the obsessive syndrome can be brought to light by pondering Kafka's inaccessible door. One important indication here is Goppert's discussion of obsession and the door phenomenon.[20] He argues that the predominant feature of obsession is the desire to control. When leaving a room, for example, the obsessive person must check and recheck whether the door was closed, the light turned off and the heater extinguished. If the person does not follow this impulse to control, he is overwhelmed by anxiety. These impulsive acts to control, topographically considered, all take place at the point of crossing a border. For the obsessive, the border or threshold is a critical place of transition where he is confronted with his inability to either commence or terminate a relationship to someone, something or somewhere. He experiences the impossibility of transitions which characterize this syndrome. In another context, von Gebsattel describes a patient identified as H. H., who suffers from this same threshold disturbance in the capacity to act. While standing in his room with his coat on, H. H. is unable to go out because he does not "know" whether he has really put on his coat. We see that an action can be literally executed and yet not be experienced as being completed in a full sense. At this door of doing/undoing, the obsessive is in the grip of incessant doubt.[21]

One of the earliest, historically observed features of obsession was that of obsessive doubt.[22] Before the inaccessible door, we are radically severed from others. Denied a secure and trusted common world, we begin to doubt ourselves. In doubting, we become a double self, divided into both self and other. We move into a closed pseudo-self-sufficient universe, condemned to live the impoverishment of a pseudo-dialogue with ourselves. In doubt, our activity and progress are fundamentally interrupted and things come to a deadly standstill. Our attention is drawn to irrelevant acts and insignificant details to ward off the encroaching anxiety and stagnation.

The obsessive world is a universe at a standstill where we are blocked off from others and constructive activity. Without the purifying circulation of things, the world becomes polluted and we are threatened by the omnipresent encroachment of decay, disease, germs, dust, feces, urine, sweat, dirt, and death.[23] Waiting at the inaccessible door dramatically depicts the obsessive predicament: here, the door appears as destructive dam and the self, stagnant pond.

Coda

The door is the access to the other, the site of human meeting, the place of dialogue, of judgment. The door is radically *intersubjective*, for it shelters the revelation of self and other. Psychologically, a door is most meaningfully disclosed when we are standing before it. To be before a door is in its deepest significance to be a sensitive attendant waiting for the manifestation of the other, for the appearance of the real. Our ritual of knocking on the door is the embodiment of respectful waiting or pause; it is not an empty gesture. With this respectful hesitation at a door demarcating difference, we provoke a life of community, of being together with others-in-difference. We celebrate the vital difference between self and other and thereby make possible a meeting. At the doorway, we respectfully wait for the other. In its purest mythic form, the person before the door is the stranger who journeys from afar, who solicits the real, who asks for admission. The dweller offers this stranger hospitality, and the door becomes the meeting place of host and guest, of person and world.

Notes

1. See Maurice Merleau-Ponty, *The Phenomenology of Perception*, Colin Smith, trans. (New York: Humanities Press, 1962).
2. Don Miguel de Unamuno, *Tragic Sense of Life*, J. Flitch, trans. (New York: Dover Publications, 1954), p. 1.
3. Maurice Merleau-Ponty, *The Structure of Behavior*, Alden Fisher, trans. (Boston: Beacon Press, 1963), p. 168.
4. Alphonson Lingus, *Before the Visage*, unpublished manuscript, Duquesne University, 1963, p. 56.
5. Ibid., p. 57.
6. See Alphonso De Waelhens, quoted in Frederik Buytendijk, *Prolegomena to an Anthropological Physiology* (Pittsburgh: Duquesne University Press, 1974), p. 19.
7. See Robert Romanyshyn, *Psychological Life: From Science to Metaphor* (Austin: University of Texas Press, 1982).
8. Merleau-Ponty, *Phenomenology of Perception*, p. 383.
9. J.H. van den Berg, *The Phenomenological Approach to Psychiatry* (Springfield, Massachusetts: Charles Thomas, 1955), p. 32.
10. The following section is drawn in part from Val Clery, *Doors* (New York: Penguin Books, 1978), p. 12.
11. Gaston Bachelard, *The Poetics of Space*, Maria Jolas, trans. (Boston: Beacon Press, 1964), p. 224.
12. Robert Ogilvie, *The Roman and Their Gods in the Age of Augustus* (London: Chatto and Windus, 1969), p. 11.
13. Martin Heidegger, "Language," in *Poetry, Language, Thought*, Albert Hofstadter, trans. (New York: Harper and Row, 1971), p. 204.
14. Mircea Eliade, *The Sacred and the Profane*, Willard Trask, trans, (New York: Harcourt, Brace and World, 1959), p. 25.
15. Bernd Jager, "The Gilgamesh Epic: A Phenomenological Exploration," in *Review of Existential Psychology and Psychiatry* 12 (1973): 13–16.
16. Robert Venturi, *Complexity and Contradiction in Architecture* (New York: Museum of Modern Art, 1967), p. 71.
17. Eliade, *The Sacred and the Profane*, p. 25.
18. Franz Kafka, *The Trial*, Willa and Edwin Muir, trans. (New York: Alfred Knopt, 1956), p. 269.
19. Ibid.
20. Hans Goppert, "Die Bedeutung der Schwelle in der Zwangskrankheit," in *Werden und Handeln* (Stuttgart: Hippokrates-Verlag, 1963), pp. 408–418.
21. V.E. von Gebsattel, "The World of the Compulsive," in *Existence*, Rollo May, Ernest Angel and Henri Ellenberger, eds. (New York: Basic Books, 1958), pp. 170–187.
22. H. Laughtin, *The Neuroses* (Washington: Butterworths, 1967), p. 35.
23. V.E. von Gebsattel, "The World of Compulsive," p. 178.

13. Body, house and city:
The intertwinings of embodiment, inhabitation and civilization

BERND JAGER

The house, body and city form a priviledged unity of mutual implication.[1] It is here that human life becomes situated and centered; from here it unfolds and comes to encompass a temporal and spatial world. It is only as *situated* life – as life arched by a sky, supported by a welcoming earth and sheltered by an environment – that past, present and future can announce themselves. It is only as surrounded by a physiognomic world, by things and beings attractive and repellent, by things to do and to avoid, that a primitive geography can first emerge, that a forward and a backward, a high and a low, an up and a down, a left and a right can first come into being. There can be no true house, body or city for a robot; consequently, there can be no true forward and backward within the reach of any mechanical device, nor can there be things near or far, up or down, nor a yesterday or tomorrow.

The house, body and city do not so much occupy space and time as generate them. It is only as inhabiting, embodied beings that we find access to a world. The house, body and city are the places where we are born or reborn and from which we step out into a larger world. One of the most interesting challenges of our time is to intertwine these three primordial terms, to rekindle their long forgotten interrelationship, to reexperience their underlying unity anew in modern thought and in modern architectural practice.

Within the Christian tradition, the homology between building and body can be traced to St. Paul's letter to the Colossians. He speaks here of Christ as "the head of the body which is the church" and of his own willingness to suffer "for the sake of Christ's body which is the church."[2] It is in the light of this understanding that a cross-shaped basilica came to symbolize the body of Christ crucified. In the Middle Ages, the choir came to symbolize the head of Christ; the transept, his outstretched arms; and the nave, his body and legs.

The history of St. Peter's Cathedral reflects clearly an abiding concern with this symbolism. The original wood-roofed basilica was redesigned in the 15th Century by Rossellino under Pope Nicholas V. A description of the plans at that time indicate a clear concern for a detailed correspondence between the building and the image of the crucified Christ.[3] It is said that under Clement VIII, the centrally planned buildings of Bramante and Michelangelo were condemned because they failed to reflect clearly this correspondence.[4] And, when in the seventeenth century Bernini created the Piazza St. Pietro, it met with severe criticism because the design would not clearly accomodate a human figure with outstretched arms.[5]

The correspondence between the church as the house of the congregation and the town as the house of a larger secular community did not escape the notice of the medieval builders.[6] Moreover, from the beginning of Christian civilization the church had been felt to refer not only to the body of Christ, but equally to constitute a link between an earthly and a heavenly city. Norberg-Schulz brings attention to the paleo-Christian basilica as a representation of the Heavenly Jerusalem envisioned as a city of antiquity. The facade of the church was experienced as the city gate; the nave and transept as the main streets; and the apse with the throne of Christ as the imperial aula.[7]

The Gothic cathedral continued and even intensified this reference to the city. But where the Christian basilica had emphasized the urban character of the heavenly city, the cathedral came to stress the heavenly aspects. Alberti's great church at Mantua, the St. Andrea, presents a facade in which the triumphal arch expresses the role of the church as portal, opening upon the heavenly city.[8] Both Alberti (1404–1472) and Palladio (1508–1580) described the city as a kind of house and the house as a kind of city. In particular, Palladio strove in all his buildings towards a symmetry inspired by the human body; he spoke at times of the spine of a house, of its nose and mouth, and of its legs, eyes and ears.[9] In the work of Francesco di Giorgio Martini, the theme of the mutual implication of body, house and city assumes an almost obsessive quality. In his detailed city plans, each part of the city is made to recall an analogous part of the human body. The anthropomorphic theme is also applied to individual buildings and even to aspects of these buildings such as the cornices and columns.[10]

In all of these architectural developments, the Renaissance builders echoed the concerns of the masters of antiquity. Vitruvius clearly took the body as a starting point for the contemplation of order and proportion as it was to be applied to building. He wrote:

> For nature has so planned the human body that the face from the chin to the top of the forehead is a tenth part, also the palm of the hand from the wrist to the top of the middle finger is as much . . . the other limbs also have their own proportionate measurement.
>
> In like fashion the members of temples ought to have dimensions of their several parts answering suitably to the general sum of the whole magnitude.[11]

In a similar vein, Galen wrote about the Greek theory of proportion:

> Chrysippus holds that beauty does not consist in the elements but in the harmonious proportion of the parts, the proportion of one finger to the other, of all the fingers to the rest of the hand, of the rest of the hand to the wrist, of these to the forearm, of the forearm to the whole arm, or finally, of all parts to all others, as it is written in the canon of Polyclitus.[12]

These classical canons of beauty are not of direct concern within the present context except as they point to the perenially felt connection between embodiment and inhabitation. It has always been impossible to speak of building without either explicit or silent reference to the human or animal body. These early aesthetic theories used in the visual arts all point to the fact that neither the Romans, the Greeks nor the Egyptians could think about the beauty of a building without at the same time also recalling the beauty of the human or animal form.

After a period of aesthetic barrenness extending into the twentieth century, this sensibility is now finding renewed expression in the visual arts. In his book on post-modern architecture, Charles Jencks concludes that:

> the overriding metaphor which recent architects have just started to express grows out of the organic tradition of modernism and relates very closely to body images and man's continuity with the natural and animal kingdoms. The human body, the face, the symmetry of animal forms are becoming the foundation for a metaphysics that man finds immediate and relevant.[13]

An interesting challenge presents itself to the human sciences. It would promise to be instructive to think through the interrelationships maintained among the body, house and city or village at various times and in different cultural settings. We could pose the question whether attitudes towards the body are frequently or perhaps invariably reflected in attitudes towards buildings, and vice versa. Would, for example, a purely functional, mechanistic approach to the body find an echo in an equally functional approach to the building of houses and cities? Would a conception of the body as a material envelope of an immaterial soul reappear in an architectural conception of house and city as mere material containers of a human cargo? Could a professed disinterest in the beauties of the flesh find its parallel in a loss of esteem for wood and stone? Could there be a relationship between the modern medical view of the body and the fact that so many modern apartment buildings look like hospitals and so many universities, like surgical wards? Would it be possible to establish a cultural link between de la Metrie's *l'homme machine* and Le Corbusier's *machine à vivre*? Might it be legitimate, even though it might appear as slightly humorous, to view Baron Haussmann in a new light as a medical pioneer preparing the way for modern heart bypass surgery?

And would such a careful study not shed more light also on Freud's anguished cry in his *Civilization and its Discontents* to the effect that modern man has become *ein Prothesengott* – i.e., a god by virtue of painful, ill-fitting prosthetic devices designed by an ever more powerful, mechanized, artificial civilization? No doubt this remark has its painful autobiographical import, but the image Freud evokes is thereby strengthened and moves us with a greater impact. His comment points to the possibility of thinking about buildings as ill-fitting artificial devices, but, by contrast, it also makes it possible to think of a more natural inhabitation where the cruel line of division between our flesh and the flesh of the material world is not a source of frustration and pain but becomes itself a spur to thought, to thoughtful action and to celebration in the arts.

The body as visible and a source of sight

If we ask what it means to inhabit or embody the world, we come upon what we may experience with Merleau-Ponty as the central mystery of the body – viz., that it belongs to the visible and can be seen, while at the same time it also remains a source of vision.[14] The body is a visible source of vision. This duality is also visited upon that part of the world we inhabit or use. A house or a city, when properly inhabited, not merely remains something seen; it itself becomes a source of vision and light according to which we see. Inhabitation and dwelling transform a world of *confronted* things, of objects inspected and judged into a realm that is supportive of vision. Dwelling sheds a light on unknown things and then slowly transforms these things into a light that radiates out to other things.

A stick held by a blind man or a pen grasped by a writer ceases to remain a material foreign object that is indifferent to our projects. To write means among other things to transform a material writing instrument into a quasi-part of the body, to incorporate it into the general scheme of bodily existence, to make it a channel through which the currents of human life can flow out to others. To feel our way without the aid of sight by means of a stick, we must transfer the borders or our sensiblity outwards and extend the tactile sense of our hands outward towards the tip of the stick. To feel our way in this manner means to flood the blindman's stick with the sensibility of our body, to use it as we would our hands or fingers to replace the function of our eyes. Such a complete appropriation of a material object could serve us as a paradigm for inhabitation.

We should note that in both instances – that of the writer's pen and the blindman's stick – the process of inhabitation cannot be instantaneously accomplished. We are seldom immediately at home in a new place, and we all need a period of apprenticeship with tools before they can become fully useful to us – before they can fully function as extensions of our body. *Inhabitation* always includes within itself a form of *habitation*. ''To inhabit'' refers to a kind of having (*habere*) that permits us a radical access to material objects and allows us to treat these objects as extensions of our own body.

To approach inhabitation in this way means to be able no longer to make such a radical distinction between flesh and matter, between bodies and mere things. Bodily existence floods over into things, appropriates them, infuses them with the breath of life, draws them into the sphere of daily projects and concerns. A fully inhabited world is at the same time also a fully embodied world. Alienation – painful discordant embodiment – is itself a loss of access to the flesh of nature; it means the suffering of a ''no'' of things. Alienation is the fatal enclosing of the powers of the body within its own skin – a forced, brooding selfishness. Alienation is ultimately the failure of inhabitation and embodiment.

To enter and finally to come to inhabit a house or a city means to come to assume a certain stance, to surrender to a certain *style of acting upon* and of *experiencing* the surrounding world. To enter a building means to come under the sway of a certain choreography and at the same time to become the subject of a certain disclosure. Like a certain bodily attitude, a building opens a particular world of tasks, outlooks, and sensibilities. The windows guide and frame our outwardly directed glance; they may offer us the possibility of seizing a majestic surrounding landscape or they may gently place before us a secret spot of nature, an inner court, a protected pond, or a colorful garden. To enter and come to inhabit a place fully means to redraw the limits of our bodily existence to include that place – to come to incorporate it and to live it henceforth as ground of revelation rather than as panorama. An environment seen thus is transformed into a place which opens a perspective to the world.

This miracle of appropriation, this transformation of something visible into something that supports vision, this subtle alchemy whereby *things* are etherealized to the point of becoming a light that guides our vision, this ceaseless transubstantiation – all remain as the mysterious core of our thought concerning the human body and the place of dwelling. How is it that the body can recede in such a way that a world can come to appear? How is it that my hand when it touches something becomes itself transparent; effaces itself to reveal the hardness, softness, warmth, roughness or delicacy of an object? How is it possible that the sound of words or the sight of letters can effectively withdraw so that a clearing is created in which we can come to contemplate the sights and sounds of past and present worlds? How is it that a kitchen table we once admired in a shop window can later become the stable, silent foundation of family meals and conversation with friends? How can a house lose its status as a confronted object to become a virtual foundation of our life? All these questions lead us back to the body and to its dual nature as visible, tangible object and power of vision, receding from the visible to reveal a world.

It is for this reason, no doubt, that for contemporary psychologists, the child's confrontation with his mirror image has assumed such great importance. It is as if the strange dual nature of our bodily existence as both power of vision and as something visible, comes to the fore through this confrontation. Through the mirror, the child comes to realize that others see him and that this image is something quite different from his own prereflective awareness of himself as a source of initiatives, as the holder of a certain undifferentiated outlook on the world. The experience of the mirror can bring to a crisis the simultaneous awareness of being both *outlook* and *object* of others' vision.

The way that a person incorporates this dual nature sets the foundation for many aspects of human life. Some people resolve to live their life as mirror images: they decide to conduct their life from the outside through a constant external awareness of how one sounds, looks and behaves. Here, the power of life has been transferred to the mirror; all initiatives and involvements are controlled by a vigilant outside perspective. On the other hand, it is also possible to deny implicitly the power of others' vision and to hang curtains over mirrors. In this style of being, one goes about one's life as if one did not offer a visible, perceptible exterior to others. This, in turn, can lead to a compulsive immersion in an unending series of tasks, to ruminations, preoccupations or addictions, the ultimate aim of which is to avoid the pressure of others' looks.

Wherever the mirror is embraced as the central issue in a life, we may expect an artificial look, a lifelessly correct appearance, and an uninviting perfection. In contrast, where the mirror is denied, we may see nothing but a disheveled mask, an absent stare, a set jaw, a preoccupied look, or a haggard face full of worry. In both instances, whether we are dealing with those who make the mirror the sole law of their life or with those who ignore its presence, we find our own existence denied in their presence. In both cases, we experience a lack of access, a denial of our power of vision, a sense that we have been either too rigidly anticipated or summarily dismissed. In both cases, we are prevented from playing a full role in the emergence of the visible.

Building as tension between the festive and the mundane

Our discussion of the interrelationship among body, house and city now moves in a direction where it becomes possible to speak of buildings as quasi-bodies and to experience the material presence of a house or a city as we would the carnal presence of a person. It then becomes possible to formulate demands on buildings which are not unlike the demands we make on people. We will then not only speak architecturally of canons of beauty or of functionality, but we will find it legitimate to ask ourselves how a building makes us feel as we walk past, use it, or come to live in its neighbourhood. It will no longer be quite so ridiculous to think of buildings as narcissistic – as self-absorbed images forever performing before the camera without giving much genuine attention to the living needs of the inhabitants and passers-by.

A great deal of recent architecture, including interior design, has often managed to perform admirably before the camera without giving much aid or comfort to inhabitants after the photographers of *House Beautiful* or *Architectural Digest* have left. It is not surprising that many modern architects enjoy living *close* to the buildings they design rather than living *in* them. The best position in respect to a narcissistic building is from behind a window or a camera lens. All this should inform us that a house, neighbourhood or city is never merely a visual object. But nor is it a mere tissue of functions. A building that is too preoccupied by its functions – that is, forever too busy to look up from its tasks – is merely a bore and a nuisance besides. Those who pass by buildings have the right to be acknowledged, received and greeted.

The narcissistic building, forever worried about losing its good looks, awaiting any day the ruin of a weather mark upon its perfect, endless facade; and the so-called functional building, perpetually flexing its tubes and wires in exaggerated fake servility – both remain oblivious to their context. Both are formally closed in upon themselves, incapable of gracefully receiving rain and wind, too frigid to shelter birds and cats and kids, too preoccupied to respond to passers-by, too removed from the true world of civilization to become for pedestrians or inhabitants the starting point of an interesting revery or a novel plan of action, of a poem or an equation.

Both types of building, while catering to abstract needs, disembody those who attempt to inhabit them because these buildings have themselves forgotten that they are bodies, that they must become flesh of our flesh if there is to be a living city, an inhabitable home and a truly human body. Both types of building remain entirely caught within a defensive stance. Narcissism, in buildings as well as in persons, constitutes a defense against the possibility of being frozen as an object of vision; it constitutes an attempt to conquer the mirror, and with it, the glance of the other. It seeks to anticipate this intrusive, congealing glance by anticipating its every move, by checkmating its dangerous activity. Narcissism attempts to escape the fate of being visible. It lives as unseen activity, as the restless, furtive anticipation of the direction and intention of the other's look. As such, narcissism opposes itself fundamentally to disclosure and manifestation. At its core it is refusal to make visible, palpable, understandable.

If narcissism protects itself from becoming a disclosed object of vision by paradoxically never stopping to create an image, functionalism seeks the same goal by deflecting all glances away from the body or the building and guiding them towards an unending stream of tasks. Where narcissism offers us an empty artificial mask, functionalism involves us in a network of activities that all lead us away from the source and the center. Both draw us away into the mundane, away from festive and original showing and shining.

At this point we need to remind ourselves that building is itself first and foremost a form of inhabiting. The word "building" refers us to the Indo-European base *bhu* for "to dwell" and is related to our English "to be." Heidegger has drawn the inference from this relationship, pointing out the many strands that link dwelling to being.[15] Building is first a *being near* a place, a haunting of a site, an eagerness for a manifestation and an obedience to what presents itself there. Building already begins in this approach to a site. Its fundamental activity is that of *situating*. This first building is a reflecting on a site – a preoccupation with a piece of nature as it is being framed and drawn within a human context.

This first building maintains within itself the tension of a creative contradiction and fundamental opposition between the realm of the festive and the world of the mundane. This first building is truthful revelation, obedience to the given, but it is also an act of violence that disturbs a virginal expanse, that rouses something boundless from its sleep and yokes it to the wheel of human tasks. Building is not merely worship of a site – a guiding path to mysterious origins. It is also the creation of domes and domiciles, it is the work of domestication and domination; it is a lordly craft. In the stories of creation it is the task of the gods to do this first building, to transform a chaos into cosmos, to frame a boundless nature so that people can begin to feel at home.

Whatever is truly built must always guide us back to these two divergent aspects of inhabitation; it must lead us to an original act of obedience and contemplation and to one of violence and appropriation. All great buildings remain organically connected with the earth, the sky, and the surrounding landscape; but they equally stand apart and present us with a definite upsurge of initiative and understanding. All great buildings present us with an environing world from which they nevertheless stand out and apart. All situating and building, therefore, comes to participate in a dual perspective. If we look with the building towards the origins we enter the realm of the *festive*. If we temporarily turn our backs upon these origins and look with the building towards the midst of life, to confront there our tasks, we have entered the *mundane*. Within the festive, the building is a pathway to origins; within the realm of the mundane, it becomes a silent, solid foundation from which we emerge and move forward into the world. And the very body that in the festive becomes a source of delight and a place of boundless mystery becomes in the realm of the mundane a dependable foundation – a beast of burden that quietly supports our tasks. And our language which in the festive mode trails off the beaten path and stirs the earth and approaches music – this "same" language becomes in the world of daily work a tool for transmitting messages.

Inhabitation, embodiment and building forever move between these twin poles of the festive and the task-oriented habitual. The festive gives us the mysterious body, the enchanting landscape, the language of poetry, the building and the site that draws into play our entire sensibility and gives direction to our search for the miraculous origins. Within the festive, we seek and celebrate the sources: the elusive body of the dancer, the outline of a great building against the sky, the shimmering light of a busy street after the rain. All these experiences are so many invitations to a restorative contemplation.

The mundane gives us access to a world of tasks, of infinite mediation and instrumentalization. Here the grain is placed in storage, gold is locked away in vaults, movements are trimmed to keep only what is essential, language is reduced to a code. All buildings and bodies draw us here inexorably in the direction of purpose, rationality and productivity.

Our human lives continually move between the festive and mundane; each realm always already anticipates the other. All inhabitation moves between the dual possibilities of a continuity and discontinuity with the past, of a celebrative obedience to a site and its laborious appropriation. All flesh, whether it be brick, stone or muscle, essentially refers to the possibility of movement between the poles of celebration and practicality. If we freeze this movement at the pole of practicality, we come upon mere matter and find the human and animal body of physiology and medicine, together with buildings that are mere equipment and cities that are only places of production and transport. If we freeze the world at the opposite pole, we come upon narcissistic bodies, the overly self-preoccupied cultural monuments, the "photogenic" but sterile tourist attractions. A fully human building, be it body, house or city, refers us fundamentally to a movement between the poles of a self-evident foundation and a mysterious source of revelation. All the places where we can truly be at home point rhythmically toward these two directions.

Notes

1. This paper was originally presented at the annual meetings of the Society for Phenomenology and the Human Sciences, Evanston Illinois, October, 1981, for a special session, "Phenomenologies of Place," organized by David Seamon and Katharine Mulford.
2. Colossians 1: 18, 24.
3. R. Wittkower, *Studies in Italian Baroque* (Boulder, Colorado: Westview Press, 1975), p. 79.
4. Ibid.
5. Ibid., p. 62.

6. K. Bloomer and C. Moore, *Body, Memory and Architecture* (New Haven: Yale University Press, 1977), p. 11.
7. C. Norberg-Schulz, *Intentions in Architecture* (Cambridge, Massachusetts: MIT Press, 1965), p. 124.
8. Ibid.
9. G. Bedaert, *Omtrent Wonen* (Deurne-Antwerpen: Kluwer, 1976), p. 103.
10. Francesco di Giorgio Martini, *Trattati di Architettura* (Milano: Ed. Il Polifilo, 1967).
11. Vitruvius, *On Architecture*, F. Granger, trans. (London: Granger, 1931), Bk. III, chap. I, p. 159.
12. E. Panofski, *Meaning in the Visual Arts* (Garden City, New York: Vintage, 1957), p. 64.
13. C. Jencks, *The Language of Post-Modern Architecture* (New York: Rizzoli, 1977), p.113.
14. M. Merleau-Ponty, *The Visible and the Invisible* (Evanston: Northwestern University Press, 1968).
15. Martin Heidegger, "Building Dwelling Thinking," in *Poetry, Language, Thought* (New York: Harper and Row, 1971), pp. 145 ff.

14. Reconciling old and new worlds: The dwelling–journey relationship as portrayed in Vilhelm Moberg's "Emigrant" novels

DAVID SEAMON

In an era when alienation, malaise and homelessness make their presence increasingly felt in the Western World, themes such as community, at-home-ness and sense of place take on renewed significance in both academic discussions and daily conversations.[1] One way in which these themes can be considered is through a phenomenological perspective, which explores the underlying, taken-for-granted patterns of human experience and behavior.[2] The *rest-movement relationship* and its associated polarities of home and reach, center and horizon, dwelling and journey, is one valuable phenomenological focus.[3] Movement is associated with newness, un-familiarity, exploration and courage. It extends awareness of distance, place and experience. Movement is linked with *journey*, which over geographical distance or in the mind, carries the person away from a stable home base outward along a path toward confrontation with place, experience or ideas.[4] Rest, the opposite of movement and journey, relates to a basic human need for spatial and environmental order and familiarity. Rest anchors the present and future in the past and maintains an experiential and historical continuity. From the vantage point of human experience, the deepest manifestation of rest is *dwelling*, which involves a lifestyle of regularity, repetition and cyclicity all grounded in an atmosphere of care and concern for places, things, and people.[5] A pure form of dwelling is probably never possible in practice, but this fact does not dilute its significance for daily life. Dwelling can be seen as an aim to strive for, and one need is for people to become more self-consciously aware of their degree and mode of dwelling and to seek ways in which they might better dwell: "The real dwelling plight lies in this, that mortals ever search anew for the nature of dwelling, that they *must ever learn to dwell*."[6]

The relationship between dwelling and journey is dialectical and identifies the need for both stability and change in people's dealings with places and environments. The whole of a person, group, or society's existence can be viewed as a series of pendulum swings between the need for center, at-homeness and continuity on the one hand, and the need for change, variety and reach on the other. Considered in a temporal sense, the dwelling–journey relationship signifies a process which occurs over time: the experience of leaving one place and going to another. This essay explores the *dwelling–journey process* at perhaps its most visible and comprehensive level: the experience of leaving one's native land and moving to a foreign place. The empirical context is Vilhelm Moberg's four "Emigrant" novels, which describe sixteen Swedes from the same home parish who leave their native country and proceed to make new homes in the St. Croix Valley of Minnesota.[7] In a broader sense, these novels depict the dwelling–journey process at the level of leaving a place, journeying, and settling in a new place. This essay uses the novels as an empirical context in which to identify underlying, more general stages of the process.[8]

The pattern revealed by a phenomenological examination of Moberg's novels is the seven-stage *dwelling–journey spiral* of Figure 1: lack of dwelling and a decision to go, preparation, journey and arrival, settling, becoming at home, coming together, creating community, and finally, reestablishment of dwelling. The novels suggest that a successful completion of this spiral is affected by two important external impacts: first, the land to be settled, appearing, obviously, after the journey; second, additional people, becoming more significant after individual families settle and become at home for themselves. One important phenomenological question is whether the pattern suggested by Moberg's account has meaning beyond the specific historical context, thus pointing to a generalizable structure applicable to the dwelling–journey process as it relates to similar experiences such as migration, tourism or traveling.

The novels indicate that a successful reestablishment of dwelling is at least partially grounded in a satisfactory reconciliation of *expectation* and *memory*. Expectation, associated with journey, provides an impetus to begin relocation and motivates the emigrants to make their new place better than the old. Memory, associated with dwelling, guarantees that the old world will guide and underlie construction of the new. On one hand, the emigrants must become free of their old world yet use it as a groundstone for creating a new place of dwelling. On the other hand, they must let the new world speak and determine itself. If they impose their expectations on that world, forcing it to be something it is not, their reestablishment of dwelling will ultimately be inauthentic, and reconciliation of memory and expecta-

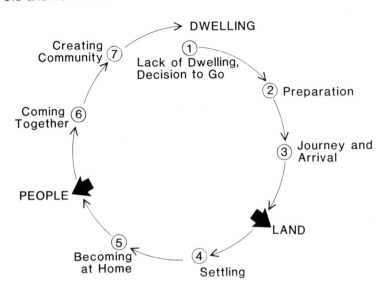

Figure 1. The dwelling–journey spiral.

tion, old and new, will not be successful. An understanding of this reconciliatory process becomes more clear as one examines the seven stages of the dwelling–journey spiral.

1. Dwelling, difficulties and a decision to go

The world that the Swedish emigrants leave behind had for centuries housed dwelling. At-homeness is thoroughly taken for granted, and one's way of life is neither questioned nor made the object of explicit attention. People born in place live there the rest of their lives. Memories in this world arise from events of locality and intertwine with communal history and tradition. This lifestyle involves the deepest form of *existential insideness*, a situation of complete and unself-conscious immersion in place.[9] The phenomenologist Jager explains that the world of dwelling is a "round world," offering "the reoccurring times of seasons, of the cycles of birth and death, of planting and harvesting, of meeting and meeting again, of doing and doing over again."[10] This "roundness" is clearly present in the world of the Swedes, who

> came from a land of small cottages and large families. They were people of the soil, and they came from a stock which for thousands of years

had tilled the ground they were now leaving . . . . The farm was a world of its own, beholden to no one. The cottages nestled low and gray, timbered to last for centuries, and under the same roof of bark and sod the people lived their lives from birth to death. Weddings were held, christening and wake ale was drunk, life was lit and blown out within these same four walls of rough-hewn pine logs. Outside of life's great events, little happened other than the change of seasons . . . . Life was lived quietly while the farmer's allotted years rounded their cycle.[11]

In the middle of the nineteenth century, however, this world of insideness and dwelling is severely shaken by developments in transportation and communication. Railroads and steamships connect distant parts of the globe, while books and newspapers, seen by a new generation who can read, describe worlds beyond the home place, particularly the new land of America, which has "soil without tillers and called for tillers without soil."[12] At the same time, the emigrants' world of dwelling is less secure. A cluster of conditions, including poverty, bad weather, famine, and societal intolerance, impinge on the world of insideness and lead some individuals to consider the unheard-of idea of moving elsewhere.

The difficulties and needs of Moberg's sixteen Swedes reflect the complexity of this initiating step in the dwelling–journey process. Some people make the decision to emigrate, as Moberg puts it, "*from* something:"[13] forty-six-year-old householder Danjel Andreasson, to escape religious persecution; seventeen-year-old farmhand Robert Nilsson, to be free of servitude; thirty-seven-year-old town whore Urika of Västergohl, to escape social ostracism; forty-eight-year-old Jonas Petter, to be free of his wife. These people leave more because of flaws in their world of dwelling than from attractions beyond that world. They seek freedom from the past and its memories.

In contrast, twenty-seven-year-old householder Karl Oskar Nilsson, one of two pivotal characters in the novels, emigrates, in Moberg's words, "*to* something."[14] He is, of course, disillusioned with his life in Sweden – with debts and the small size of his farmstead. Yet the force behind his decision arises more from expectation; the journey, he thinks, will improve the future: "I seek a land where through my work I can help myself and mine."[15] Throughout the novels, Karl Oskar represents qualities associated with expectation and journey – action, strength, certainty and boldness. Interpreted phenomenologically, his pronouncement indicates how Karl Oscar confronts the events and challenges that the journey and resettlement introduces. These confrontations are successful at least partially because he journeys to rather than from and interprets his new place in terms of the future rather than the past. He looks forward to the future and is active and aggressive with his land, believing that hard work and diligence will lead to a successful new home in the wilderness.

If Karel Oskar represents qualities of expectation and journey, his twenty-five-year-old wife Kristina, the novels' other central character, symbolizes aspects of memory and dwelling – continuity, tradition, piety and acceptance of the world as it was and is. She represents the forces that sense the potential dangers of the journey and feel intuitively the difficulties of creating a new home. "I go with my husband," she declares, "but I do so with hesitation and half in regret."[16] She first opposes emigration vehemently, fearing that Karl Oskar's boldness has interfered with his clear thinking: "He was never satisfied with anything in this world: he reached for the impossible, the little-known."[17] She fears their ignorance of North America and the long, dangerous sea voyage. Through a fall and winter, she and Karl Oskar discuss their conflicting views. Ultimately, it is not a compromise on their part but a severe external shock in their world of dwelling – the death of their four-year-old daughter because of famine – that leads Kristina to agree to the emigration plan. "She would never," says Moberg of her home, "feel the same in this place again."[18]

2. Preparation

Lack of dwelling and a decision to go is followed by a second step – preparation, which involves providing for the journey and breaking satisfactorily with homeplace. Providing for the journey is no easy task for the emigrants, since they distrust the few written accounts they have of the New World and know no one who has been there before them. Their main sources of information are infrequent newspaper reports, which often emphasize the unpleasant and tragic aspects of emigration; and a book, *A Description of the United States of North America*, which contains considerable misinformation but is significant because it gives the emigrants a sense of destination – the fertile farming regions surrounding the upper end of the Mississippi River and its tributaries.

Karl Oskar and Kristina select implements for the New World which have been crucial in their old world of dwelling – timber and carpentry tools, hunting and fishing gear, cloth, sewing needs, woolen garments, bedclothes, and many other items. The materials to be taken, comprising "one small cartload," are packed in a knapsack, two four-bushel cloth sacks, and a large oaken chest painted black.[19] This chest, several hundred years old, had been passed down from father to son for many generations and approached "mostly at life's great happenings: baptisms, weddings, and funerals."[20] Now the chest becomes the Nilsson family's "most treasured piece of furniture;" it and other chests like it become the symbol of the emigrants' journey:[21]

> This was the dawn of a great era in the lives of the old clothes chests throughout the peasant communities. After centuries of neglect in dark loft corners they were now being scrubbed and polished and prepared for their voyage across the great sea. These chests were to be in the vanguard of history's greatest migration. To them would be entrusted the emigrants' most cherished belongings.[22]

Before they depart, Karl Oskar arranges for his family's sea journey and separates cleanly from his homeplace. He sells his farm and cattle for prices less than he originally paid and books his family's passage. He visits the church dean to break openly from the parish. By that time, 1850, any person of good character could leave Sweden without petitioning the Church or king, but Karl Oskar wishes to leave his place honestly and in good standing: "[He] did not wish to leave as if he had done wrong."[23] The dean looks quizzically at the first parishioner to come on such an errand and proceeds to give a short sermon on the dangers and temptations of the New World. Karl Oskar is unswayed and the dean grudgingly gives his blessing: "I pray God to bless you and yours during your voyage to a faraway land. May you never regret your bold decision."[24]

Jager suggests that the successful start of a journey requires a thoughtful remembrance of the world from which the journey arises: "The traveller can leave behind only that which he has truly faced."[25] In officially breaking with parish affairs and trusting their future to the tools and materials supporting their old world of dwelling, Karl Oskar and Kristina seek to face the past honestly. They begin a journey which breaks them loose irrevocably from their former sphere of dwelling, from "the self-evident, the habitual, the familiar, the reoccuring."[26]

3. Journey and arrival

The third stage of the dwelling–journey process is a series of journeys and arrivals ending with a final destination at the new place. Jager points out that the journey is a series of confrontations with the terrain and situations through which the traveller must pass.[27] The emigrants' first confrontation is the sea voyage: "The earth was known to them, intimate, reliable, but they mistrusted the sea; it was unknown and dangerous."[28] The unknown quality of the voyage points to a first characteristic of the journey's confrontations: they are unpredictable, often happening in a manner that one could not imagine in his world of dwelling. "We are on the voyage," thinks Karl Oskar, "and very little is actually the way I had thought it would be."[29] Second, the difficulties of the confrontations cause a certain degree of misgiving. "I should never have given in," thinks Kristina. "I feel it can never go well."[30] Even the confident Karl Oskar harbors doubts. "Perhaps I have brought unhappiness upon us – we may have to suffer a great deal; and all is on my shoulders. I insisted on the emigration – if it turns out badly, I can blame only myself."[31]

After voyaging for ten weeks, the emigrants, now immigrants, arrive in New York and are "overtaken by surprise at their first meetings with the unknown country."[32] They experience *existential outsideness*, a sense of separation and alienation from their environment.[33] The confusions of place are many: the hot weather; the strange English language; the shorter length of daylight; some of their own kinsmen, now Americans, ready to cheat them. At the same time, however, a safe arrival offers energy and hope. The captain of the vessel observes that when the sick and dying aboard his ship see land "they returned to life."[34] Kristina, now pregnant, realizes that "not only had she herself come to life, again, but the child within her seemed to have gained new life now that she had carried it into the New World."[35] The journey offers many confrontations, but a successful completion of one segment provides fresh energy for continuation.

An overland journey by train, canal boat and steamer is the next confrontation. Much about this trip, like the sea voyage before, confuses and frightens the Swedes – the unfamiliar modes of transportation, the strange people, the changing environment, especially the prairie, which "stung their hearts with its might and emptiness."[36] Among the group themselves, however, a sense of separation is replaced by togetherness. Several individuals had felt mutual dislike at the start of the emigration, but confronted by the New World's strangeness and dangers, people forget old differences and accept each other: "they realized that in their situation they could be of help to each other."[37]

Near the end of their journey, as a river steamer delivers them to their destination in Minnesota, the immigrants come to feel their fragility and insignificance in relation to the larger world. As outsiders and onlookers severed from their former taken-for-granted world of insideness, they can momentarily view their situation through the objectivity of distance. They profoundly realize that they can not turn back, that they must make of their new place what they can:

> They shuddered when they tried to comprehend the whole distance they had travelled across land and water. Trying to remember, they were unable to reach back – not even their imagination could undertake a return journey. The distance was too overwhelming; the earth which God had created was too large and too wide to fathom.

> A realization which their minds had long resisted became fixed in their hearts and souls: this road they could never travel again; they could never return. They would never see their homeland again.[38]

4. and 5. Settling and becoming at home

An important new factor – the land for which the journey was made – enters the dwelling–journey process after a successful arrival. A new home is no longer a remote image but a tangible possibility. The land triggers an important new input of motivation and energy to drive the settling process ahead: "The very sight of the fertile land," writes Moberg about Karl Oskar, "stimulated him and egged him on to work."[39]

After arrival, settling and becoming at home are the next two stages in the dwelling–journey process. They are usefully discussed together, since the former reflects the physical actions and adjustments necessary to turn an unknown environment into a home, while the latter reflects the required inner, psychological changes. Moberg's account indicates that the two stages are intimately connected, and their separation here is more a heuristic convenience than a clear division in the world of experience.

The settling stage is best represented by Karl Oskar. Symbolizing the energy and drive of the journey, he takes it to its most successful conclusion, searching longer and farther than other members of his party for the land that will provide the best material possibilities for a new place: "Earlier in the day, he had seen the next best [land]; he had gone on a little further and now he had found the best. He had arrived."[40] Feeling comfortable in place for Karl Oskar is largely the completion of the settling process – i.e., satisfying material needs and gaining physical mastery over place. Building a house and moving his family in, Karl Oskar feels relatively at ease: "Beginning this very day, he felt settled and at home in North America."[41]

plementarily of stages for both indicates that any planned attempt at community should take these relationships into account, providing time for personal orientation before community organization is officially attempted.

In its most general form, the dwelling–journey spiral asks the essential nature of the experience of changing places. The argument is that underlying any mode of this experience – migrating, touring, traveling, and so on – are common characteristics. The seven-stage spiral suggested by Moberg's novels is a first attempt at delineating these general characteristics, and even in its preliminary form appears to have relation to other modes of changing places. Consider traveling versus tourism. The modern tourist's experience of place is considerably different from a traveler's situation, and the seven stages described in Table 1 give several clues as to why. The traveler has a serious need for going to a place, he undertakes extensive preparation, he attempts to penetrate beneath the surface of a place to discover deeper qualities and the human dimension. He seeks *empathetic insideness* in terms of place – i.e., through concern, interest and receptivity, he works to enter into that place and understand its essential meanings and qualities.[61] In contrast, the tourist's reasons for travel are usually less serious and motivated by advertising, peer pressure, or vacation time. Someone else often arranges the journey, which is usually relatively comfortable. The resulting experience of place is typically shallow, grounded in stereotypes, attractive scenery, and pre-arranged events. Whereas a successful traveler moves through the spiral's seven stages, the tourist rarely passes step 4. Experientially, he has not journeyed, only moved over physical distance.

In relation to today's world situation, the dwelling–journey spiral is valuable because it presents a picture of human place-making occurring without a large degree of external mechanized assistance. Today, because of an advanced technological and societal infrastructure, people readily move about and change places; a trans-Atlantic journey, for example, seems inconsequential and easy. People forget that in past generations, dwelling and, especially, journeying were arduous; travel was not begun without long consideration and planning. Exploring Moberg's novels phenomenologically is valuable because he presents a picture of dwelling and journey which is *existentially* accurate. The immigrants lived in a world which compared to modern standards is in many ways primitive, yet because they had responsibility for survival *in their own hands* without the assistance of technological or societal backup, their situation is in one sense more authentic *experientially*. One sees human place-making for people left to their own human devices.

Table 1. Traveling vs. tourism experientially

Stage	Traveling	Tourism
1) Wish to go	arises from within the person; authentic, genuine need	often motivated by external factors, e.g., peer pressure, cheap prices, luxurious accommodations, package arrangements, etc.
2) Preparation	thorough, done out of interest and wish, organized, created by the person actively, perhaps learning language of new place	less thorough, accepted passively, provided by outside sources, predefined itinerary
3) Journey and arrival	often difficult and long, possible dangers, sense of having covered distance	relatively comfortable, short as possible, assistance from outside, often no sense of having covered distance
Place	chosen, not interchangeable, the *only* destination	one possible destination, not necessarily crucial for itself; often interchangeable
4) Learning physically	necessary to move about, done actively and requires time, enjoyed but sometimes difficult	often not needed; rather, transportation and directions provided by buses, tour guides, etc.
5) Becoming at ease	requires time but done to accomplish one's goal	not usually happening
People	crucial to help with traveler's goal, may need language	not usually happening, little real contact with people; people seen often imitate stereotypes
6) Getting to know people	time required, sense of need may help	not usually happening
7) Penetrating place	difficult	not possible
Empathetic insideness	seeing in terms of the place, allowing place to "be"	not possible

Today, unless some major global disruption occurs, people have little chance to experience such a situation directly, but Moberg's novels, considered phenomenologically, allow people to consider that situation vicariously. In this sense, a phenomenology of changing places promotes self-sensitization: students can ponder the considerable difference in living between the Swedish immigrants' world and ours. The novels provide a sobering relevation. How intimately connected these earlier people were with space, time and environment! Normally, today, people do not recognize their human smallness and fragility. A phenomenological look at Moberg's novels can awaken this realization and provoke the individual to explore self-consciously his existential relationship with the worlds of dwelling and journey in situations where he has only himself and immediate environmental resources.

Such sensitization places attention on the direction of humankind's present historical course. Our modern era cultivates journey, horizon and reach often at the expense of dwelling, centers and homes. One out of every three Americans changes place of residence every three years. Can we afford to continue this pattern? Do we want the interchangeable, artificial environments that Relph has called placelessness or should we consider the reestablishment of places, localities and communities grounded in landscapes and natural environments?[62]

Dwelling, according to Heidegger, involves a wish to care for and preserve the things, people and events which join to make the place where one chooses to live.[63] This care and concern is obvious and often brutally necessary in the immigrants' world, where the loss of a tool, seed or animal can mean hardship or catastrophe. In the modern world, however, environments are frequently interchangeable, and people less often take part in their place or care for it. Environmental responsibilities are often left to some outside caretaker such as custodian, administrator or public committee. People experience a tremendous freedom from time and physical environment, but they often misuse this advantage, caught up in titillation, boredom or restlessness. A phenomenological consideration of Moberg's novels offers no certain answer to the modern Western world's dilemma. But through the themes of dwelling and journey, a phenomenological perspective does bring the dilemma to our attention, asking us to ponder where the future takes us and where we take the future.

Notes

1. This essay is a revised version of a paper entitled "The Dwelling–Journey Relationship: Its Portrayal in Vilhelm Moberg's 'Emigrant' Novels," presented at the national meetings of the Institute of British Geographers, Lancaster, England, 4 January 1980, for a special session, "Geography and Literature," organized by Douglas C.D. Pocock. The author would like to thank Katharine Mulford and Douglas Pocock for their invaluable criticisms of earlier drafts.
2. On the methods of phenomenology and a demonstration of its use, see David Seamon, *A Geography of the Lifeworld* (New York: St. Martin's, 1979).
3. See, for example, Bernd Jager, "Theorizing, Journeying, Dwelling," in A. Giorgi, C. Fischer and E. Murray, eds., *Duquesne Studies in Phenomenological Psychology*, vol. 2 (Pittsburgh: University of Duquesne Press, 1975), pp 235–260; Seamon, *Lifeworld*; Anne

Buttimer, "Home, Reach, and a Sense of Place," in A. Buttimer and D. Seamon, eds., *The Human Experience of Space and Place* (London: Croom Helm, 1980), pp. 166–187.

4. Jager, p. 251.
5. See, especially, Martin Heidegger, "Building Dwelling Thinking," in *Poetry, Language, Thought* (New York: Harper and Row, 1971), pp. 145–161.
6. Ibid., p. 161, italics in original.
7. Vilhelm Moberg, *Utvandrarna* (1949), *Invandrara* (1952), *Nybyggarna* (1956), *Sista brevet till Sverige* (1959). These volumes are published by Bonniers in Stockholm. The English translations, available from the Popular Library in New York, are *The Emigrants* (1951), *Unto a Good Land* (1954), *The Settlers* (1956), *Last Letter Home* (1959). Page references in this essay are to the English texts. On Moberg's life and work, see Philip Holms, *Vilhelm Moberg* (Boston: Twayne Publishing, 1980). On the use of imaginative literature in environmental research, see Douglas C.D. Pocock, ed., *Humanistic Geography and Literature* (London: Croom Helm, 1981).
8. The establishment of dwelling for one new group often means the deterioration or destruction of dwelling for other groups, in this case, the Sioux Indians of Western Minnesota. Moberg gives some attention to this destruction in his novels. Since his main concern is the Swedes, however, most of his narrative is devoted to their experiences. On the Sioux's situation, see especially *Last Letter Home*, Part II.
9. Edward Relph, *Place and Placelessness* (London: Pion, 1976), p. 55.
10. Jager, p. 251.
11. Moberg, *The Emigrants*, p. 7.
12. Ibid., p. 8.
13. Ibid., p. 8.
14. Ibid., p. 8.
15. Ibid., p. 189.
16. Ibid., p. 189.
17. Ibid., p. 109.
18. Ibid., p. 123.
19. Ibid., p. 170.
20. Ibid., p. 150.
21. Ibid., p. 150.
22. Ibid., p. 169.
23. Ibid., p. 174.
24. Ibid., p. 179.
25. Jager, p. 250.
26. Ibid., p. 251.
27. Jager, p. 251.
28. *Emigrants*, p. 216.
29. Ibid., p. 245.
30. Ibid., p. 248.
31. Ibid., p. 246.
32. *Unto a Good Land*, p. 28.
33. Relph, p. 51.
34. *Unto a Good Land*, p. 16.
35. Ibid., p. 35.
36. Ibid., p. 119.
37. Ibid., p. 153

38. Ibid., p. 123.
39. Ibid., p. 252.
40. Ibid., p. 224.
41. Ibid., p. 275.
42. Ibid., p. 240.
43. Ibid., p. 278.
44. Ibid., p. 410.
45. *Settlers*, p. 472.
46. Ibid., p. 24.
47. Ibid., p. 27.
48. Ibid., p. 179.
49. Ibid., p. 60.
50. Ibid., p. 180.
51. Ibid., p. 179.
52. Ibid., p. 179.
53. Ibid., pp. 179–180.
54. Jager, p. 259.
55. Ibid., p. 259.
56. *Settlers*, p. 474.
57. *Last Letter Home*, p. 249.
58. Other discussion on the role of memory in reconciling the elderly person's old and new worlds, though at a different temporal and environmental scale, is found in Graham D. Rowles, "Growing Old 'Inside': Aging and Attachment to Place in an Appalachian Community," in N. Daton and N. Lohmann, eds., *Transitions of Aging* (New York: Academic Press, 1980), pp. 153–170.
59. *Last Letter Home*, p. 261.
60. Ibid., p. 11.
61. Relph, pp. 54–55.
62. Ibid., David Seamon, "Heidegger's Notion of Dwelling and One Concrete Interpretation as Indicated by Hassan Fathy's *Architecture for the Poor, Geoscience and Man* 24 (1984): 43–53.
63. Heidegger, note 5.

15. The role of spiritual discipline in learning to dwell on earth

MICHAEL E. ZIMMERMAN

Western people, particularly North Americans, are action-oriented and voluntaristic. For two centuries at least, we have sought to alter our social and economic conditions to bring about a new and better world. Today, faced with an environmental crisis that results largely from the attempt to improve the world through industrialization, we hear much talk about the need to learn how to dwell in harmony with the earth. What is required, we are told, is a new way of thinking, a 'paradigm shift' that will lead to socio-economic behavior more compatible with both the biosphere and the spiritual needs of humanity.[1] With increasing frequency, writers turn to the thought of Martin Heidegger as a source for such a new understanding of who we are. Heidegger speaks of our need to "dwell" on earth appropriately by "sparing and preserving" beings, by "letting beings be."

The problem, however, is whether we understand what Heidegger means. Many of us like to think we do. Despite our talk about the need for a paradigm shift in thinking, we tend to think this shift merely involves a reorientation of certain concepts or an adoption of a new vocabulary that will lead to more efficacious action. We are not convinced that a real change in thinking requires a fundamental change in our very existence, a change that would not be comprehensible to the ways in which we currently think.

Because of our strong commitment to action in the face of the present crisis, we assume that it was enough for Heidegger to have undergone this existential shift. We, however, do not need to do so. For us, it is enough to put into practice what this great thinker and others like him had to say. "Letting beings be" becomes a slogan to guide our planning and organizing in ways that decrease the impact of human activity on the biosphere. We even try to design houses in line with what Heidegger supposedly means by true "dwelling." Everywhere, people are attempting to put into practice the new idea of harmonious living. Yet, who of us knows what is really meant by "letting beings be" and by "harmonious living?"

In this essay, I examine some passages often unnoticed from "Building Dwelling Thinking," one of Heidegger's essays most frequently cited as providing a guide for living in harmony with the earth.[2] The argument is that in order for people to be heirs of a new way of thinking, more may be required than learning a new vocabulary. A paradigm shift does not occur by our reading books about it; nor does it happen when we set about to put into practice what we have heard preached. Action is not unimportant, but the problem is that it is very difficult to perceive clearly, let alone alter, the motives for our actions. I am taking a cue here from the philosopher Jacob Needleman, who argues that in our present condition, we cannot understand the message of either Eastern or Western religions. We are so caught up in egocentric ways of thinking, he says, that we can hardly be expected to hear the call of grace even if it is offered.[3] Similarly, the philosopher of religion Houston Smith maintains that true understanding requires a kind of spiritual discipline or practice that is largely unknown in the modern Western world.[4] Such discipline does not of itself produce the insight or transformation, but instead prepares us to receive it or, as Castaneda's Don Juan says, makes us "accessible to power."[5]

The point here is that if we go into action believing that we know what Heidegger means by dwelling and letting beings be, while in fact we do not, we risk an even greater confusion in the world. We have been raised in a tradition that emphasizes will and action, and we insist on finding immediate practical applications for the ideas that show an alternative to that tradition. If one approaches Heidegger's writings as a guide for action, one will find such a guide, but it will probably be the reader's own aims re-expressed in Heideggerean terminology. Most of us are caught up in a web of egoistic self-understanding that seeks to manipulate reality in ways that promote our ideals and goals. Given this state of mind, we ought not to be surprised if, after reading Heidegger, we come away full of ideas about how to replace the "bad" old scheme with a "good" new one. Our understanding of and impulse to action, however, need critical examination. In his "Letter on Humanism," Heidegger remarks:

> We are still far from pondering the essence of action decisively enough. We view action only as causing an effect. The actuality of the effect is valued according to its utility. But the essence of action is accomplishment. To accomplish means to unfold something into the fullness of its essence, to lead it forth into this fullness – *producere*. Therefore only

what already is can really be accomplished. But what "is" above all is Being. Thinking accomplishes the relation of Being to the essence of man. It does not make or cause the relation. Thinking brings this relation to Being solely as something handed over to it from Being. Such offering consists in the fact that in thinking Being comes to language. Language is the house of Being. In its home man dwells. Those who think and those who create with words are the guardians of this home.[6]

Before we can dwell harmoniously and appropriately with other beings on earth, we must learn to dwell within the "house of Being" and learn to hear and understand the language of Being. But what is this "house of Being," and how can learning to live in something so apparently abstract provide us with the insight needed to change the world? To answer this question suitably, we must be prepared to entertain the possibility that our most cherished goals and ideals may not be consistent with what Heidegger understands by dwelling in the house of Being. As Nietzsche once suggested, what is important is not so much the courage of one's convictions, but the courage for an attack on one's convictions. Let us now turn to "Building Dwelling Thinking" in order to examine what Heidegger says about dwelling that is appropriate to our present questions.

This essay, first given as a lecture in 1951, addresses itself in part to the severe housing shortage in a post-war, defeated Germany. The housing shortage was, for Heidegger, a concrete expression of a far more fundamental and serious problem – the homelessness of modern humanity. World War II, the proximate cause of the destruction of so much German housing, was itself a symptom of modern humanity's disease of homelessness. We are not at home because we no longer understand who we are. One can live peacefully or dwell appropriately only if one knows, at some profound level, who one really *is*.

We moderns define ourselves as humanists. Having rejected Biblical and classical forms of authority during the Enlightenment, we installed ourselves in the place of a dead God and practice human self-worship. Nineteenth-century scientific naturalism allegedly did away with human pretentions to supernatural status and put us on the same level as other animals. In spite of all claims made about the "natural" status of the human animal, however, we think that "some animals are more equal than others." We see ourselves as the most clever animal of all, the one capable and deserving of becoming lord of the earth.[7] Beings have become commodities or raw materials for our purposes. Lacking any divine or transcendent conception of the purpose of human existence, we inevitably identify our goals egoistically: security, power, wealth, and survival. Western technological rationality, when it is severed from a deeper wisdom, is egoism on a planetary scale.[8] Just as the individual ego sees things and people primarily as instruments to further the ego's survival and desire for pleasure, so, too, modern humanity sees everything as an object to promote the security and power of the human subject. Capitalists and communists alike seek to transform nature into a suitable home for godlike humanity.[9] As Hegel allegedly said, it is either Nature or us. The high ideal of unfolding all human potential has the curious effect of making human beings into the most important raw material in that unfolding.[10] In the quest for total self-realization, power, and security, we turn ourselves into things that serve these heralded goals.

If we conceive ourselves and treat ourselves as things, we can hardly expect to be "at home". Instead, we feel lost, even if the "house" turns out to be materially comfortable. Obsessive-compulsive people turn themselves into machines to organize everything so that safe living can finally occur – at some point in the future. Western humanity is as obsessive and constricted as any neurotic individual. Even when faced with environmental disaster that clearly results from our compulsion to act, build, or change, our response to the crisis is to call for more action. This call is not what Heidegger recommends in "Building Dwelling Thinking." More important, rather, is *listening and hearkening*. We need to rediscover who we really are. Also, we must continue to act in ways that hold the world together as best we can in accordance with our present way of thinking. Such action, however, only addresses itself to the symptoms of the underlying disease that can be treated only by taking a step back from our current identity.

Heidegger notes wryly that "Man acts as though *he* were the shaper and master of language, while in fact *language remains the master* of man. Perhaps it is before anything else man's subversion of *this* relation of dominance that drives his nature into alienation."[11] By language, Heidegger does not mean mere words and propositions, for they are made possible only by language understood as primordial *Logos*, that gathering which opens up a world in which beings can manifest themselves. *Logos*, language in the highest sense, lets beings be revealed or disclosed *as* beings, as things that *are*. *Logos* appropriates human existence so that beings can be revealed, and also so that this event of revelation can *itself* be revealed. A great thinker or poet is one who, revealing the awesome event of the sheer presencing or Being of beings, also calls to mind the marvelous qualities of the beings that are so presented. Hearing a great poem reminds us of our highest obligation: to bear witness to presencing (Being) and to think things that are present (beings). To bear witness requires that we dwell as mortals on earth. In dwelling, we care for and preserve all beings. But here we move too quickly, I fear, to the acts – i.e., to the caring and preserving – that we think are needed to solve present problems. In thinking this way, however, have we really heard the *Logos*? Let us look more deeply into what is required for us to dwell rightly on earth.

Heidegger claims that language, or *Logos*, has retracted the real meaning of the word "dwelling" so that we are left to ponder mere 'foreground' meanings. "Language withdraws from man its simple and high speech. But its primal call does not thereby become incapable of speech; it merely falls silent. *Man, though, fails to heed this silence.*"[12] We think we know what Heidegger means by dwelling, but we probably do not, any more than the Athenians questioned by Socrates really knew who they were, or what virtue meant. We cannot hear the *Logos* because it has withdrawn itself and because we are too caught up in the use of language as a device of the ego. Heidegger maintains that to hear the *Logos*, we must first heed silence. But who of us is capable of this? We are almost constantly carrying on an internal dialogue of judgments, evaluations, and concepts that are largely culturally acquired aids for survival. Far from heeding silence, we usually flee from it into the noisy distractions of everyday life, including scholarly work.

To heed the silence means coming home to ourselves, for we humans are essentially the silent, open realm in which Being – revelation and disclosure of beings – takes place. According to Heidegger, to be means to be present or manifest. Presencing, however, requires an "absencing" or a clearing or opening in which to occur. We are that opening. The voice in our heads, the birds in the sky, the chair in the house first reveal themselves and thus "are" within the silent absencing called human existence. Our bodies, egos, feelings, thoughts, perceptions, goals, memories, objects – all beings, in fact – reveal themselves within the silent clearing we are called on to be. This opening that we are is a gift.[13] Giving thanks for it simply means being open, receptive, prepared to hear what we are called on to hear. But here is the rub: being open includes being aware of our mortality. Yet the whole function of the ego, with which we mistakenly identify ourselves, is to escape from and deny death. To let our mortality reveal itself, as in the the mood of anxiety, requires that we somehow be released from the ego's resistance to any such revelation. Precisely because we are unwilling to accept our mortality, we cannot be fully alive, open, and human. Heidegger tells us that

Mortals dwell in that they initiate their own nature – their being capable of death as death — into the use and practice of this capacity, so that there may be a good death. To initiate mortals into the nature of death in no way means to make death, as empty Nothing, the goal. Nor does it mean to darken dwelling by blindly staring toward the end.[14]

Already in Plato's *Phaedo*, Socrates tells us that philosophy is the practice of dying. For Heidegger, this practice consists in a willingness to let go into the silence and openness that constitute our very Being. We are so entrenched in the *contents* of awareness that we fail to notice awareness or openness as such. Awareness itself, of course, is not a thing, but instead constitutes the open realm in which things can be revealed. Within the open realm of awareness, both ego-subject and objects can first reveal themselves and thus "be". This awareness is not the property of my ego; instead, the ego "belongs" to the open awareness. But we must not be misled by the metaphor of ownership. Awareness is not a thing that possesses another thing, "me". The point here is that human existence involves something more fundamental than the ego-subject. Heidegger suggests that a human being becomes "authentic" when released from the compulsive activity of the ego. When it is authentic, human existence functions to serve, not to dominate. In the moment of releasement, enlightenment, or authenticity, things do not dissolve into an undifferentiated mass. Instead, they stand out or reveal themselves in their own unique mode of Being. Aware of the Being of beings, authentic human existence is also profoundly aware of the beings as such.[15]

Further insight into what Heidegger means by our silent openness can be gained by examining his discussion of space. Ordinarily, we think of ourselves as egos located in bodies, and these bodies in turn located in a container called space. My thoughts are supposedly representations of objects or people "out there." This view of the self as encapsulated in a body is untenable, according to Heidegger. Subject-object dualism cannot explain our experience. When, for example, we think of the old bridge in Heidelberg, our thinking is not merely a picturing or representing of the bridge in our so-called "minds": "From this spot right here, we are there at the bridge — we are by no means at some representational content in our consciousness."[16] Human existence opens up the clearing in which spaces and space can first reveal themselves. "I" am not an enclosed ego-subject, nor am "I" a self-contained body. "I" am the clearing or opening in which my ego, object, and space can appear. I am not in my body; my body is "in" me as the clearing. Human existence is the non-thinglike realm, the nothingness, in which beings can be manifest:

> To say that mortals *are* is to say that in *dwelling* they persist through spaces by virtue of their stay among things and locations. And only because mortals pervade, persist through, spaces by their very nature are they able to go through spaces. But in going through spaces we do not give up our standing in them. Rather, we always go through spaces in such a way that we already experience them by staying constantly with near and remote locations and things. When I go toward the door of the lecture hall, I am already there, and I could not go to it at all if I were not such that I am there. I am never here only, as this encapsulated body; rather I am there, that is, I already pervade the room and only thus can I go through it.[17]

To dwell, then, means to be the silent openness that we always already are – a curious feat! In learning to be this open realm, we become attuned to *Logos*. We learn to be in the service of the Being of beings. That is, we learn to let beings bring themselves to appearance by giving voice to themselves through us. Learning to be silent, open, and receptive, however, requires a discipline and practice foreign to our present ways. In another essay, I have examined in detail how Heidegger interpreted Heraclitus as a guide for spiritual practices, such as stilling the mind, patiently observing, and proper breathing – practices usually thought to belong only to Eastern thinkers.[18] If we hope to understand what Heidegger means, we may need to be willing to practice the kinds of disciplines necessary for hearing the *Logos* if and when it speaks through us. Crucial to such disciplines is an acceptance of the ego's mortality, for until such acceptance comes the ego will do all it can to continue thinking and acting in the mode of domination and survival. An acceptance of mortality, however, cannot be willed or grasped, but comes as a gift to those willing to prepare themselves to receive the gift. The meditative practices needed to prepare ourselves are neither easy nor painless, and those individuals capable of guiding us are few. Nor do such practices seem to constitute the kind of "action" we seem to think is imperative today. Yet like Lao Tsu, Heidegger warns us against action that tends to make matters worse.[19] Homelessness will not be cured even if we see to it that every family on earth has clean air and water and a six-room house with lawns.

No action will cure homelessness because homelessness is despair, and despair is a sign that we still believe that our actions can somehow save us from death and the need to renew our understanding of who we really are. Heidegger says that

> The real dwelling plight lies in this, that mortals ever search anew for the nature of dwelling, that *they must ever learn to dwell*. What if man's homelessness consisted in this, that man still does not even think of the *real* plight of dwelling as *the plight*? Yet as soon as man *gives thought* to his homelessness, it is a misery no longer. Rightly considered and kept well in mind, it is the sole summons that *calls* mortals into their dwelling.[20]

Kierkegaard once noted that the essential feature of despair is not knowing that you are desperate. Acknowledging our despair is the first step beyond it. For Buddhism, too, life involves suffering for as long as we understand ourselves as substantial egos who can somehow find a way to avoid suffering. As soon as we see that we are not separate substances but the openness in which phenomena appear, there is an end to the suffering that stems from clinging, grasping, and manipulating. For Heidegger, in becoming aware of our homelessness, we become aware of our constant tendency to flee into false homes and false identities, away from the true home of silent openness. Homelessness and alienation are symptoms of a lack of self-understanding. When we are able to recall who we really are, we are home again. And by coming home, we become capable of taking wise steps toward dwelling appropriately on earth.

At the same time, we humans can never simply be at home as a bird is at home in its nest. We must constantly remind ourselves that we are not mere things, but instead we are the openness in which things can be revealed. In becoming at home in the silent openness, we also become at home with the beings that reveal themselves therein. These beings include not only animals, plants, mountains, stars, and other people – but also our own bodies, wishes, feelings, memories, hopes, and thoughts. When we are at home with our mortal openness, we no longer have to be enemies of the events – the pain, loss, and death – that occur within the clearing. If we no longer identify ourselves with the ego that craves security and gratification, we do not have to resist what things are, nor do we feel compelled to manipulate them solely to suit our desires. Because we are essentially mortal, learning to be at home means accepting mortality. Learning to be mortal is the essence of homecoming and dwelling.

In preparing every day for coming home, we learn to be at home here and now on the earth. Preparing for death does not mean yearning for some new place after this life. We are always already where we are headed. We are already home here on earth, but we must be willing to be mortal in order to dwell appropriately here. We must be careful to avoid the dualistic tendency to distinguish between "me" as silent openness and "me" as ego. The clearing is not a thing or entity at all; the clearing constitutes no-thingness in which things can be. When human existence is silently open, there are only beings. My ego becomes a problem only when I think my life is about doing what it tells me. When silently attuned to the openness that is essential to human existence, I am no longer identified with the ego, for the ego goes into action only to insure its survival. If I accept and acknowledge my mortality at the deepest level, the motive for egoism and its will to power is undermined. Becoming open means becoming the clearing in which the beings of the world can display or manifest themselves. Here ends the suffering that stems from subject–object dualism. Out of such openness, and only out of it, emerges the possibility for genuine action. The action of attunement to *Logos*, or of becoming open for the Being of beings, is the prerequisite for practical action that is in harmony with what *is*.

None of us knows whether modern technological culture can avoid the terrible suffering and dislocation that seem to loom ahead in the form of environmental disasters, over-population, financial collapse, or nuclear war. What seems to be dawning on us is that actions taken to avert disaster tend to make the original situation worse in wholly unexpected ways, and the problems facing us are usually "solutions" to previous problems. What we need is a more profound understanding of who we are, so that we can behave more appropriately on earth. In the meantime, we must do our best to alleviate the symptoms of the disease of anthropocentric humanism. And perhaps even more importantly, we must be willing to do what is needed to prepare ourselves to hear the healing *Logos* that brings a new self-understanding. Who among us is prepared to make such preparations? Does the fate of the earth depend on our willingness to ready ourselves for a new disclosure of who we really are?

Notes

1. See Alan R. Drengson, "Shifting Paradigms: From the Technocratic to the Person–Planetary," *Environmental Ethics* 3 (1980): 221–240; Theodore Roszak, *Person/ Planet* (New York: Doubleday, 1978); Morris Berman, *The Re-enchantment of the World* (Ithaca: Cornell University Press, 1981); Fritjof Capra, *The Turning Point* (New York: Simon and Schuster, 1982); Huston Smith, *Beyond the Post-modern Mind* (New York: Crossroads, 1982).
2. Martin Heidegger, "Building Dwelling Thinking", in *Poetry, Language, Thought*, Albert Hofstadter, trans. (New York: Harper and Row, 1971), pp. 145–161.

3. Jacob Needleman, *Consciousness and Tradition* (New York: Crossroads, 1982); Jacob Needleman, *Lost Christianity: A Journey of Rediscovery to the Center of Christian Experience* (New York: Bantam, 1982); Jacob Needleman, *A Sense of the Cosmos: The Encounter of Modern Science and Ancient Truth* (New York: Dutton, 1975). Needleman says that "philosophical speculation may be anything but a help toward the attainment of wisdom. For the very idea of what knowledge is and the purposes it may serve is, in unregenerate man, a direct or distant product of his desires and fears . . . . If philosophical speculation is presented or given to the appetites, which have their own utilitarian manner of thinking, it may lead to the illusion that wisdom or the ability to know is already present in a man when in fact he may have never had the real experience of certainty about anything . . . ."

4. See Huston Smith, "Perennial Philosophy, Primordial Tradition," in *Beyond the Post-Modern Mind*.

5. See Carlos Castaneda, *Journey to Ixtlan* (New York: Simon and Schuster, 1972).

6. Martin Heidegger, "Letter on Humanism" in *Basic Writings*, Frank A. Capuzzi, trans., in collaboration with J. Glenn Gray and David Farrell Krell (New York: Harper and Row, 1977), p. 193.

7. On how modern naturalism helps to justify the domination of nature, see S.R.L. Clark, *The Moral Status of Animals* (New York: Oxford University Press, 1977).

8. On the topic of technology, see chapter seven in Michael Zimmerman, *Eclipse of the Self: The Development of Heidegger's Concept of Authenticity* (Athens: Ohio University Press, 1981); also see Michael Zimmerman, "Beyond Humanism: Heidegger's Understanding of Technology," *Listening* 12 (1977): 74–83; Michael Zimmerman, "Heidegger on Nihilism and Technique," *Man and World* 8 (1975): 399–414; Michael Zimmerman, "Technological Culture and the End of Philosophy," in *Philosophy and Technology*, Paul T. Durbin and Carl Mitcham, eds. (Greenwich, Connecticut: Jai Press, 1978).

9. See Michael Zimmerman, "Heidegger and Marx on the Technological Domination of Nature," *Philosophy Today* 23 (1979): 99–112.

10. See C.S. Lewis, *The Abolition of Man* (New York: Macmillan, 1947).

11. Heidegger, "Building Dwelling Thinking," p. 146.

12. *Ibid.*, p. 148; emphasis added.

13. See Martin Heidegger, *What Is Called Thinking?*, Fred D. Wieck and J. Glenn Gray, (New York: Harper and Row, 1968). Heidegger writes: "We receive many gifts, of many kinds. But the highest and really most lasting gift given to us is always our essential nature, with which we are gifted in such a way that we are what we are only through it. That is why we owe thanks for this endowment, first and unceasingly" (p. 142).

14. Heidegger, "Building Dwelling Thinking," p. 151.

15. On the topic of releasement (*Gelassenheit*), see Martin Heidegger, *Discourse on Thinking*, John M. Anderson and E. Hans Freund, trans. (New York: Harper and Row, 1966). Also see chapter eight of Zimmerman, *Eclipse of the Self*.

16. Heidegger, "Building Dwelling Thinking," p. 157.

17. Ibid., p. 157.

18. See Michael Zimmerman, "Heidegger and Heraclitus on Spiritual Practice," in *Philosophy Today* 27 (1983): 87–103.

19. For a Heideggerean interpretation of the *Tao Te Ching*, see *Tao: A New Way of Thinking*, Chang Chung-yuan, trans. (New York: Harper and Row, 1976).

20. Heidegger, "Building Dwelling Thinking," p. 161.

Part IV

Discovering wholes

16. Nature, water symbols, and the human quest for wholeness

ANNE BUTTIMER

Few words so commonplace in everday vocabulary are so elusive to grasp as "the whole."[1] Like mirrors, notions of what constitutes a "whole picture" may reflect quite as much of what is in the eye of the beholder as they do about reality. Herein lies a profound dilemma. Once a person, group, or culture articulates its own conception of the whole, immediately antennae on other possible wholes become fixed; receptors to foreign insights become restricted to those categories which are familiar and, therefore, limited.

Martin Heidegger's reflections on thought and being prod imaginations toward horizons beyond those of the taken-for-granted.[2] They evoke a thirst for more holistic ways of understanding than can be achieved via reductionist or scientific ways.[3] Favored among human scientists is his concept of *dwelling* as "gathering of the fourfold" – Earth, Heavens, Mortals and Divinities – as the essential feature of humanness.[4] Inevitably, however, his whole idea is couched in the myth and symbolism of European civilization; it may be best exemplified in the agrarian landscapes of the Black Forest or Rhineland. His "mortals" are exclusively human, his "divinities' presenced in cathedral and shrine; a momentary glimpse may be snatched at the interplay of "earth" and "sky" via the march of seasons and such artifacts as bridges, buildings, and artisan crafts. Ocean and tide, island and beach, seem remote.

Despite this focus on European experience, one of Heidegger's enduring gifts is the invitation to probe worlds beyond one's own – to reach beyond whatever whole may have sedimented itself in cultural consciousness and gaze attentively at others. It is in this spirit that this essay draws attention to water, an element which does not play an explicit role in Heidegger's fourfold, but is nevertheless one of the most fundamental elements in Creation

– a *sine-qua-non* for terrestrial life. Through reflections on water symbolism in various civilizations, this essay seeks broader horizons on nature, thought, and being than those which our anthropocentric and settled worlds of the West have deemed edifying, ideologically defensible, or rationally arguable. Indirectly, the aim is to elucidate neglected aspects of human dwelling, a central aim of this volume.

If one is justified in construing Heidegger's notion of dwelling as metaphor for stability and settlement in space, then one can surely construe water symbols as metaphors for adventure and journey, for an element which lubricates, emancipates, renews and recreates human existence through time. In fact, if there can be a universal conception of dwelling on the earth relevant to all world civilizations, it must include this fluid, liberating element. If not, the conception must fall short of that wholeness toward which Heidegger himself pointed when he wrote, "poetically, man dwells . . . ."[5]

At the outset, then, let me define wholeness as horizon rather than destination: a horizon which recedes as the journey through life unfolds. I wish to share some reflections on water symbols in diverse milieux, regarding these as horizons which people have charted in their own quests for wholeness. Against the background of this cross-cultural and historical evidence, albeit filtered through the lenses of a Westerner, I propose some categories through which our own taken-for-granted "wholes" can be evaluated. The challenge, as I see it, in these later years of the twentieth century, is not so much one of rationalizing or analyzing how particular "wholes" are constituted or held together; rather, it is one of discovering ways beyond them toward a broader vision of humanity and world.

Symbols, experience, and the whole

Most Western academics use symbols – texts, maps, equations, diagrams – to unravel and analyze parts; symbols to put the parts back together again. A distinction should, of course, be made between signs and symbols: the equations and acronyms which scholars use to facilitate unequivocal meanings in conversation should more appropriately be called *signs*, while insignia, shrines, art and architecture, myth and metaphor, should be regarded as *symbols*. The latter point beyond themselves, and appeal to imagination, intuition, and memory, as well as to intellect; the former can function with just the sensory-motor or mechanical capacities of humanness.[6] We share one of the most characteristic habits of anthropoids, viz., the transformation of direct experience into symbols, be they articulated via sound, taste, literature or algebra. Symbolic transformations are the stuff of human creativity.[7] To use one's own categories in interpreting the symbols of another is also a universal human trait. The interpretation of signs and symbols, however, so clear and efficient for the insider, may be a matter of shock, scandal, or puzzlement for the outsider. Consider the Dragon, sacred symbol of palace and temple in China, symbol of evil to European eyes.[8] The painting of Saint George and the Dragon which for English eyes represented the triumph of virtue over vice, when once displayed in Beijing, was not surprisingly construed as a symbol of European imperialism. When Western eyes alight on a Japanese painting of water turbulence, how is it to be interpreted? As art to be evaluated in aesthetic terms, as an invitation to research on hydro-dynamics, or as a story about the cosmos?

Symbols per se are obviously not adequate to facilitate mutual understanding. In the case of water symbolism, the potential for confusion is especially so, for the symbol cannot be interpreted correctly until placed in the context of a civilization's physical milieu and cosmology. A higher level of symbolic transformation from experience to language is clearly needed: what one seeks is some horizon for discourse which could enable each of us to come to appreciate diverse images of wholeness.[9] It is in this emancipatory, lubricating sense that water symbolism may yield its greatest gift, viz., a thirst for something beyond those circumscribed wholes in which we all now "dwell" in our worlds of experience and expertise.

Let me offer an illustration from intellectual history. The progress of scientific knowledge is commonly documented via the record of major products, by author and date, as well as via the labelling of theories and models. Historians of thought, however, be they idealist or materialist in orientation, when describing or interpreting this story, resort to metaphors such as "currents of thought," "watersheds," "convergence of streams," "cycles," or "phases" of knowledge production and diffusion. Literature on human creativity is permeated with water symbolism. When individual scholars are asked specifically about their own moments of insight they often speak in metaphors like "wellspring of inspiration," "flood of insight" or "stream of consciousness."[10] Isaac Newton, reflecting on his life's work, described his own experience as that of "a little boy playing on the seashore and diverting myself in now and then finding a smoother pebble or a prettier shell than ordinary, whilst the *great ocean of truth* lay all undiscovered before me."[11] Sabres clash in the verbal sportmanship over "internalist" versus "externalist" interpretations of Western intellectual history, but few discussants acknowledge how culturally confined the whole theater is.[12] None of the signs and symbols used by either contending party is really understandable until it is placed in the context of deeper myths, e.g., Promethean or Faustian myths of progress which hold the conviction that through time there has been a progressive refinement of thought and an inevitable trajectory toward "truth." Few seem aware that this very practice of entertaining discourse on intellectual developments per se, apart from their connections with other, material, political, or emotional developments in human experience, may be quite incomprehensible to fellow humans in other civilizations. In short, if one is to seek understanding of water symbols, one has to recognize that they probably make sense within a cultural and geographical context whose guiding myths are imbibed and mutually affirmed without rational analysis or reflection.

If it is human to make symbols, one can justifiably argue that it is quintessentially human to create and live by myths. Even Western philosophers today claim that the mythopoetic mode of knowing is the necessary complement to the rational.[13] It would appear, for example, that one of the guiding myths of Euro-American university life is failing, viz., that a rational division of labor and functional specialization among knowledge experts will eventually yield understanding of "the whole." In the last few decades, the result has been a turn toward the humanities, with a hope that something could be learned from an exploration of aesthetic, intuitive, or volitional dimensions of our humanness. Perhaps the time has come for a rediscovery of the dialectic nature of wholeness: that no structure makes sense without process, that functional specialization can only lead to a Tower of Babel if provision is not made for communication among those who occupy its well-engineered rooms. Even from a rational vantage point, the West already senses a thirst for symbolism which connotes lubrication, flow, and dynamism of a circulatory system which could connect parts and wholes.[14]

In the late twentieth century, problems of water resources − their use, abuse, scarcity or abundance − evoke something more than metaphysical speculation. There is obviously a sense of problem felt among hydrologists and political scientists throughout the world. The United Nations announces a decade of research on water; a recent report from an eminent group of hydrologists assembled at Zurich warns that by the year 1990 only half the world's population will have access to unpolluted drinking water.[15] In Rio de Janeiro live more than two million *favelados* without access to running water or sewage disposal.[16] The world of research busies itself in the quest for solutions, and the quest seems worthwhile for reasons beyond those of intellectual curiosity.

A sensitivity about life as a whole and the motivation to explore problems and seek solutions belong to realms of humanness which transcend the purely rational. They could be regarded as religious, for *religio* (literally, "to bind") refers to a felt bond among creatures, and its opposite is negligence (from *negligio*, "to unloosen"). Concern about water resources might be one of the best entrances to reality which other civilizations take for granted, viz., that nature, cosmos, and humanity form a whole, and that whole means holy.

If water symbolism is to be catalyst for holistic understanding, or a potential facilitator of improved communication between those who now find themselves in the roles of victim or oppressor in the international drama of water resources, one needs to reflect not only on the everyday experiences of humans in diverse milieux; not only on the scientific explanations of water dynamics and use; but also on the contexts of faith in which perceptions, uses, and abuses of water are formed and sanctioned.

Water symbols in experience, expertise, and myth

At the basic level of sensory experience, water appeals to the whole: it can be seen, felt, smelled, touched, and tasted. What would the day be like without the morning shower, the cool drink of water after a hike, the refreshment of a swim, or the beauty of falling snow? Socially speaking, the beach, oasis, river or stream has been the meeting place for humans and animals throughout history. Water functions as magnet and shrine, in whose presence all kinds of communication barriers seem to dissolve. The fixing of international boundaries – one of the most significant challenges for mankind's symbolic interaction – has nearly always used watersheds, rivers, straits and sounds. In 1982, the United Nations Law of the Sea Conference could still not reach agreement on offshore limits or provisions for deep-sea mining. The survival of humanity may depend upon whether agreements can be reached about access to and use of water.

At the scientific level, one is today much better informed than ever about the nature and dynamics of water, a theme which in Judson's phrase, "has tempted the eye of the artist, the sinews of the engineer, the intelligence of the scientist, and its mysteries are not yet fathomed."[17] A better theme on which interdisciplinary communication could be fostered could scarcely be found. There is the factual as well as the fictional, hard data and soft, which could be shared among our fields. Why the enormous fascination of the ocean in human history? On any globe one can see that ninety seven percent of all the world's water lies in the oceans and seas; only three percent on land. And of this three percent, seventy-seven percent is locked up in

icecaps and glaciers, twenty-two and a half percent is underground, and only a tiny one and a half percent is available for plants, animals, and
humans.[18] The West has long sought explanation for the disposition of land
and water. The theory of continental drift which speculated about Pangaea,
Tethys Sea, Gondwanaland, and Laurasia − a theory readily dismissed as
"myth" by hard-nosed scientists in this century − is now resurrected thanks
to the discovery of tectonic plates. Intellectual historians are today less
cavalier about dismissing the role of myth in scientific discovery.

Thales, one of the earliest Western philosophers, once hypothesized that
"all is water." In this brief statement, one finds perhaps the best symbolic
prototype of that perennial quest for simple propositions and unifying principles of the "whole" which has characterized our Western intellectual
heritage. Spinoza later sought to explain the whole in terms of one Ultimate
Cause and thus reduce multiplicity to unity. What a contrast this perspective
is to the Oriental approach, where imagination and aesthetics played a far
greater role than intellect, but where the Absolute was identified with nature,
in all its multifarious forms, rather than in One Supreme Being existing outside or above nature.[19]

The West, of course, has no monopoly on monistic thinking. *Varuna*, the
Vedic god, was monarch of the universe, upholder of both physical and
moral orders (*rta*).[20] A distinction can also be discerned between the
philosophy of *Tao*, which advocated sensitivity to nature's own "nature," as
it were, and a variety of Confucianism which justified the mastering of it. The
Western world, however, albeit its impressive record of monasticism and
mysticism, has stubbornly pursued the route of empirical and hypothetico-
deductive reasoning in its investigations of nature, whereas other civilizations have appealed to art, music and poetry in their journeys toward
understanding the world. Parallels can be found, of course, between the
lyrical expressions of *Fraticelli* and Romantic poets in Europe and the
homilies of a Shintō priest, e.g., Takasumi Séngé: "There is no place in
which a god does not reside, even in the wild waves' eight hundred folds or
in the wild mountain's bosom."[21]

Western architecture would celebrate One (albeit Triune) God, but
Chinese landscape artists would seek to display "the principle of organization connecting all things."[22] Already, superficial evidence seems to suggest that what sets the West apart from other civilizations in its journey
toward wholeness is (a) emphasis on the intellectual and rational; (b) visual
perception as somehow more reliable than the other senses; and (c) mythological grounds for a hierarchical conception of power in the design and
dynamism of reality. In other civilizations, one finds a blending of the in-

tellectual with aesthetic, emotional, and volitional faculties of understanding wholeness; indeed, it seems that water symbolism has served to generate this multi-sensory array of perceptions, as well as openness to a plurality of styles in which order could be found in various social settings.

A more radical difference between the Western and other worlds is, of course, that of underlying *myth*. The lessons to be learned from nature for a Chinese scholar of the Han or Sung dynasties were not only to be gleaned via aesthetic rather than calculative methods – they were to be learned from natural events themselves. The human and cosmic orders were intimately interconnected, so hurricanes, storms and floods were signs of divine displeasure with a particular regime: wise government was something which nature patrolled. The term for revolution, *Ko-ming*, literally meant a "cutting off" or "taking away" of that mandate from Heaven from some particular ruler.[23]

It is far easier to speak of symbolism with respect to experience or expertise than it is to delve into the world of myth. Ever since Xenophanes chided Homer and Hesiod for their "mythological" expressions, the main thrust of Hellenistic thought has been to empty *mythos* of all possible religious or metaphysical value.[24] Myth has come to connote all that is false. Proper knowledge – "truth" – required *Logos*, or at least *historia*. In our Western tradition, both Socratic and Christian, myth has become suspect, the very opposite of truth. One might well wonder whether those capacities to regain touch with a mytho-poetic level of understanding have atrophied beyond repair? Atrophy, one hopes, does not signify death; to reawaken tired muscles, one appeals to emotion as well as aesthetics in gazing at how other civilizations have construed their "wholes."

Water plays a cardinal role in most Creation myths, frequently associated with the female element, in reciprocal relationship with the male elements of Sky and Earth. But the story is usually suited to the normal life experience of men and women within particular physical milieux. In the arid and semiarid Navajo world, for example, the process of creation is seen to emerge through the conjunction of Mother Earth and Father Sky, the basic ingredients being cornmeal, pollen, and powdered plants or flowers.[25] In Polynesia, where the Ocean is the ubiquitous horizon of life, one reads the following account of creation:

> In the beginning there were only the Waters and Darkness. Io, the Supreme God, separated the waters by the power of thought and of his words, and created the Sky and the Earth. He said: Let the waters be separated, let the heavens be formed, let the earth be.[26]

People still utter those powerful words when faced with serious problems in life; they are believed to be effective in shedding light into secret places, in providing inspiration for composing songs, and in times of despair or war.[27] Buddhism, which has diffused throughout a great variety of physical milieux in Asia, recognizes a heterogeneity of deities (*kami*) and levels of being.[28] In Japan, the sacred lotus, floating on the ocean, holds a key symbolic role in creation.[29] In the Judaeo-Christian account of creation, it is the Spirit which breathes over the waters. When people disobeyed, a great flood came to cleanse the world. The symbolism of universal flood, of course, is as old as Gilgamesh, oldest perhaps of human records.[30]

A provocative contrast can be discerned between the Western account of Noah who, after the flood, gathered specimens of all living creatures into the Ark, and the Hindu account of Vishnu, incarnated as a Fish-God, who salvaged specimens of all vegetables and their seeds as well as all animal species.[31] "Since the Fish-God was incarnated in water," a contemporary Hindu scholar writes, "people believe that water is sacred."[32] Might one not speculate that for the Western mind sacredness is symbolized in fixed property (the Ark) whereas for the Hindu the sacred flows like water? For the West, wholeness (holiness) may consist of reaching a clearly defined destination, whereas for the Hindu it emerges from pilgrimage? On the level of myth, then, two contrasting images of wholeness emerge: one implying home, enclosure, and protection in time and place; the other implying movement, flow, and immersion within the stream of life.[33] For the nomadic forebears of Judaeo-Christian symbolism, The Ark of the Convenant was a sealed box, eventually to be enshrined, enthroned, within temple or cathedral, whereas for the Hindu, holiness flowed within the waters, particularly in the sacred waters of the Ganges.

Stereotypes, of course, are hazardous. In the Christian liturgy, water symbolizes the Holy Spirit who comes to dwell within the believer upon Baptism. To the Samaritan woman at the well, Christ said: "Whoever drinks the water that I will give him will never be thirsty again. The water that I will give him will become in him a spring which will provide him with living water, and give him eternal life."[34]

Cosmology and metaphor in Western conceptions of nature

Within the Western world, it would seem relatively easy to discern connections among myth, symbol, and attitudes toward the whole. The taken-for-granted is more complex, however, than might appear at first glance. Even a cursory look at Western history shows how myths have been used to justify, baptize, and steer our ways of life. Nor is it possible to separate out the cosmologies of the West from the peculiar kinds of environmental experiences which Europeans have known over the past two-thousand years. Permeating Western symbols and myths are certain key images of nature, varying over time, which have provided a kind of canvas, or framework, for the creative work of artists and scientists during successive periods.

More specifically, one could claim that symbols, arising from experience or myth, have been harvested via *metaphor* in the pursuit of cognitive certainty. From Greece the Western tradition has inherited the conviction that intellect was queen among human faculties, and that human reason (*logos*) should provide the ultimate criteria for assessing truthfulness. From Greece, as well as from the Hellenic stream of the Judaeo-Christian tradition, has come a legacy of suspicion about the emotional, sensory, and intuitive features of our humanness. The distinction, and eventual separation, of intellectual and moral virtues in education is one which split Western approaches to thought and being, truth and goodness.

Yet one suspects that in those key metaphors for the whole which were built on symbols of nature – particularly those of water – one could find lurking assumptions about the nature of being itself. The intellectual history of the West has been variously interpreted. I draw here mainly on the works of Glacken, Yi-Fu Tuan, and Mills[35] and add a further consideration, viz., that of "root metaphor" as expounded by Pepper.[36] Pepper describes four world hypotheses in Western intellectual history which claim to give the "whole picture" about reality, and it seems worthwhile to examine how the nature of water was construed in each. The fit is scarcely comfortable, but as a heuristic exercise, this interpretation may help to unmask connections between cosmology, science, and wholeness in our Western traditions. A rendering of Pepper's four root metaphors in terms relevant to understanding water is: (1) nature as appropriate *form*, designed by Divine Providence as fit abode for mankind – a fitness evidenced, for example, in the balancing of moistures; (2) nature as *organism*, demonstrated primarily in the analogy to the human body; (3) nature as *machine*, evidenced through scientific experiments in alchemy and hydrology; and (4) nature as *theatre of events*, which staged spontaneous and unpredictable happenings, such as floods, droughts, and storms. In each of these "whole pictures" lurks implications about truth and rightness; each bears implicit or explicit guidelines for how humans should deal with nature. These examples make no claims to exhaustiveness, nor shall I confine them to the West. Wherever possible, some parallels with non-Western thought will be drawn.

1. Nature as appropriate form

Babylonians considered the stars as the "writing of the sky." Arabs calculate time according to the stars. For the first millenium of European history, one could say that nature was "read" in terms of how well it displayed God's ultimate plan for humanity on earth.[37] In *Romans*, Paul claims that because God's truths are so plainly written in his Creation, pagans could not plead ignorance of Him. "Some peoples, in order to discover God, read books," Augustine wrote, "but there is a great book: the very appearance of created things. Look about you. Look below you. Note it, read it."[38] Viewing Nature as a book implies that there is an author, therefore natural forms were legible, and reflective of that author's intentions. This theocentric view contrasts, for example, with Hindu and Buddhist traditions where each natural form was, as it were, its own author. The Dogen (Japan) says: "There are many thousands of worlds comparable to the *sutras* within a single speck of dust. Within a single dust there are innumerable Buddhas. A single stalk of grass and a single tree are both the mind and body of us and Buddhas."[39] Zen gardens and miniaturized natural forms are "not merely symbols but ways of pointing immediately at what is called in Chinese the *Tao*."[40] The Meghaduta of Kalidasa ascribes conscious individuality, a real personal life, to all forms of nature; in fact, the poet describes aspects of nature that correspond to various human emotions.[41] What seems to be common to all these diverse approaches to nature is the attempt to explain visible forms in terms of some underlying set of rules or norms. The root metaphor of *form* implies a world of diversity, a mosaic of variegated pattern and fitness.

In Medieval times, European geographers were considered the "anatomists of the great world."[42] They described the visible patterns of land and water, human landscapes and social forms, all in terms of "fit," viz., how human civilizations adapted themselves to the natural environment. The Greeks had already paved the way by classifying the earth into zones (*klimata*) of varying appropriateness for human life. The role of water symbolism in this formistic conception appealed directly to life experience. Health of mind and body, as well as that of society, demanded a careful balance of the humors (moistures), and this, in turn, demanded a sensitive attunement to milieu, especially to climate.

Largely because of its role in balancing the humors, climate was linked with all forms of deformity, insanity, greed and warlike habits. Health meant the wholeness of the organism. So, too, a healthy society operated like an organism. A vast literature developed around the question of the optimal climate for human life.[43] It was first considered to be Greece and, later, northwestern Europe; all other societies were stereotyped in terms of their tempers and their ability to lead a healthy life. What is intriguing is the consistent curiosity about appropriate social forms, appropriate government, for people with different temperaments, viz., inhabitants of different climatic milieux. Bodin usually wound up his essays with a plea for strong central monarchy as the only means of dealing with the schisms and strife of the sixteenth century French world about which he wrote.[44]

2. Nature as organism

In the sixteenth century a vast new world opened up for the West as the ocean was gradually mastered. Political imaginations flew to the prospect of world empires: Portugal, Spain, Belgium, Holland, France and England sent out their antennae for conquest. Throughout European history, of course, the sea had always offered horizons of opportunity for Greek, Viking, Hansa and Goth – counterpoint symbol to that settled, land-based agrarian civilization which ruled "at home." Skills for overcoming physical constraints of mountain and moor could be passed on orally from generation to generation, but to build cumulative knowledge of the sea demanded a scientific attitude.[45] The sixteenth century also witnessed enormous upheavals in religious, military, and economic life. The Renaissance was dawning and the Reformation moved full steam ahead; with both came a radically altered image of nature. Before the sixteenth century, people may have looked to nature for signs of what lay beyond; now they studied it for its own sake.[46] The world was viewed from an anthropocentric rather than a theocentric vantage point. The human body became the symbol of perfection: men and women were themselves the image of the cosmos.[47]

In the Renaissance version of water symbols and the whole, nature's work of art could be understood from one's body. The human body provided an excellent model: composed of many parts, it is still one. Analogy to the life cycle could enable one to conceptualize change over time; the same principles of order could be postulated for both natural and human life. "In every man ... a world, a universe, regards itself," said Bruno.[48] Adherents to this view include such eminent figures as Leonardo, Gilbert, Kepler, Bruno, Harvey and, possibly, Newton. In many ways this view echoes elements of Arab thought, imported possibly via Aquinas and developed by Albert.[49] The cosmos now possesses life, intelligence and soul; it goes through the stages of infancy, youth, maturity and old age; it has skin, hair, a heart, stomach, veins, and arteries.[50]

Two aspects of this Renaissance image seem particularly relevant to water symbolism and metaphor. First, the extraction of precious stones was considered somewhat like abortion: alchemists believed that all minerals, left to themselves, eventually "ripened" into gold.[51] Secondly, an enormous curiosity arose about the hydrologic cycle and the role of water in the workings of the earth as a whole.[52] Leonardo wrote: "The body of the earth, like the bodies of animals, is intersected with ramifications of veins which are all in connection and are constituted to give nutriment and life to the earth and its creatures. These come from the depths of the sea and, after many revolutions, have to return by the rivers created by the bursting of these veins high up."[53]

The "scientific" puzzle was to figure out how water moved from the oceans to the tops of mountains:

> The waters circulated with constant motion from the utmost depths of the sea to the highest summits of the mountans, not obeying the nature of heavy matter; and in this case they act as does the blood of animals which is always moving from the sea of the heart and flows to the top of their heads; and he who bursts veins – as one may see when a vein bursts in the nose, that all the blood from below rises to the level of the burst vein. When the water rushes out of a burst vein in the earth it obeys the nature of other things heavier than air, whence it always seeks the lowest places.[54]

It was this parallelism between body and earth which evidently inspired Harvey's discovery of the blood circulation system – a discovery appreciated more by geologists than it was by medical authorities at the time.[55] Geologists sought some central fire in the earth that performed a role analogous to that of the heart in man.

3. Nature as machine

To introduce the post-Galilean view of the world as a giant machine, water symbolism also helps. In contrast to Leonardo's "organic" explanation of water circulation, the "machine" metaphor suggested the alembic, or alchemist's alternative. In his distillation flask, water is heated to boiling point and the steam so generated is then cooled to produce condensation in the head of the flask.[56] The earth is seen to operate in similar fashion: inside there is a central fire that heats the incoming water flowing downward through subterranean passages from the oceans. Water then rises as steam to the earth's surface, where it condenses – for example, in mountains and hills. The alembic model could explain clouds, rain, thunder, and lightning – even earthquakes. The geologist Hutton (familiar with James Watt, inventor of the steam engine) saw the world in mechanist terms – the earth as a perfectly constructed machine, bearing the marks of its Creator's power and wisdom.[57] Whatever in it is subject to decay must, through its own internal mechanisms, also be restored. Its mechanisms are, however, to be distinguished from those of its creation, which remain beyond speculation. The most favored metaphor which ushered in this new image was, of course, the clock.[58]

The use of water and water symbols in the "clocking" of time is perhaps one of the most famous examples of metaphor in science and technology. One commentator claims that Galileo and his generation inaugurated "a new attitude for man before nature: he ceased to regard her as a child watches his mother, modelling himself after her; he wishes to conquer her, to make himself 'lord and possessor'."[59] There is a certain Oedipal aspect to this interpretation of the sudden adoption of the "machine" metaphor in various parts of Europe by scholars of widely different background. The violation of nature which ensued was accompanied by feelings of guilt and anxiety to which we are still heir.

Mechanism is, of course, traceable to early sources in Greek and Roman philosophy, and Cicero eulogized the power of mechanist thought and *techne* already in the first century B.C.[60] Mechanism probably arose, like other metaphors, from the attempt to explain the unfamiliar in terms of the familiar. Instead of the human body, however, the analog arose from experiences with objects – carpentry, architecture, clocks, levers and pulleys; and later with steam engines and computers.[61] Throughout the seventeenth century mechanism actually supported a teleological and a religious conception of the universe: there was still a maker, and objects were made for a purpose. An added nuance, however, came through the Enlightenment faith in human ingenuity: the well-constructed object – for example, the clock in the Strasbourg Cathedral – did not need constant maintenance. In fact, the better the construction, the more it could be left to its own devices. If there was a God, then, His Omnipotence would be best shown by his absenting himself. God became a "retired engineer," and the environment could become secularized.[62] People believed they could tinker with and ultimately control nature; what had been put together could easily be taken apart. Attitudes of analysis and dissection joined those of curiosity about how mechanisms might be controlled. Nature became a reservoir of poten-

tially exploitable resources, and each major technological innovation –
dams, pumps, irrigation, and so forth – brought with them a changed image
of the environment.

4. Nature as theater of events

In marked contrast to the integrated pictures of the whole offered by the
metaphors of organism and machine, a fourth view returns to the plurality
of events and phenomena on the earth.[63] A contextual view sees the world
as stage for spontaneous and possibly unique events. Each flood, hur-
ricane, earthquake or storm is seen as a unique occurrence, each to be
analyzed and described holistically in its own terms.

In many non-Western civilization, natural events are construed as signs
of something else, or as "personalities" in their own right. During the early
Han period in China, it was believed that natural events and human institutions were mutually interrelated, and if the king governed well, weather,
wind and rain would be favorable, whereas if the king's reign was bad,
natural calamities would arise.[64] Greek myth also personified storm and
drought, and these signified not only part of nature's drama but were also
indicators of how appropriate the earth's *klimata* were for human dwelling.

The contextual approach to particular events in the modern West bears
little relationship to the Chinese and Greek versions. It may be more typical
of the trans-Atlantic corner of the West – from the land where Pilgrims
sought to finally make the Reformation work and rid human consciousness
of old dogmatisms and intellectual effetism.[65] The emerging natural
philosophy would be pragmatic: the truth of yesterday would no longer suf-
fice for today and would most probably be false tomorrow. The ultimate test
of credibility was whether something would work.[66] To understand an event
meant to look at it contextually, and build a whole picture from the strands
and textures of references surrounding that particular event.[67]

Here, then, is a fourth version of the cognitive whole which does not demand an integrated picture of the cosmos, but promises a synthetic
understanding of particular problems and situations. Tensions, of course,
arise when this holistic mode of reaching understanding of an event is
stretched toward normative ends, viz., as base for solving problems.
Researchers with applied aims in mind often move from the event itself to
the "systems" in which that event appears to be implicated; they then draft
plans for its management or monitoring, which may eventually become insensitive to context. On the North American continent, for example, the

United States Corps of Engineers had already spent millions trying to harness the Mississippi River before they discovered that Flood Plain Indians had in many cases already understood how to adapt their ways of life to the giant stream and its floods.[68] A contextual view of the world could only work if all were to agree on the principle of cultural pluralism and geographic autonomy — i.e. that in each valley people had responsibility to and for its own niche.

Identity, order and niche

What lessons may be derived from these four world views and the patterns of water symbolism they suggest? How do Western conceptions of water relate to those of other civilizations? What guidelines for a journey toward a wider horizon on wholeness can be gleaned from this comparative sketch?

A central theme in this essay is that the key metaphors for "wholeness" in any civilization may be best elucidated in terms of mythological foundations and physical milieux. At the same time, their endurance could scarcely be explained without reference to those institutional structures and power arrangements which prevail between political regimes and scholars in a society. In the modern West, for example, there can be little doubt that academic fields of expertise must somehow demonstrate their value in terms of society's ongoing public interests. Let me conclude with some suggestions about how water symbolism enters explicitly or implicitly in the discourse between expertise and experience on three distinct levels of public interest, viz., *identity, order,* and *niche*.

Water as symbol of identity

Naming is one of the ubiquitous techniques used by mankind to establish and maintain a sense of personal and social identity. Scandinavia offers ample illustration: consider how many place and family names include water symbols (e.g., *-sjö, -ström,-å, -bro*). Lakes, rivers, oceans and seas have served the interests of human identity in most human cultures, and the earth's toponymy yields deeper insight into the history of civilizations than does its topography. Even today, Merseyside, Clydeside, Östersjön can provide symbols of home for emigrant or native, more effectively than Liverpool, Glasgow, or towns around the Baltic Sea. Mediterranean and Levant — despite all the vicissitudes of political history — still resonate the music of a particular region. Similarly, the Rhineland, Danubian Plain and Po Valley offer symbols of cultural identity which transcend the many discrete "wholes" which inhabit those regions. Hydrological projects from Tigris-Euphrates through Tennessee Valley to Mekong all bear out the practical as well as ideological implications of "river valley identity": to be effective, the whole valley has to be involved, whatever the realignments of political or administrative structures which this might necessitate. A shining example in Europe is, of course, the Dutch *wattenschaffen* dating from the twelfth century.[69] Today, as pollution and other problems mount in the North Sea and invasions of the Baltic steel strains international nerves, it becomes clear that the definitions of political "whole" and regional identity might well align themselves with those of water.

All humans presumably develop an identity which involves elements of "home" and "reach." River valleys and seas can provide horizons for different homes. Today's challenge seems to demand global horizons of concern as well as knowledge, but the legacy of symbolism in this respect is marred with the record of imperial conquest (political or economic) and its scientific support, which Heidegger called *Herrschaftswissen*.[70] A challenge outlined not only by him but by many others is to conceive an identity (home and reach) which could emerge from *Besinnliches Nachdenken*: how water works and how it is symbolized in various civilizations could be the wellspring for such an approach to our fields of knowledge.

Water as symbol of order

A sense of identity is intimately associated with implicit conceptions of optimal order in society as well as in spatial and temporal affairs. Wittfogel's hydraulic civilizations exercised autocratic control over highly diverse pockets of local order; the Nile valley, by contrast, had a loose federation of village communities. The Swedish tradition of *lag* burgeoned around marine operations; the Admiralty in Britain provided symbols for team work on municipal as well as military operations. Even in everyday language, we often speak of "launching" or "piloting" a project, "pooling resources," a "wave of success," work "flowing smoothly," leadership "running a tight ship," workers "inundated" or "swamped" with agenda. The everyday language of teamwork, social management and policy is permeated with terms drawn from human experience with water and sea during precisely that period when Europeans sought to conquer ocean and ports.

At an earlier time and in other civilizations, water symbolism pointed to alternative models of order: models of community life adapted to different cultural, natural, and historical milieux. In the West, the vast literature on connections between health, climate, and human behavior was readily dismissed as "environmental determinism," but it contained many provocative ideas about the appropriateness of political form to particular milieux. If there is one realm of contemporary life that really thirsts for creative imagination, it is surely politics, in the radical meaning of the term; public life needs the irrigation and free flow of political energies throughout all parts of society. A body politic modelled on hydrological symbolism could make an interesting alternative to those grotesque charades of mechanism which reduce the citizen to an automation to be policed rather than a potential co-creator of political life.

Water as symbol of niche

To substantiate and maintain one's sense of identity and order — personally and socially — humans require a *niche*. In this ecological term, one could embrace not only livelihood and resource base, but all the proxemic and sensory elements of the everyday milieu. Throughout the record of farming and fishing societies, of artisan and industrial economies, of empires desirous to expand their *Lebensraum*, water symbolism has been used to connote both "home" and "horizon." It is scarcely possible to understand the history of Viking, Hansa, Phoenician, Portuguese or English without understanding how their language symbolized water as horizon for adventure. All over the world one finds in art and poetry, in science as well as fiction, water as symbol for home and reach, security and adventure. For so many writers and artists, the very presence of water — lake or ocean — was an indispensable condition for creative work. Vilhelm Moberg, it is claimed, always sought a view over lake or sea for his working milieu. Dan Andersson, writing in Värmland, spoke of "något bakom bergen . . ." [something beyond the mountain], but the cargo cults of his Polynesian or Caribbean counterpart would have sung of something beyond the horizon.[71] It could be that creative insight is peculiarly sensitive to the milieu in which it dawns. Could one not compare the record of maritime civilizations with that of continental ones, in terms of water symbolism? For example, could not one compare the gentle Shinto symbols with those of the Hydraulic civilizations, those of the mounted nomad or those of the peasant, and find how wise or vain were the dreams of *niche* which have shaped the surface of the earth?

Niche implies both ecological and economic resources whose quality and scale reflect different societies' images of identity and order. The great irony in today's discussions about water resources in the West revolves around an ethno- and egocentrism. As long as one portion of humanity frames for itself an identity which surpasses its own geographical horizons and employs experts to chart its strategies of order without acknowledging the rights of all humanity to its own niche, all the rhetoric of peace and justice remains hollow.

An enduring challenge

Any experientially grounded probe using symbols to identify the "whole" is understandable in the context of particular cosmologies, and needs to be interpreted with rational as well as mythopoetic lenses. This enormous hermeneutical challenge is confounded by the ever present shadow of Narcissus. During the era when nature was regarded as the handiwork of God, I presume theology was without question the interpreter. When the secrets of civilization and climate were to be studied in terms of the human body, geographers could be regarded as "the anatomists of the great world." In the machine era, I presume the technologist has felt at home. But the rejection and succession of basic metaphors was never a function of epistemology alone; such changes were born and steered from aesthetic, moral, and emotional judgements; in short, they were due to changing mythological horizons – horizons which receded as knowledge and experience unfolded. Can water symbolism, in cross-cultural perspective, help us to interpret these shifting horizons and reach toward higher levels of symbolic transformation which I claimed at the outset were needed? If we can not manage to transcend our own institutionally-defined pools of expertise, how can we imagine that we have anything useful to offer in the resolution of problems relating to world water resources?

The most brilliant analyses and rational plans in the world do not motivate people to change their actual behavior with respect to water use and abuse. Ways of life are built upon taken-for-granted habits and practices, most of which are not consciously considered. European farmers are not asked to question or change their daily practices every time a new machine arrives or when efficiency in agribusiness unleashes massive doses of fertilizer and mechanized systems on a formerly subsistence-base economy. Nor does the housewife who always counted on chickens, dogs, or pigs to consume leftovers change her habits when plastics and canned foods replace the home-grown kind. Habits "cling;" they are not moralized about but are simply taken-for-granted. A great deal of venom and rhetoric has been aired at huge capitalistic enterprises which are so apparently insensitive to ecology; legal mechanisms are gradually being implemented to muzzle the giants. Yet I suspect that on a global scale, it is the farmers and nomads of the world, now suddenly finding themselves in a radically changed economic and technological world, who are the worst offenders and victims of water pollution. One could say that their technosphere has been radically altered with damaging effects on their biosphere, and yet their images and values have not changed concomitantly.

It is much easier, however, to blame others than to look at ourselves and our academic *genres de vie*. It may well be that fragmentation and specialization of our expertise reflects itself in the landscapes and life forms within which we pursue our everyday agenda. A look at water symbolism and its cardinal role in world cosmologies helps here: *ceteris* are never *paribus*. Water symbolism beckons us beyond our academic niches, offering a cleansing of encrustated routines, and suggests some alternative ways of perceiving ourselves and our world. Like a river flowing past a rich diversity of landscapes and regions, the contemporary world sweeps past our traditional "boxes" of expertise which seem in many ways like oxbow lakes and levees of forgotten relevance. Water permeates the whole of life, inviting all to ongoing creation.

So might one dare to dream of a theology where Eros rejoins Logos, where spirituality, emotion, and worship rejoin intellect as equally valuable sources of insight into truth and goodness? Might one dream of a technology where Prometheus is reconciled with Epimetheus, and the drama of Faust and Gretchen rewritable? Can we envision environmental and human sciences ready to be tamed of their managerial hybris and listening to a reading of the earth's surface in terms of the accumulated wisdom of civilizations – and thereby led to a sense of Creation as a whole? Teilhard de Chardin's poetic vision of the universe has something to offer us all: a vision of humanity finally become conscious of itself and aware of a Unity, founded on Infinite Love, which supports diversity and the integrity of all things.[72] Few metaphors could be more helpful in the journey toward understanding the whole.

Notes

1. This essay is an abbreviated version of a presentation to theologians and hydrologists at a symposium on water problems, Lund University, October 1982; see Anne Buttimer,

"Water Symbolism and the Understanding of Wholeness," in Reinhold Castensson, ed., *Vattnet bär livet* (Linköping, Sweden: University of Linköping, 1984), pp. 57–92.

2. See Martin Heidegger, *Being and Time* (New York: Harper and Row, 1962); *On the Way to Language* (New York: Harper and Row, 1971); *Poetry, Language, Thought*, (New York: Harper and Row, 1971). Also, see J.J. Kockelmans, *On Heidegger and Language* (Evanston, Illinois: Northwestern University Press, 1972).

3. Heidegger, *Being and Time*; Heidegger, *Poetry, Language, Thought*. Also, see W. Biemel, *Martin Heidegger* (New York: Harcourt-Brace Jovanovich, 1976).

4. Heidegger, "Building Dwelling Thinking," in *Poetry, Language, Thought*, pp. 143–162.

5. Heidegger, "Poetically, Man Dwells . . .," in *Poetry, Language, Thought*, pp. 211–229.

6. See C.G. Jung, *Man and His Symbols* (New York: Doubleday, 1965), pp. 20–21.

7. Ernst Cassirer, *The Philosophy of Symbolic Forms* (New Haven, Connecticut: Yale University Press, 1944); Ernst Cassier, *Language and Myth* (New York: Dover, 1946); Suzanne Langer, *Philosophy in a New Key: A Study in the Symbolism of Reason, Rite, and Art* (Cambridge, Massachussetts: Harvard University Press, 1957).

8. See F. Huxley, *The Dragon: Nature of Spirit, Spirit of Nature* (London: Thames and Hudson, 1979).

9. One allegory from the Judaeo-Christian world may illustrate the prospect: on that first Pentecost Day, after the pouring out of the Holy Spirit, thousands of people from diverse civilizations could suddenly communicate as though they possessed a common vernacular language.

10. See H.F. Judson, *The Eighth Day of Creation* (New York: Simon and Schuster, 1979); H.F. Judson, *The Search for Solutions* (New York: Holt, Rinehart and Winston, 1980).

11. Cited in Judson, *Search for Solutions*, p. 5.

12. See E. Mendelssohn, *The Social Production of Scientific Knowledge: Sociology of Sciences Yearbook* (Dordrecht: Reidel, 1977); S. Lilley, "Cause and Effect in the History of Science," *Centaurus* 3 (1953): 58–72.

13. C.O. Schrag, *Radical Reflection and the Origin of the Human Sciences* (Lafayette, Indiana: Purdue University Press, 1980).

14. I have attempted a sketch in "Reason, Rationality, and Human Creativity," *Geografiska Annaler* 61B (1978): 43–49.

15. See Norman and Dorothy Myers, "From the Duck Pond to the Global Commons: Increasing Awareness of the Supranational Nature of Energing Environmental Issues," *Ambio* XI (1982): 195–201.

16. Janice Perlman, *The Myth of Marginality: Urban Poverty and Politics in Rio de Janeiro* (Berkeley: University of California Press, 1976).

17. H.F. Judson, *Search for Solutions*, p. 12.

18. *The Illustrated Encyclopedia of Planet Earth* (New York: Exeter Books, 1979), p. 106.

19. See Hajime Nakamura, *The Idea of Nature, East and West* (London: Encyclopedia Britannica, 1980), p. 284.

20. See John B. Noss, *Man's Religions* (New York: Macmillan, 1956), p. 98; and Nakamura, pp. 262 ff. A provocative critique of the assertion that only Western thought can claim universality is articulated in Hajime Nakamura, *Ways of Thinking of Eastern Peoples: India-China-Tibet-Japan*, P.P. Wiener, trans. (Honolulu, Hawaii: East-West Center Press, 1964), pp. 25–29.

21. Cited in Nakamura, *The Idea*, p. 253.

22. See Judson, *Search for Solutions*, p. 14.

23. Nakamura, *The Idea*, for 260 ff.

24. See Mircea Eliade, *Myth and Reality* (New York: Harper, 1963), pp. 1–4.
25. D. McClagan, *Creation Myths: Man's Introduction to the World* (London: Thames and Hudson, 1977), pp. 56–57.
26. E.S.C. Handy, *Polynesian Religion* (Honolulu: University of Hawaii Press, 1927), pp. 10–11; also, see Richard Cavendish, ed., *Mythology: An Illustrated Encyclopedia* (London: Orbis Publishers Ltd., 1980); and A. Cotterell, *A Dictionary of World Mythology* (New York: G.P. Putnam's Sons, 1980).
27. Eliade, *Myth and Reality*, p. 31.
28. Nakamura, *The Idea*, p. 243.
29. McClagan, *Creation Myths*, p. 46.
30. N.K. Sanders, ed., *The Epic of Gilgamesh* (Hamondsworth, Middlesex: Penquin Books, 1960).
31. Rana P.B. Singh, "Sacred Space, Sacred Time, and Pilgrimage in Hindu Society: A Case of Varanasi City," in R.H. Stoddart and E.A. Morinis, eds., *The Geography of Pilgrimages* (London: Academic Press), in press.
32. Ibid.
33. Rana P.B. Singh, "Geographical Approaches Towards the Lifeworld in Indian Context," in *Professor M.R. Chaudhuri Felicitation Volume* (Calcutta: Indian Geographical Society), in press.
34. *New Testament*, Gospel of John 4:13. For a discussion of water symbolism in oceanian, monsoonal and Moslem worlds, see Buttimer, "Water Symbolism."
35. Clarence Glacken, *Traces on the Rhodian Shore* (Berkeley: University of California Press, 1868); Yi-Fu Tuan, *The Hydrological Cycle and the Wisdom of God: A Theme in Geoteleology* (Toronto: University of Toronto, Department of Geography, 1968); W.J. Mills, "Metaphorical Vision: Changes in Western Attitudes to the Environment," *Annals of the Association of American Geographers* 72 (1982): 237–253.
36. Stephen Pepper, *World Hypotheses* (Berkeley: University of California Press, 1942); Anne Buttimer, "Musing on Helicon: Root Metaphors in Geography," *Geografiska Annaler* 64 B (1982): 89–96.
37. Mills, "Metaphorical Vision."
38. Cited in Glacken, p. 204.
39. Nakamura, *The Idea*, p. 283.
40. F. Spiegelberg, *Zen, Rocks and Waters* (New York: Random House, 1961), p. 19.
41. See R.M. Kale, *The Meghaduta of Kalidasa* (Bombay: Booksellers Publishing, n.d.).
42. Mills, "Metaphorical Vision," p. 241.
43. E. Leboulaye, ed., *Oeuvres complètes de Montesquieu* (Paris: Garnier Freres, 1975–1979).
44. Jean Bodin, *The Six Books of a Commonweal (The Republic)*, R. Knolles, trans. (London: G. Bishop, 1906); Jean Bodin, *Method for the Easy Comprehension of History*, B. Reynolds, trans. (New York: Columbia University Pres, 1945).
45. P. Vidal de la Blache, *Principles of Human Geography*, E. de Martonne, ed., M.T. Bingham, trans. (London: Constable, 1926), pp. 424–446.
46. Glacken; also see A.O. Lovejoy, *The Great Chain of Being: A Study in the History of an Idea* (Cambridge: Harvard University Press, 1936).
47. Mills, "Metaphorical Vision," p. 242.
48. Mills, "Metaphorical Vision," p. 242; also, see L. Barkan, *Nature's Work of Art: The Human Body as Image of the World* (New Haven: Yale University Press, 1975).
49. Glacken, pp. 254–284.
50. F.D. Adams, *The Birth and Development of the Geological Sciences* (London: Bailliere, Tindall and Cox, 1938).

51. Mills, "Metaphorical Vision," p. 244.
52. Yi-Fu Tuan, *Hydrological Cycle.*
53. J.P. Richter, ed., *The Literary Works of Leonardo da Vinci* (London: Phaidon, 1970).
54. Ibid., vol. 2, p. 158.
55. M. Nicolson, *The Breaking of the Circle: Studies in the Effect of the 'New Science' upon Seventeenth Century Poetry* (London: Oxford University Press, 1960); J. Hutton, *Theory of the Earth with Proofs and Illustrations* (Edinburgh: Cadell, Junion and Davis, 1795).
56. E.H. Duncan, "Satan-Lucifer: Lightning and Thunderbolt," *Philogical Quarterly* 30 (1951): 441–443.
57. Hutton, vol. I, p. 3.
58. E.J. Dijksterhuis, *The Mechanization of the World Picture* (London: Oxford University Pres, 1961), pp. 442–443.
59. R. Lenoble, *Esquisse d'une histoire de l'idée de nature* (Paris: Editions Albin Michel, 1969).
60. Cicero, *De natura Deorum* (London: Loeb Classical Library), II, 60.
61. Pepper, pp. 221–231.
62. Dijksterhuis, p. 491.
63. William James, *Pragmatism* (New York: New American Library, 1955).
64. Nakamura, *Idea*, p. 260.
65. M. Eliade, *The Quest* (Chicago: University of Chicago Press, 1969) pp. 94–101.
66. See James; and Pepper, pp. 268–279.
67. Pepper, pp. 232–279.
68. G. White, *Natural Hazards: Local, National, Global* (New York and London: Oxford University Press, 1974).
69. See Jean Gottman, *A Geography of Europe* (New York: Holt, Rinehart and Winston, 1969), pp. 277–279.
70. Heidegger, *Being and Time.*
71. Dan Andersson, *Visor och ballader* (Stockholm: Tidens Förlag, 1950), p. 89.
72. P. Teilhard de Chardin, *Toward the Future*, Rene Hague, trans. (London: Collins, 1975), pp. 163–208.

17. Counterfeit and authentic wholes: Finding a means for dwelling in nature

HENRI BORTOFT

What is wholeness? To answer this question, it is helpful to present a specific setting. Imagine someone not yet recognizing it asking, "what is roundness?" We might try to answer him by giving a number of instances, such as "the moon is round," "the plate is round," "the coin is round," and so on. Of course "round" is none of these things, but by adducing a number of such instances we may hope to provoke in him the recognition of roundness. This happens when his perception of the specific instances is reorganised, so that they now become like mirrors in which roundness is seen reflected. In spite of what many people might think, this process does not involve empirical generalization – i.e., abstracting what is common from a number of cases. The belief that concepts are derived directly from sensory experiences is like believing that conjurors really do produce rabbits out of hats. Just as the conjuror puts the rabbit into the hat beforehand, so the attempt to deduce the concept by abstraction in the empiricist manner presupposes the very concept it pretends to produce.

I attempt the same procedure in this essay with the aim of understanding wholeness. I adduce a number of examples of wholeness, with the aim of learning more about wholeness itself by seeing its reflection in these particular cases. I distinguish authentic wholeness from counterfeit forms in terms of the relationship between whole and part. The result leads to an understanding of how the whole can be encountered through the parts. Finally, I argue that the way of science developed by the poet and student of nature, Johann Wolfgang von Goethe (1749–1832), exemplifies the principle of authentic wholeness. Goethe's mode of understanding sees the part in light of the whole, fostering a way of science which dwells in nature.

Two examples of wholeness: Holograms and the universe of light and matter

The advent of the laser has made possible the practical development of a radically different kind of photography. *Hologram* is the name given to the special kind of photographic plate produced with the highly coherent light of a laser − i.e., light which holds together and does not disperse, similar to a pure tone compared to noise. Whereas the ordinary photographic plate records and reproduces a flat image of an illuminated object, the hologram does not record an image of the object photographed but provides an optical reconstruction of the original object. When the hologram plate itself is illuminated with the coherent light from the laser with which it was produced, the optical effect is exactly as if the original object were being observed. What is seen is to all optical appearances the object itself in full three-dimensional form, being displaced in apparent position when seen from different perspectives (the parallax effect) in the same way as the original object.

A hologram has several remarkable properties, in addition to those related to the three-dimensional nature of the optical reconstruction which it permits. The particular property which is of direct concern in understanding wholeness is the pervasiveness of the whole optical object throughout the plate.[1] If the hologram plate is broken into fragments and one fragment is illuminated, it is found that the same three-dimensional optical reconstruction of the original object is produced. There is nothing missing; the only difference is that the reconstruction is less well defined. The entire original object can be optically reconstructed from any fragment of the original hologram, but as the fragments get smaller and smaller the resolution deteriorates until the reconstruction becomes so blotchy and ill-defined as to become unrecognizable. This property of the hologram is in striking contrast to the ordinary image-recording photographic plate. If this type of plate is broken and a fragment illuminated, the image reproduced will be that recorded on the particular fragment and no more. With orthodox photography the image fragments with the plate; with holography the image is undivided with the fragments.

What can be seen straightaway about wholeness in this example of the hologram is the way in which the whole is present in the parts. The entire picture is wholly present in each part of the plate, so that it would not be true in this case to say that the whole is made up of parts. This point will be explored in detail shortly, but the advantage of beginning with the hologram is that it is such an immediately concrete instance of wholeness.

A second example of wholeness involves the ordinary experience of looking up at the sky at night and seeing the vast number of stars. We see this nightime world by means of the light "carrying" the stars to us, which means that this vast expanse of sky must all be present in the light which passes through the small hole of the pupil into the eye. Furthermore, other observers in different locations can see the same expanse of night sky. Hence we can say that the stars seen in the heavens are all present in the light which is at any eye-point. The totality is contained in each small region of space, and when we use optical instruments like a telescope, we simply reclaim more of that light.[2] If we set off in imagination to find what it would be like to be light, we come to a condition in which here is everywhere and everywhere is here. The nighttime sky is a "space" which is one whole, with the quality of a point and yet including all within itself.

Matter also turns out to behave in an unexpectedly holistic way at both the macroscopic and the microscopic level. We tend to think of the large-scale universe of matter as being made up of separate and independent masses interacting with one another through the force of gravity. The viewpoint which emerges from modern physics is very different to this traditional conception. It is now believed that mass is not an intrinsic property of a body, but it is in fact a reflection of the whole of the rest of the universe in that body. Einstein imagined, following Ernst Mach, that a single particle of matter would have no mass if it were not for all the rest of the matter in the universe.[3] Instead of trying to understand the universe by extrapolating from the local environment here and now to the universive as a whole, it may be useful to reverse the relationship and understand the local environment as being the result of the rest of the universe.[4]

Similarly, at the microscopic level, we tend to think of the world as being made up of separate, independent sub-atomic particles interacting with one another through fields of force. But the view which emerges from physics today is very different. Particle physicists, as they are called, have found that sub-atomic particles cannot be considered to be made up of ultimate, simple building blocks which are separate and outside of each other. Increasingly, it becomes clear that analysis in this traditional way is inappropriate at the microscopic level. Thus, in the "bootstrap" philosophy of Geoffrey Chew, the properties of any one particle are determined by all the other particles, so that every particle is a reflection of all the others. This structure whereby a particle contains all other particles, and is also contained in each of them, is expressed succinctly by the phrase, "every particle consists of all other particles."[5]

Just as there are no independently separate masses on the large-scale, then, there are also no independent elementary particles on the small-scale. At both levels, the whole is reflected in the parts, which in turn contribute to the whole. The whole, therefore, cannot simply be the sum of the parts – i.e. the totality – because there are no parts which are independent of the whole. For the same reason, we cannot perceive the whole by "standing back to get an overview." On the contrary, because the whole is in some way reflected in the parts, it is to be encountered by going further into the parts instead of by standing back from them.

The hermeneutic circle

A third instance of wholeness is externally somewhat different from the previous two. It is concerned with what happens when we read a written text. If reading is to be meaningful, it is not just a matter of repeating the words verbally as they come up in sequence on the page. Successful reading is not just a matter of saying the words. It is an act of interpretation, but not interpretation in the subjective sense. True interpretation is actively receptive, not assertive in the sense of dominating what is read. True interpretation does not force the text into the mould of the reader's personality, or into the requirements of his previous knowledge. It conveys the meaning of the text – "conveys" in the sense of "passes through" or "goes between." This is why a reader sometimes can convey to others more of the meaning of a text than he may understand himself.

Authentic interpretation, and hence successful reading, imparts real meaning, but the question becomes, what or where is this meaning? We often say, "I see," when we wish to indicate that we have grasped something. If we try to look at what we imagine is in our grasp, however, we find ourselves empty-handed. It does not take much experimentation here to realize that meaning cannot be grasped like an object.

The meaning of a text, therefore, must have something to do with the whole text. What we come to here is the fundamental distinction between whole and totality. The meaning is the whole of the text, but this whole is not the same as the totality of the text. That there is a difference between the whole and the totality is clearly demonstrated by the evident fact that we do not need the totality of the text in order to understand its meaning. We do not have the totality of the text when we read it, but only one bit after another. But we do not have to store up what is read until it is all collected together, whereupon we suddenly see the meaning all at once in an instant. On the contrary, the meaning of the text is discerned and disclosed with progressive immanence throughout the reading of the text.

We can begin to see how remarkably similar the meaning structure of a text is to the optical form of the hologram. The totality of the text can be compared to the pattern of marks on the hologram plate. But the meaning of the text must be compared to the whole picture which can be reconstructed from the hologram plate. This is the sense in which the meaning of the text is the whole. The whole is not the totality, but the whole emerges most fully and completely through the totality. Thus, we can say that meaning is hologrammatical. The whole is present throughout all of the text, so that it is present in any region of the text. It is the presence of the whole in any region of the text which constitutes the meaning of that region of the text. Indeed, we can sometimes find that it is just the understanding of a single passage which suddenly illuminates for us the whole meaning of the text.

What we come to here is the idea of the hermeneutical circle, which was first recognized by Friedrich Ast in the eighteenth century and subsequently developed by Schleiermacher in his program for general hermeneutics as the art of understanding.[6] At the level of discourse, this circle says that to read an author we have to understand him first, and yet we have to read him first to understand him. It appears we have to understand the whole meaning of the text "in advance" to read the parts which are our pathway towards the meaning of the text as a whole. Clearly, this is a contradiction to logic and the form of reasoning which is based thereon. Yet it is the *experience* we go through to understand the meaning of the text, as it is also the experience we go through in writing a text. The same paradox for logic can be found at the level of the single sentence. The meaning of a sentence has the unity of a whole. We reach the meaning of the sentence through reading the words, yet the meaning of the words in that sentence is determined by the meaning of the sentence as a whole.

The reciprocal relationship of part and whole which is revealed here shows us clearly that the act of understanding is not a logical act of reasoning because such an act depends on the choice of either/or. The paradox arises from the tacit assumption of linearity − implicit in the logic of reason − which supposes that we must go either from part to whole or from whole to part. Logic is analytical, whereas meaning is evidently holistic and hence understanding cannot be reduced to logic. We understand meaning in the moment of coalescence when the whole is reflected in the parts so that together they disclose the whole. It is because meaning is encountered in this "circle" of the reciprocal relationship of the whole and the parts that we call it the hermeneutical circle.

The whole and the parts

The hologram helps us to see that the essence of the whole is that it is whole. If we had begun our discussion of the whole with the statement that the whole is whole, it would have seemed to be vacuous or trivially pedantic. But the optical instance of the hologram enables us to see that, far from being a trivial tautology, this statement expresses the primacy of the whole. No matter how often we break the hologram plate, the picture is undivided. It remains whole even while becoming many.

This essential irreducibility of the whole is so strong that it seems inconceivable that there is any way in which the whole could have parts. This is very much opposite to the view we usually have of the relation between parts and whole, which is a view that effectively denies the primacy of the whole. We are accustomed to thinking of going from parts to whole in some sort of summative manner. We think of developing the whole, even of making the whole, on the practical basis of putting parts together and making them fit. In this conventional way of working, we see the whole as developing by "integration of parts." This way of thinking, however, places the whole secondary to the parts, though usually we do not notice this error. Such a way of seeing places the whole in secondary relationship because it necessarily implies that the whole comes after the parts. It implies a linear sequence: first the parts, then the whole. The implication is that the whole always comes later than its parts.

Faced with the primacy of the whole, as seen in the hologram, we may want to reverse the direction of this way of thinking of the whole. This we would do if we thought of the parts as being determined by the whole, defined by it, and so subservient to the whole. But this approach is not the true primacy of the whole, either. It puts the whole in the position of a false transcendental which would come earlier than the parts, and so would leave them no place. This approach effectively considers the whole as if it were a part, but a "superpart" which controls and dominates the other, lesser parts. It is not the true whole, and neither can the parts be true parts when they are dominated by this counterfeit whole. Instead, there is only the side-by-sideness of would-be parts and the counterfeit whole. This is a false dualism.

In as much as the whole is whole it is neither earlier nor later. To say that the whole is not later than the parts is not to say that we do not put parts together. Of course we do — consider the action of writing, for example. But the fact that we often put parts together does not mean that in so doing we put the whole together. Similarly, to say that the whole is not earlier than the parts is not to deny the primacy of the whole. But, at the same time, to assert the primacy of the whole is not to maintain that it is dominant, in the sense of having an external superiority over the parts.

We can see the limitation of these two extreme approaches to the whole if we look at the act of writing. We put marks for words together on a page by the movement of the pen to try to say something. What is said is not the resultant sum of the marks, nor of the words which they indicate. What is said is not produced automatically by the words adding together as they come. But equally, we do not have what is said fixed and finished in front of us before it is written. We do not simply copy what is already said. We all know the familiar experience of having the sense that we understand something and then finding that it has slipped away when we try to say it. We seem to understand already before saying, but in the moment of expression we are empty. What appears is not ready-made outside the expression. But neither is expression an invention from a vacuum.

The art of saying is in finding the "right parts." The success or failure of saying, and hence of writing, turns upon the ability to recognize what is a part and what is not. But a part is a part only inasmuch as it serves to let the whole come forth, which is to let meaning emerge. A part is only a part according to the emergence of the whole which it serves; otherwise it is mere noise. At the same time, the whole does not dominate, for the whole cannot emerge without the parts. The hazard of emergence is such that the whole depends on the parts to be able to come forth, and the parts depend on the coming forth of the whole to be significant instead of superficial. The recognition of a part is possible only through the "coming to presence" of the whole. This fact is particularly evident in authentic writing and reading, where something is either to come to expression or come to be understood.

We cannot separate part and whole into disjointed positions, for they are not two as in common arithmetic. The arithmetic of the whole is not numerical.[7] We do not have part *and* whole, though the number category of ordinary language will always make it seem so.[8] If we do separate part and whole into two, we appear to have an alternative of moving in a single direction, either from part to whole or from whole to part. If we start from this position, we must at least insist on moving in both directions at once, so that we have neither the resultant whole as a sum nor the transcendental whole as a dominant authority, but the emergent whole which comes forth into its parts. The character of this emergence is the "unfolding of enfolding," so that the parts are the place of the whole where it bodies forth into presence.[9] The whole imparts itself; it is accomplished through the parts it fulfills.

We can perhaps do something more to bring out the relationship between whole and part by considering the hologram again. If we break the hologram plate into fractions, we do not break the whole. The whole is present in each fraction, but its presence diminishes as the fractioning proceeds. Starting from the other end, with many fractions, we could put the fractions together to build up the totality. As we did so, the whole would emerge; it would come forth more fully as we approached the totality. But we would not be building up the whole. The whole is already present, present in the fractions, coming fully into presence in the totality. The superficial ordering of the fractional parts may be a linear series – this next to that, and so on. But the ordering of the parts with respect to the emergent whole, the essential ordering, is nested and not linear. Thus the emergence of the whole is orthogonal to the accumulation of parts because it is the coming into presence of the whole which is whole, the whole which is immanent.

This process tells us something fundamental about the whole in a way which shows us the significance of the parts. If the whole presences within its parts, then a part is a place for the presencing of the whole.[10] If a part is to be an arena in which the whole can be present, if cannot be "any old thing." Rather, a part is special and not accidental, since it must be such as to let the whole come into presence. This speciality of the part is particularly important because it shows us the way to the whole. It clearly indicates that the way to the whole is into and through the parts. The whole is nowhere to be encountered except in the midst of the parts. It is not to be encountered by stepping back to take an overview, for it is not over and above the parts, as if it were some superior, all-encompassing entity. The whole is to be encountered by stepping right into the parts. This is how we enter into the nesting of the whole, and thus move into the whole as we pass through the parts.

This dual movement, into the whole through the parts, is demonstrated clearly in the experience of speaking and reading, listening and writing. We can see that in each case there is a dual movement: we move through the parts to enter into the whole which presences within the parts. When we understand, both movements come together. When we do not understand, we merely pass along the parts. Consider, for example, the interpretation of a difficult text, say, Kant's *Critique of Pure Reason*. At first encounter, we just pass along the parts, reading the sentences without understanding. To come to understand the text, we have to enter into it, and we do this in the first place by experiencing the meaning of the sentences. We enter into the text as the medium of meaning through the sentences themselves, putting ourselves into the text in a way which makes us available to meaning. We do not stand back to get an overview of all the sentences, in the hope that this will give us the meaning of the text. We do not refer the text to some other, external text which will give us the meaning. There is no superior text which can be an authority in interpretation because there is no access to the meaning of Kant's book other than through the text itself. Even for Kant, there was no pure "meaning in itself," present as an object in his consciousness, which he then represented in language. The original text is already an interpretation, and every text written about Kant's book is itself an expression of the meaning which that book was written to make evident. The hermeneutic approach must recognize, as Heidegger said, that " . . . what is essential in all philosophical discourse is not found in the specific propositions of which it is composed but in that which, although unstated as such, is made evident through these propositions."[11] Authentic interpretation recognizes the way in which the whole, which is the meaning of the text, comes to presence in the parts which are the sentences.

Encountering the whole: The active absence

Everything we encounter in the world can be said to be either one thing or another, either this or that, either before or after, and so on. Wherever we look, there are different things to be distinguished from one another: this book here, that pen there, the table underneath, and so on. Each thing is outside the other, and all things are separate from one another. But in recognizing the things about us in this way we, too, are separate from and outside of each of the things we see. We find ourselves laid out side by side, together with and separate from, the things we recognize. This is the familiar spectator awareness. In the moment of recognizing a thing we stand outside of that thing, and in the moment of so standing outside of that thing we turn into an "I" which knows that thing, for there cannot be an "outside" without the distinction of something being outside of some other thing. Thus, the "I" of "I know" arises in the knowing of something in the moment of recognition of the thing known. By virtue of its origin, the "I" which knows is outside of what it knows.

We cannot know the whole in the way in which we know things because we cannot recognize the whole as a thing. If the whole were available to be recognized in the same way as we recognize the things which surround us, then the whole would be counted among those things as one of them. We could point and say "here is this" and "there is that," and "that's the whole over there." If we had the power of such recognition, we would know the whole in the same way that we know its parts, for the whole itself would simply be numbered among its parts. The whole would be outside its parts in the same way that each part is outside all the other parts. But the whole comes into presence *within* its parts, and we cannot encounter the whole in the same way that we encounter the parts. We should not think of the whole as if it were a thing.

Awareness is occupied with things. The whole is absent to awareness because it is not a thing among things. To awareness, the whole is no-thing, and since awareness is awareness of *something*, no-thing is nothing. The whole which is no-thing is taken as mere nothing, in which case it vanishes. When this loss happens, we are left with a world of things, and the apparent task of putting them together to make a whole. Such an effort disregards the authentic whole.

The other choice is to take the whole to be no-thing but not nothing. This possibility is difficult for awareness, which cannot distinguish the two. Yet we have an illustration immediately on hand with the experience of reading. We do not take the meaning of a sentence to be a word. The meaning of a sentence is no-word. But evidently this is not the same as nothing, for if it were we could never read! The whole presences within parts, but from the standpoint of the awareness which grasps the external parts, the whole is an absence. This absence, however, is not the same as nothing. Rather, it is an *active* absence in as much as we do not try to be aware of the whole, as if we could grasp it like a part, but instead let ourselves be open to be moved by the whole.

A particularly graphic illustration of the development of a sensitivity to the whole as an active absence is to be found in the experience of writing, where we saw earlier that we do not have the meaning before us like an object. Another illustration of the active absence is provided by the enacting of a play. An actor does not stand away from his part as if it were an object to be captured by awareness. He enters into his part in such a way that he enters into the play. If the play is constructed well, the whole play comes into presence within the parts so that the actor encounters the play through his part. But he does not encounter the play as an object of knowledge over which he can stand like the lines he learns. He encounters the play in the part as an active absence which can begin to move him. When this happens the actor starts to be acted by the play, instead of trying to act the play. The origin of the acting becomes the play itself, instead of the actor's subjective "I." The actor no longer imposes himself on the play, as if it were an object to be mastered, but he listens to the play and allows himself to be moved by it. In this way he enters into the part in such a way that the play speaks through him. This is how, his awareness occupied with the lines to be spoken, he encounters the whole which is the play – not as an object but as an active absence.

Developmental psychology now offers considerable support for this notion that the whole is "nothing" to our ordinary awareness, as well as for the notion that we can develop a sensitivity to the whole as an "active absence." Psychologists have discovered that there are two major modes of organization for a human being: the action mode and the receptive mode.[12] In the early infant state, we are in the receptive mode, but this is gradually dominated by the development of the action mode of organization which is formed in us by our interaction with the physical environment. Through the manipulation of physical bodies, and especially solid bodies, we develop the ability to focus the attention and perceive boundaries – i.e. to discriminate, analyze and divide the world up into objects. The internalization of this experience of manipulating physical bodies gives us the object-based logic which Henri Bergson called "the logic of solids."[13] This process has been described in detail by psychologists from Helmholtz down to Piaget. The result is an analytical mode of consciousness attuned to our experience with solid bodies. This kind of consciousness is institutionalized by the structure of our language, which favors the active mode of organization. As a result, we are well prepared to perceive selectively only some of the possible features of experience.

The alternative mode of organization, the receptive mode, is one which allows events to happen – for example, the play above. Instead of being verbal, analytical, sequential and logical, this mode of consciousness is non-verbal, holistic, non-linear and intuitive. It emphasizes the sensory and perceptual instead of the rational categories of the action mode. It is based on taking in, rather than manipulating, the environment.

For reasons of biological survival, the analytic mode has become dominant in human experience. This mode of consciousness corresponds to the object world, and since we are not aware of our own mode of consciousness directly, we inevitably identify this world as the only reality. It is because of this mode of consciousness that the whole is "nothing" to our awareness, and also that when we encounter it we do so as an "active absence." If we were re-educated in the receptive mode of consciousness, our encounter with wholeness would be considerably different, and we would see many new things about our world.

Wholeness in science

There are many hermeneutic illustrations of the active absence – speaking, reading, playing a game, and so on – which are similar to the actor playing his part in the play. These examples can each demonstrate the reversal which comes in turning from awareness of an object into the encounter with the whole. This turning around, from grasping to being receptive, from awareness of an object to letting an absence be active, is a reversal which is the practical consequence of choosing the path which assents to the whole as no-thing and not mere nothing.

It is because of this reversal that the authentic whole must be invisible to the scientific approach, as currently conceived. The paradigm for modern scientific method is Kant's "appointed judge who compels the witnesses to answer questions which he has himself formulated."[14] Science believes itself to be objective, but is in essence subjective because the witness is compelled to answer questions *which the scientist himself has formulated.* He never notices the circularity in this because he believes he hears the voice of "nature" speaking, not realizing that it is the transposed echo of his own voice. Modern positivist science can only approach the whole as if it were a thing among things. Thus the scientist tries to grasp the whole as an object for interrogation. So it is that science today, by virtue of the method which is its hallmark, is left with a fragmented world of things which it must then try to reassemble.

The introduction of a quantitative, mathematical method in science led to the distinction between primary and secondary qualities.[15] The so-called primary qualities – like number, magnitude, position and so on – can be expressed mathematically. But such secondary qualities as color, taste, and sound cannot be expressed mathematically in any direct way. This distinction has been made into the basis for a dualism in which only the primary qualities are considered to be real. Any secondary quality is supposed to be the result of the effect on the senses of the primary qualities, being no more than a subjective experience and not itself a part of "objective" nature.

The result of this dualistic approach is that the features of nature which we encounter most immediately in our experience are judged to be unreal – just illusions of the senses. In contrast, what is real is not evident to the senses and has to be attained through the use of intellectual reasoning. Thus, one group of qualities is imagined to be behind or beneath the other group, hidden by the appearances, so that a secondary quality is understood when it is seen how it could have arisen from the primary qualities. The reality of nature is not identical to the appearances which our senses give, and a major aim of positivist science is *to replace the phenomenon* with a mathematical model which can incorporate only the primary qualities. This quantitative result is then supposed to be more real than the phenomenon observed by the senses, and the task of science becomes a kind of "metaphysical archaeology" which strives to reveal an underlying mathematical reality.

The way this approach is done in practice can be illustrated by Newton's treatment of the colors produced by a prism. His method was to correlate all observations of secondary qualities with measurements of primary qualities, so as to eliminate the secondary qualities from the scientific description of the world.[16] Newton eliminated color by correlating it with the "degree of refrangibility" (what we would now call "angle of refraction") of the different colors when the sun's light passes through a prism. Furthermore, refraction can be represented numerically, thus the ultimate aim of substituting a series of numbers for the sensory experience of different colors is achieved (later the wavelength of light would replace refrangibility). Hence, something which can be measured replaced the phenomenon of color, and in this way color as color was eliminated from the scientific account of the world.

Goethe's way of science

Newton's approach to light and color illustrates the extraordinary degree to which modern science stands outside of the phenomenon, the ideal of understanding being reached when the scientist is as far removed as possible from the experience.[17] The physics of color could now be understood just as well by a person who is color-blind. There is little wonder that the successful development of physics has led to an ever-increasing alienation of the universe of physics from the world of our everyday experience.[18]

Goethe's approach to color was very different from Newton's analytic approach. Goethe attempted to develop a physics of color which was based on everday experience. He worked to achieve an authentic wholeness by *dwelling in the phenomenon* instead of replacing it with a mathematical representation.

Goethe's objection to Newton's procedure was that he had taken a complicated phenomenon as his basis, and tried to explain what was simple by means of something more complex.[19] To Goethe, Newton's procedure was upside down. Newton had arranged for the light from a tiny hole in a window shutter to pass through a glass prism onto the opposite wall. The spectrum of colors formed in this way was a well-known phenomenon at the time, but Newton's contribution was to explain it in a new way. He believed that the colors were already present in the light from the sun coming through the hole, and the effect of the prism was to separate them. It would be quite wrong to say, as is said so often in physics textbooks, that *the experiment showed* Newton this, or that he was *led to believe* this by the experiment. Rather, it was Newton's way of seeing which constituted the experiment's being seen in this way. He saw the idea (that white light is a mixture of colors which are sorted out by the prism) "reflected" in the experiment, as if it were a mirror to his thinking; he did not derive it from the experiment in the way that is often believed.

In contrast to Newton, Goethe set out to find the simplest possible color phenomenon, and make this his basis for understanding color in more complex situations. He believed Newton erred in thinking colorless light was compounded of colored lights because colored light is darker than colorless light, and this would mean that several darker lights were added together to make a brighter light. Goethe looked first at the colors which are formed when the prism in used with light in the natural environment, instead of the restricted and artificial environment which he felt Newton had selected as the experimental basis for his approach. By doing this, Goethe recognized that the phenomenon of prismatic colors depended on a boundary between light and dark regions. Far from the colors somehow being already *contained* in light, for Goethe they *came into being* out of a relationship between light and darkness.

To Goethe, the prism was a complicating factor, and so to understand the arising of colors, he looked for the more simple cases, which meant looking for situations where there are no secondary factors, only light and darkness. Such a case is what Goethe first called *das reine Phänomen* (the "pure phenomenon"), and for which he later use the term *Urphänomen* ("primal or archetypal phenomenon").[20] He found the primal phenomenon of color in the color phenomena which are associated with opaque or semitransparent media. When light is seen through such a medium, it darkens first to yellow, and then orange and red as the medium thickens. Alternatively, when darkness is seen through an illuminated medium, it lightens to violet and then blue. Such a phenomenon is particularly evident with atmospheric colors, such as the colors of the sun and the sky and the way that these change with atmospheric conditions. Thus, it was in the natural environment that Goethe first recognized the primal phenomenon of color to be the lightening of dark to give violet and blue, and the darkening of light to give yellow and red. He expressed this process poetically as "the deeds and sufferings of light."[21]

Once Goethe had found this primal phenomenon he was in a position to see how the colors change from one to another as conditions change. He could see how these shifts were at the root of more complex phenomena such as the prismatic colors. One result is that a dynamic wholeness is perceived in the prismatic colors – a wholeness totally lacking in Newton's account. In other words, Goethe's presentation describes the origin of colors whereas Newton's does not. The colors of the spectrum are simply not intelligible in Newton's account because there is no inherent reason why there should *be* red, or blue, or green, as there is no reason why they should appear in the order that they do in the spectrum. But with Goethe's account, one can understand both the quality of the colors and the relationship between them, so that we can perceive the wholeness of the phenomenon without going beyond what can be experienced. Goethe's method was to extend and deepen his experience of the phenomenon until he reached that element of the phenomenon which is not given externally to sense experience. This is the connection, or relationship in the phenomenon which he called the *law (Gesetz)*, and which he found by going more deeply into the phenomenon instead of standing back from it or trying to go beyond it intellectually to something which could not be experienced.[22] In other words, Goethe believed that the organization or unity of the phenomenon is real and can be *experienced*, but that it is not evident to sensory experience. It is perceived by an intuitive experience – what Goethe called *Anschauung*, which "may be held to signify the *intuitive knowledge gained through contemplation of the visible aspect.*"[23]

In following Goethe's approach to scientific knowledge, one finds that the wholeness of the phenomenon is intensive. The experience is one of entering into a dimension which is in the phenomenon, not behind or beyond it, but which is not visible at first. It is perceived through the mind, when the mind functions as an organ of perception instead of the medium of logical thought. Whereas mathematical science begins by transforming the contents of sensory perception into quantitative values and establishing a relationship between them, Goethe looked for a relationship between the perceptible elements which left the contents of perception unchanged. He tried to see these elements themselves holistically instead of replacing them by a relationship analytically. As Cassirer said, "the mathematical formula strives to make the phenomena calculable, that of Goethe to make them visible."[24]

It seems clear from his way of working that Goethe could be described correctly as a *phenomenologist* of nature, since his approach to knowledge was to let the phenomenon become fully visible without imposing subjective mental constructs. He was especially scathing towards the kind of theory which attempted to explain the phenomenon by some kind of hidden mechanism. He saw this style of analysis as an attempt to introduce fanciful sensory-like elements behind the appearances, to which the human mind then had to be denied direct access. He thought Descartes' attempt to imagine such mechanical models behind the appearances was debasing to the mind, and no doubt he would have felt the same way about Einstein's picture of the impregnable watch as an analogy for the situation facing the scientific investigator.[25] Goethe did not examine the phenomenon intellectually but, rather, tried to visualize the phenomenon in his mind in a sensory way – by the process which he called "exact sensorial fantasy" (*exakte sinnliche Phantasie*).[26] Goethe's thinking is concrete, not abstract, and can be described as one of dwelling in the phenomenon.[27]

The Ur-Phenomenon

The notion of the *Urphänomen* is an invaluable illustration of the concrete nature of Goethe's way of thinking which dwells in the phenomenon. The primal phenomenon is not to be thought of as a generalization from observations, produced by abstracting from different instances something that is common to them. If this result were the case, one would arrive at an abstracted unity with the dead quality of a lowest common factor. For Goethe, the primal phenomenon was a concrete instance – what he called "an instance worth a thousand, bearing all within itself."[28] In a moment of intuitive perception, the particular instance is seen as a living manifestation of the universal. What is merely particular in one perspective is simultaneously universal in another way of seeing. In other words, the particular becomes symbolic of the universal.[29]

In terms of the category of wholeness, the primal phenomenon is an example of the whole which is present in the part. Goethe himself said as much when he called it "an instance worth a thousand," and described it as "bearing all within itself." It is the authentic whole which is reached by going into the parts, whereas a generalization is the counterfeit whole that is obtained by standing back from the parts to get an overview. Looking for the *Urphänomen* is an example of looking for the right part – i.e. the part which contains the whole. This way of seeing illustrates the simultaneous, reciprocal relationship between part and whole, whereby the whole cannot appear until the part is recognized, but the part cannot be recognized as such without the whole.

For example, Goethe was able to "read" how colors arise in the way that the colors of the sun and the sky change with the atmospheric conditions throughout the day. Because there were no secondary, complicating factors, this was for him an instance of the primal phenomenon of the arising of colors. This phenomenon was perceived as a part which contained the whole, and it was, in fact, through the observation of this particular phenomenon that Goethe first learned to see intuitively the law of the origin of color. Yet, the way that the colors of the sun and sky change *together* does not stand out as a phenomenon until it is seen as an instance of how colors arise. The search for the primal phenomenon is like creative writing, where the need is to find the right expression to let the meaning come forth. By analogy, we can say that Goethe's way of science is "hermeneutical." Once the primal phenomenon has been discovered in a single case, it can be recognized elsewhere in nature and in artificial situations where superficially it may appear to be very different. These varying instances can be compared to the fragments of a hologram.

Newton, in contrast, tried to divide light into parts: the colors of the spectrum from red through to blue. But these are not true parts because each does not contain the whole, and hence they do not serve to let the whole come forth. Colorless light, or white light, is imagined to be a summative totality of these colors; whole and parts are treated as separate and outside of each other. Newton tried to go analytically from whole to parts (white light separated into colors), and from parts to whole (colors combined to make white light). In contrast, Goethe encountered the wholeness of the phenomenon through the intuitive mode of consciousness, which is receptive to the phenomenon instead of dividing it according to external categories.[30]

Conclusion

The experience of authentic wholeness requires a new style of learning largely ignored in our schools and universities today. Typically, modern education is grounded in the intellectual faculty, whose analytical capacity alone is developed, mostly through verbal reasoning. One notes, for example, that science students are often not interested in observing phenomena of nature; if asked to do so, they become easily bored. Their observations often bear little resemblance to the phenomenon itself.[31] These students are much happier with textbook descriptions and explanations, a fact readily understandable once one recognizes that most educational experience unfolds in terms of one mode of consciousness – the verbal, rational mode.

The experience of authentic wholeness is impossible in this mode of consciousness, and a complementary style of understanding could usefully be developed. This can be done, first by learning to work with mental images in a way emulating Goethe – i.e. forming images from sensory experiences. In turn, this process requires careful observation of the phenomenon. Authentic wholeness means that the whole is in the part, hence careful attention must be given to the parts instead of to general principles. In contrast, an intellectual approach to scientific education begins by seeing the phenomenon as an instance of general principles.

Working with mental images activates a different mode of consciousness which is holistic and intuitive. One area where this style of learning is now used practically is in transpersonal education.[32] Experiments with guided fantasy indicate that a frequent result is the extension of feelings, whereby the student experiences a deeper, more direct contact with the phenomenon imagined.[33] In this way, a more comprehensive and complete encounter with the phenomenon results, and aspects of the phenomenon otherwise unnoticed often come to light. In addition, students feel themselves to be more in harmony with the phenomenon, as if they themselves were participating in it. This leads to an attitude toward nature more grounded in concern, respect and responsibility.[34]

Goethe's way of science is not the only direction for a way of learning grounded in authentic wholeness. In most general terms, such a style of education and science is phenomenological, letting things become manifest as they show themselves without forcing our own categories on them. This kind of learning and science goes beyond the surface of the phenomenon, but not behind it to contrive some causal mechanism described by a model borrowed from somewhere else. A contemporary illustration of such an approach is the work of biologist Wolfgang Schad in his zoological study, *Man and Mammals*.[35] Schad shows how all mammals can be understood in terms of the way in which the whole is present in the parts. In addition, he demonstrates how each mammal can be understood in terms of its own overall organization.

Schad begins with the direct observation of the immediate phenomena, working to rediscover the uniqueness of individual animals. According to Schad's approach, every detail of an animal is a reflection of its basic organization. Thus, he does not begin by replacing the phenomenon with a stereotype, but rather searches for the animal's unique qualities. This approach does not lead to fragmentation and multiplicity. Instead, it leads to the perception of diversity within unity, whereby the unique quality of each mammal is seen holistically within the context of other mammals. With a wealth of drawings and photographs, Schad demonstrates how going into the part to encounter the whole leads to the perception of multiplicity within a holistic perspective. He shows that multiplicity in unity means seeing uniqueness without fragmentation.

The counterfeit approach to wholeness − i.e. going away from the part to get an overview − leads only to the abstraction of the general case, which has the quality of uniformity rather than uniqueness. Schad indicates how a biology grounded in authentic wholeness can recognize the inner organic order in an animal in such a way that its individual features can be explained by the basic organization of the animal itself. In short, the mammal "explains" itself. For example, the formation of the hedgehog's horny quills is explained in terms of the basic organization of the hedgehog itself. Other questions for which Schad provides answers are why cattle have horns, and deer, antlers; why leopards are spotted, and zebras, striped; why otter, beavers, seals, and hippopotamuses live in water; why giraffes' necks are long; why rhinoceroses are horned. Schad convincingly demonstrates that features such as these can be explained through careful observation of an animal's organization in relation to the organization of other mammals.

Like Goethe's, Schad's way of science is phenomenological and hermeneutical. It is phenomenological because the animal is capable of disclosing itself in terms of itself. Phenomenology, said Heidegger, is the effort "to let that which shows itself be seen from itself in the very way in which it shows itself from itself."[36] Phenomenology brings to light what is there but at first may be hidden. Schad discovers in the animal the qualities which make that animal what it is rather than some other creature. In addition, Schad's work is hermeneutical, since when the point is reached where the animal discloses itself, the animal becomes its own language. In this moment, the animal *is* language. As an authentic discovery, this moment can only be experienced directly; it cannot be "translated" adequately into the verbal language of secondhand description. In this sense, Schad's way of seeing echoes the universal sense of Gadamer's hermeneutics, in which "being that can be understood is language."[37]

As Schad's work suggests, Goethe's way of science did not end with him. His style of learning and understanding belongs not to the past but to the future. It is widely acknowledged today that, through the growth of the science of matter, the Western mind has become more and more removed from contact with nature. Contemporary problems, many arising from modern scientific method, confront people with the fact that they have become divorced from a realistic appreciation of their place in the larger world. At the same time, there is a growing demand for a renewal of contact with nature. It is not enough to dwell in nature sentimentally and aesthetically, grafting such awareness to a scientific infrastructure which largely denies nature. The need is a *new* science of nature, different from the science of matter, and based on other human faculties besides the analytic mind. A basis for this science is the discovery of authentic wholeness.[38]

Notes

1. T. Leith and H. Upatnieks, "Photography by Laser," *Scientific American* 212 (1965): 24–35.
2. David Bohm, *Wholeness and the Implicate Order* (London: Routledge and Kegan Paul, 1980), p. 149.
3. C.W. Kilmister, *The Environment in Modern Physics* (London: English University Press, 1965), p. 36.
4. Jayant Narlikar, *The Structure of the Universe* (Oxford: Oxford University Press, 1977), p. 250.
5. Fritjof Capra, *The Tao of Physics* (London: Wildwood House, 1975), p. 313.
6. Richard E. Palmer, *Hermeneutics* (Evanston: Northwestern University Press, 1969), chap. 7.
7. P.H. Bortoft, "A Non-reductionist Perspective for the Quantum Theory," M. Phil. thesis, Department of Theoretical Physics, Birkbeck College, London University, 1982, chap. 5.
8. The difficulty with talking about part *and* whole is that a distinction is made which is extensive, and this leads to dualism. The difficulty disappears with the recognition that there can be an *intensive* distinction; see Bortoft, "Non-reductionist Perspective."
9. See the notion of unfolding (*explicatio*) and enfolding (*implicatio*) in the work of Nicholas of Cusa, discussed in Karl Jaspers, *The Great Philosophers*, vol. 2 (London: Rupert Hart-Daris, 1966), p. 129; also, see David Bohm, *Wholeness and the Implicate Order*, chap. 7.
10. The terminology of presence and presencing is adopted from Heidegger as an attempt to escape dualism. See G.J. Seidel, *Martin Heidegger and the Pre-Socratics* (Lincoln: University of Nebraska Press, 1964), chap. 3.
11. Martin Heidegger, *Kant and the Problem of Metaphysics* (Bloomington: Indiana University Press, 1962), p. 206.
12. Arthur J. Deikman, "Bimodal Consciousness", in *The Nature of Human Consciousness*, Robert E. Ornstein, ed. (San Francisco: W.H. Freeman, 1973).
13. Henri Bergson, *Creative Evolution* (London: Macmillan, 1911), p. ix; also, see Milic Capek, *Bergson and Modern Physics* (Holland: Reidel, 1971), pp. 56, 69, 72–74.
14. Immanuel Kant, *Critique of Pure Reason*, Norman Kemp Smith, trans. (London: Macmillan, 1964), p. 20.
15. E.A. Burtt, *The Metaphysical Foundations of Modern Science* (London: Routledge and Kegan Paul, 1980), p. 83.
16. Michael Roberts and E.R. Thomas, *Newton and the Origin of Colours* (London: Bell, 1934), pp. 60, 110.
17. Idries Shah, *The Sufis* (New York: Doubleday, 1964), p. xvi.
18. Aron Gurwitsch, "Galilean Physics in the Light of Husserl's Phenomenology", in *Phenomenology and Sociology*, Thomas Luckmann, ed. (Harmondsworth: Penguin Books, 1978).

19. Ernst Lehrs, *Man or Matter: Introduction to a Spiritual Understanding of Nature on the basis of Goethe's Method of Training, Observation and Thought*, second edition (London: Faber and Faber, 1958), p. 290.

20. H.B. Nisbet, *Goethe and the Scientific Tradition* (University of London: Institute of Germanic Studies, 1972), p. 39.

21. Ernst Lehrs, *Man or Matter*, p. 293.

22. H.B. Nisbet, *Goethe and the Scientific Tradition*, p. 36, n. 149.

23. Agnes Arber, *The Natural Philosophy of Plant Form* (London: Cambridge University Press, 1950) p. 209, italics in the original.

24. Quoted in A.G.F. Gode von Aesch, *Natural Science in German Romanticism* (New York: Columbia University German Studies, 1941), p. 74.

25. H.B. Nisbet, *Goethe and the Scientific Tradition*, p. 54; Albert Einstein and Leopold Infeld, *The Evolution of Physics* (London: Cambridge University Press, 1947), p. 33.

26. Ernst Lehrs, *Man or Matter*, pp. 99, 112.

27. The difference between these two kinds of scientific thinking illustrates, and is illustrated by, the distinction which Heidegger makes between "belonging *together*" and "*belonging* together" (Martin Heidegger, *Identity and Difference*, [New York: Harper and Row, 1969], p. 29). In the first case, belonging is determined by together, so that "to belong" means to have a place in the order of a "together" – i.e. in the unity of a framework. But in the case of *belonging* together, the "together" is determined by the belonging, so that there is "the possibility of no longer representing belonging in terms of the unity of the together, but rather of experiencing this together in terms of belonging" (ibid.). Thus, we could say that Goethe experienced the *belonging* together of the yellow sun and the blue sky, and that he did not try to make them belong *together*. This experience of *belonging* together is reached by dwelling in the phenomenon instead of replacing it with conceptual representatives.

28. Ernst Lehrs, *Man or Matter*, p. 125.

29. Ernst Cassirer, *The Problem of Knowledge* (New Haven: Yale University Press, 1974), p. 146.

30. Goethe followed the same approach in studying living things in nature. With flowering plants, for example, he proposed that "All is leaf" and that "this simplicity makes possible the greatest diversity" (Rudolf Magnus, *Goethe as a Scientist*, [New York: Collier Books, 1961], p. 45). Goethe perceived the stem leaf as the primal or archetypal organ of the flowering plant because he saw it as containing all within itself. He did not mean by this that all the further organs of the flowering plant – i.e., sepals, petals, and stamens – grew out of the stem leaves in a material sequence. Rather, he saw the plant holistically, thus seeing the intensive dimension of wholeness. His perception that all is leaf is another instance of the intuitive perception whereby the particular is seen as a living manifestation of the universal and hence in the moment of seeing is symbolic of the universal. See J.W. Goethe, *Goethe's Botanical Writings*, Bertha Mueller, trans. (Honolulu: University of Hawaii Press, 1952); and Lehrs, *Man or Matter*.

31. R.G. Stansfield, "The New Theology? The Case of the Dripping Tap," paper presented to the British Association for the Advancement of Science, September, 1975.

32. Gay Hendricks and James Fadiman, *Transpersonal Education* (Englewood Cliffs, New Jersey: Prentice-Hall, 1976).

33. Ibid.

34. See David Seamon, "Goethe's Approach to the Natural World: Implications for Environmental Theory and Education," in D. Ley and M. Samuels, eds., *Humanistic*

Geography: Prospects and Problems (Chicago: Maaroufa, 1978), pp. 238–250.

35. Wolfgang Schad, *Man and Mammals* (New York: Waldorf Press, 1977).

36. Martin Heidegger, *Being and Time* (New York: Harper and Row, 1962), p. 58.

37. Hans-Georg Gadamer, *Truth and Method* (London: Sheed and Ward, 1979), p. 432.

38. See Henri Bortoft, *Goethe's Scientific Consciousness* (London: Institute for Cultural Research Monograph, Octagon Press, 1986).

The contributors

Botond Bognar is an assistant professor of architecture at the University of Illinois, Urbana-Champaign. He has studied at the Budapest Institute of Technology and the University of California, Los Angeles. He has practiced architecture in both Budapest and Tokyo. His most recent book is *The Challenge of Japanese Architecture*.

Henri Bortoft teaches physics and philosophy and is currently writing a monograph on Goethe's scientific consciousness. He did postgraduate research at Birkbeck College (University of London) on the foundations of the quantum theory and worked for several years as a research assistant to the philosopher J.G. Bennett.

Walter L. Brenneman, Jr. teaches in the department of religion at the University of Vermont. He was trained in psychology and the phenomenology of religion. With his wife, Mary, he is currently engaged in the documentation and interpretation of the holy wells in Ireland. He is author of *Spirals: A Study in Symbol, Myth and Ritual*; and, with Stanley O. Yarian and Alan M. Olson, *The Seeing Eye: Hermeneutical Phenomenology in the Study of Religion*.

Anne Buttimer is a professor of social and economic geography at the University of Lund in Sweden. Currently, she is conducting research on the history of ideas and the sociology of knowledge. Her two latest books are *Creativity and Context* and *The Practice of Geography*.

Kimberly Dovey, a native of western Australia, teaches architecture at the Royal Melbourne Institute of Technology. He was previously a lecturer in environmental design at the University of California, Berkeley, where he is a doctoral candidate. His work has appeared in *Landscape, Places*, and the *Journal of Architectural Education*.

Joseph Grange is chairperson of the philosophy department at the University of Southern Maine in Portland. He received his doctorate from Fordham University and has published widely on the relationship between phenomenology and ecology.

Miriam Helen Hill is an assistant professor of geography at Indiana University Southeast in New Albany, Indiana. She received her Bachelor's and Master's degrees in earth science from Indiana State University and her doctorate in geography from Kent State University. Her article for this volume includes material from her dissertation, "The Non-Visual Lifeworld: A Comparative Phenomenological Geography."

Bernd Jager teaches in the psychology department at Sonoma State College in Rohnert Park, California. He studied at the University of Groningen, San Francisco State College, and received his Ph.D. from Duquesne University. His work appears, among other places, in the series, *Duquesne Studies in Phenomenological Psychology*, vols. 1–4.

Richard Lang teaches in the department of psychology at Seattle University in Seattle, Washington. His research involves the application of phenomenology to psychological themes.

Robert Mugerauer directs *Landmarks*, an environmental consulting firm in Austin, Texas, and is a Visiting Scholar in the graduate school at the University of Texas at Austin. He was trained in philosophy at the University of Notre Dame, the University of Texas at Austin, and the University of Freiburg. He has been a National Endowment for the Humanities fellow, doing research on "Heidegger and Homecoming." Presently, he is working on a hermeneutical interpretation of the American landscape.

Edward Relph is a professor of geography at Scarborough College, University of Toronto. His research involves a phenomenological approach to environmental and landscape issues. He has written the books, *Place and Placelessness* and *Rational Landscapes and Humanistic Geography*.

David G. Saile is an associate professor of architecture at the University of Kansas. He received his doctorate in architecture from the University of

Newcastle upon Tyne. His current research interests include ritual and home, the role of the built environment in community, and communication and meaning in the environment.

R. Murray Schafer is a Canadian composer and author involved with the study of sound and the sonic environment. He is author of *The Tuning of the World* and lives near Bancroft, Ontario.

David Seamon is an assistant professor of architecture at Kansas State University. Trained as a behavioral geographer and environmental psychologist, he is interested in a phenomenological approach to environmental behavior and place-making. He has written the book, *A Geography of the Lifeworld*. His most recent volume, edited with Thomas Saarinen and James Sell, is *Environmental Perception and Behavior: An Inventory and Prospect*.

Francis Violich is a professor of city planning and landscape architecture at the University of California, Berkeley. He did his undergraduate work at Berkeley and graduate studies at Harvard and The Massachusetts Institute of Technology. Concerned with the social and cultural implications of physical planning and urban design, he has conducted pioneer studies of Latin American city planning and its background in Spanish urban history. He is currently investigating methods for revealing the essential quality of existing urban places and building into urban design processes a more authentic sense of community identity.

Michael E. Zimmerman is a professor of philosophy at Newcomb College of Tulane University. He is also a clinical professor of psychiatry at Louisiana State University's School of Medicine and teaches philosophy and psychotherapy at Tulane Medical School. He has written extensively on the philosophical and cultural impact of modern technology. He is author of *Eclipse of Self: The Development of Heidegger's Concept of Authenticity*.

Index